An Accident Waiting to Happen

Philip Howard

AN ACCIDENT WAITING TO HAPPEN

a life with Ehlers Danlos Syndrome

ISBN-978-1506090832 (CreateSpace-Assigned)

Cover Design c Andrew Howard (www.andrewhoward.io)

CreateSpace Independent Publishing Platform

What my proof readers said:

"Phil. I found this very powerful. I can't wait to see what people who have your medical condition make of it."

Steve

"I couldn't put it down."

Denise

"I love your style of writing but I found the beginning hard to read because I know you and you were in pain. I'm glad I persevered because that is what the book is about; perseverance (plus courage). It is an amazing story about how you learned to find happiness and hope. Well done."

Joan

Contents

This book is dedicated to my mum and dad who lived with love

.......and fear.

"Ehlers Danlos Syndrome isn't an obstacle, nor is it something you can push aside. It's a way of life. You have no choice, but to follow its lead.❤" (taken off twitter December 2013)

Acknowledgements

I would like to thank Steve Morgan, Joan Sutton and Denise Goundrill for reading this book and making such helpful and intelligent comments. Their encouragement helped me to complete this work.

My thanks also goes to Andrew Howard for designing the cover. (**Cover Design: www.andrewhoward.io**).

Most of all I would like to thank my wife Linda. She has looked after me for 41 years. I have overcome many difficulties but I would not have done so without her love and support.

About the author

Philip is a retired teacher. Despite suffering from Ehlers Danlos syndrome he has led an active life punctuated by many injuries arising from that activity. He is married with three children and recently welcomed his twelfth grandchild into the world. He writes; tries to do gardening when it doesn't hurt and is a member of Hull Male Voice Choir.

Introduction

I was born in the northern industrial town of St. Helens on the first of June 1950 at a quarter past two; precisely one half hour after my brother, Victor. My early years were spent in a simple two up, two down terraced house that had a toilet at the bottom of the yard. By the time I'd progressed to grammar school we'd moved to a very nice house in a posher part of town; so posh in fact that it had an inside toilet.

I left school in 1969 and worked in the Health Service for ten years before becoming a teacher, a career that lasted until my retirement in 2009. I got married in 1973 and subsequently produced three children who have provided me with eleven beautiful grandchildren. To all intents and purposes I have lived a very ordinary, conventional life.

Appearances are deceptive.

I suffer from a rare and unusual medical condition and as a result I have endured a multiplicity of injuries. The first occurred when I was a baby. My father was playing with me in the front room. I crawled under a sideboard to gather a ball that had rolled past me. My parents immediately recognized that something was wrong as I began crying and did not come out from under the furniture. My father pulled me out feet first and to his horror, was greeted by my bloodied face. I had split my forehead from top to bottom in three different places. The white scars are still visible to this day. My parents checked the sideboard and found nothing untoward. I had apparently cut myself on nothing.

As a result I was referred to a consultant paediatrician who inaccurately diagnosed me as suffering from "unconfirmed haemophilia". My medical problem was so rare that they simply didn't know what was wrong with me. It was not until I was nineteen that I was finally diagnosed as having "Ehlers Danlos Syndrome" Sufferers from this condition have joints that dislocate easily causing long term damage to their joints. In addition their skin cuts or bruises at the slightest knock.

As a result of this misdiagnosis both my parents and I were not given the correct help and guidance until much damage had already been done to my body.

Photographs of my childhood all share the same feature. Some part of my body is bandaged, in a sling or a plaster cast.

Despite this the photographs show an apparently happy little boy squinting into the holiday sunshine. The pictures lie however. I was not happy. In fact I was very troubled but no one knew it. I have suffered much emotional damage as a result of the physical injuries and have only now begun to come to terms with it.

I did not experience a normal childhood. In fact large sections of my life have not been normal but it was not until I was lying at the bottom of a ladder, in my fifty eighth year, listening to the siren of an approaching ambulance and feeling fear creeping over me that I thought for the first time, "Not another one! This has got to stop; if I survive."

This has been a very difficult book for me to write. I have revisited a number of serious injuries that have occurred to me and have relived the pain of tearing flesh, bloodied limbs and smashed bones.

My life has been beset by adversity and has been full of pain but this story does more than describe these evil spirits. It paints a picture of how to overcome both of them and achieve some degree of the peace that I am now learning to enjoy.

Part One
There's Something Wrong with Our Son

Chapter 1 Bleeding

I am bleeding.

I am twelve years old and am lying slumped at the foot of a low wall with a huge hole in my leg.

I look down once more at my right shin hoping that what I have just seen is an illusion. It is very real.

I am bleeding.

The pain is indescribable.

I cry out for my mother but she is not here.

No one is here.

No one has heard my cries.

No one has sensed my loneliness.

I need to move.

I need to get help.

The bleeding won't stop.

Chapter 2 In Serious Trouble

Some memories never fade.

I knew immediately that I was in serious trouble.

Despite my youth I had already broken my right ankle, sprained my left, dislocated both kneecaps and had had over forty stitches inserted in a variety of cuts but I had never experienced anything as bad as this. This was the moment that defined the future course of my life. From now on nothing would be the same.

This was the moment when, despite being of such tender years, I grew up.

I had spent the summer holidays of 1963 playing football, rugby and cricket on the top field of Taylor Park in St. Helens. It is still a beautiful park with a paddling pool and a wood. A path lined by rhododendron bushes leads through to a boating lake edged by blue railings upon which fishermen rest their rods or weary elbows and watch the day go by.

Top field as we called it looked down quite a severe gradient onto this vista. Behind the trees lay the famous rugby ground, home of St. Helens Rugby League club and beyond that stood huge industrial chimneys belching pollution from large factories that made St.Helens the world centre of glass production.

I enjoyed sports of every kind and was a very active little lad who couldn't sit still to save his life. My mother still tells the story of my father saying to me, "I'll give you a shilling if you stay quiet for just 5 minutes." After about thirty seconds I said, "Is it 5 minutes yet dad?"

I never got the money.

I was full of life. On one morning in the summer holidays, I played cricket in the park with my friend, Terry Hayes. I won the toss and decided to bat. Terry had to bowl and field, as there was no one else. We built a stone wicket from the sandstones lumps that had been removed from an adjacent wall at the beginning of the school holidays. I stood, bat in hand as Terry began to hurtle in, in an attempt to dismantle the stones with his trusty tennis ball. 310 runs later he got me leg before.

My friend was exhausted but eagerly took up the bat, which liberated him from 2 hours toil as a bowler. He had scored ten when I bowled him. He'd only had the bat for about three minutes and he begged me to let him have another go.

"Nope. You're out, my turn."

Needless to say an exhausted Terry decided to finish some five minutes later and we went home. I had thoroughly enjoyed myself. I can't speak for Terry.

I had endless energy, drive and commitment and all of these characteristics would soon be severely tested by the sound of an ambulance bell and the flashing of its light.

We returned to school in early September. The summer sun still shone as it always does in childhood memories that forget the ugly days. I have fond memories of my school days in spite of the awful things that happened to me there. When I return to my home town I sometimes go out of my way to drive past and have a look at the ivy-covered entrance that still looks the same despite the changes that have occurred behind.

I settled back into its daily routine very quickly and all was going well until the month neared its end.

The school canteen guarded the entrance to a large playing field and every day at 12.15pm hundreds of boys made their way up the steps to enjoy either a half hour of games or first sitting for lunch. My hunger drove me to the right of those steps in an attempt to avoid the congestion.

It was only a low wall, no more than eighteen inches high and was often used as a seating area for boys watching the cricket being played on the manicured lower field. Now because of the slight drizzle that hinted at the approach of autumn, no one was sat there. It was bare and inviting. All it required was a small leap to take me onto the grass banking that led to my lunch. It was just a little jump but as I took off, my left foot slipped on the wet floor. I fell, hitting my right shin on the sharp edge of the wall.

There is a famous piece of film footage from the First World War showing soldiers climbing out of their trench to begin an attack on enemy lines. One man is shot and slides back down the banking as his comrades stream past. Just like him I recoiled from the wall as if a sniper's bullet had pierced my skull. My body arched backwards and my jaw extended open letting saliva drop to the ground. I collapsed in a heap at the foot of the wall as other foot soldiers swept past me, intent on reaching the top, oblivious to what was happening to me.

I lay there shocked and stunned for a second and then pulled down my sock and gasped. This was no simple cut requiring a few stitches and a clean up. Ripped flesh and blood stretched down from my knee towards my ankle. I had ruptured, is the word that comes to mind, my entire shin. I stared at the gaping hole in my leg and as I write now, I wretch and cry out. I could see my shin-bone.

I instinctively grabbed my leg from behind, pushing the muscle forward in order to take the weight off the wound. I was trying to hold my leg together. I had to get help.

To my left, some one hundred yards away, I could see the red wooden doors, the paintwork shining like a beacon that would take me inside the school building. Somehow I managed to drag my body off the floor. I ran, Quasimodo like, across the school yard dodging the rugby balls whizzing like enemy bullets about my head. Ignoring the shouts of players annoyed at my apparent interference, I dashed for the doors that led to salvation. I opened them, dismissive of the school regulation that said no admittance during break times. I had intended to go up the steps and hobble some three hundred yards to the school office but the sight of boys queuing for the delights of the tuck shop dragged me downwards.

I stumbled down the concrete steps, clutching the highly polished banister rail. Pushing past much larger boys I burst through the double doors that led into the dark changing rooms that doubled as the tuck shop at mid-morning break and lunch.

"Sir!" I screamed.

Mr. Fisher, Head of French was a very sophisticated man. He was intelligent and always formally polite. He possessed an extremely posh accent that suggested to his northern pupils that he came from somewhere down south. He stood there in his academic gown, supervising the sale of Mars bars and crisps.

5

"Sir!" I banged my disfigured limb onto one of the benches as I collapsed in front of him.

" Oh my goodness!" he exclaimed.

"Right."

He turned to another boy. "You, boy. Come here.' '

I had never seen this boy before despite the red wavy hair that shone on his head. I was only a child but I could tell from his reaction that he was in a state of shock, mesmerised by the sight of my leg. I thought to myself 'I don't know you but you're older than me. If I can deal with it, you can. Please do something.'

Mr. Fisher barked an order.

"Listen to me boy. Go to the office. Tell Mrs. Baines that Howard has cut his leg and needs an ambulance." Mr. Fisher, like me, must have seen the fear in his eyes.

"What's his name? Boy what's his name?'

"Er Howard Sir."

"Good' I thought. 'He knows my name.'

"Go! Now! Be quick but don't run. Just get there and tell them to get an ambulance!"

The boy nodded and with that I presume he must have left although I never actually saw him go. I had suddenly become aware of the total agony in my leg. I looked at it and I knew it was serious.

"You're being very brave. Well done! Keep it up!" Mr. Fisher smiled and stuck his thumb in the air. I reciprocated the gesture enjoying this feeling of temporary bonhomie.

In truth I wasn't being brave at all. I had no choice but to lie there and wait for help to come. I was in too much pain to cry so I returned his smile. I couldn't do anything else and I hoped a smile might make things better.

Mr. Fisher talked to me with an affection that I had never experienced from teachers who worked in the formal setting of a boys' grammar school. I don't remember the details of what passed between us. I just remember it being a very pleasant conversation, all things considered. I realize now that he was trying to divert my attention. Now, as I write, I remember that he made a purposeful move towards my left as I lay on the bench. I think he was trying to make sure I didn't look to my right. It's taken forty-five years for me to realize that.

Before I knew it, "Flash" Clifton the Deputy Head came bounding in followed by two ambulance men. Only then did I notice that the room had been cleared of boys. I wondered if they'd got their sweets. Perhaps they didn't.

I was sorry to have denied them but their inconvenience was minimal compared to mine.

Flash was, as ever, imperious, his gown flowing behind him as he moved. He took command.

As the ambulance men bandaged my leg, he spoke.

"Right Howard do you have a phone at home?"

"No sir."

"Will your mother be in?"

I didn't have a clue.

"Yes sir." I said in hope. I hadn't thought about my mum until that moment and suddenly I realized that I needed her desperately. A tear welled in my eyes.

7

"We'll take her to the hospital. She'll be there right away," he said reassuringly and stuck his thumb in the air in the same way that Fisher had done moments before. It made me smile and the tears did not fall.

It was the only time I came close to crying.

"Right. We'll send someone to get your mum."

Before I knew it the ambulance men had finished bandaging me.

"This is a big cut son so we're going to put you on the stretcher. Then we'll get you to hospital in no time".

I nodded, thankful of the burly reassurance that I would be OK

As they carried me back up the stairs to the waiting vehicle Mr. Clifton shouted behind me.

"Well done Howard. Your mum will be there soon. Be brave!" With that the ambulance men shut the doors of the beautiful cream limousine, a converted 1950s Austin Princess, and we glided regally towards the hospital.

I lay there, strapped to the stretcher with the younger of the two ambulance men watching over me. He kept smiling at me and I had the awful feeling that he was worrying about me. I chattered non-stop and even the prospect of what lay ahead could not shut me up. Ten minutes into the journey I was silenced however. I heard the ambulance's bell ring. We were going through lights on red.

"Is that the ambulance bell?"

"Yeah." He smiled.

"Ringing for me?"

"Yeah." He laughed.

"Wow!"

I tried to see out of the tinted windows but gave up.

"Where are we?"

"The Lingholme. Not long now."

The officer smiled again and then fiddled with my blanket as if tucking me in. I think he wanted to comfort me for suddenly I had fallen silent and withdrew into myself. I put my right arm behind my head and faced the side of the vehicle. I had run out of things to say.

The ringing of the ambulance bell was a source of excitement for a young boy but it couldn't disguise the reality of what I already knew. I was being transported towards a bed where many stitches would be inserted, without anaesthetic.

I had had so many injuries over the years that I was known by name in the casualty unit of The Providence hospital. I was used to hospitals and ambulances but for the first time I was frightened. I felt very alone and now I wanted my mum. I pictured her face at the front door. I could see the alarm as she recognized one of my teachers. I wondered who was delivering the bad tidings. I felt sorry for her. I was causing my parents more anxiety. It wasn't my fault but I was already beginning to feel the guilt that has stalked me all my life. Anxious questions ravaged my brain. Why was I having so many accidents? Couldn't I just be a little more sensible? Why didn't I walk up the steps like all the other boys when I knew how badly I could get hurt? It was all my fault and now I was paying the price of my apparent stupidity.

My thoughts were stopped in their tracks as the limousine came to a halt without any apparent change in engine noise. The back door opened to reveal the rear entrance of the Casualty unit, which backed out directly onto the main street. The term "Accident and Emergency" had not been developed yet. The two men grunted slightly as they lifted my stretcher out. They carried me through the green wooden gates past the long narrow rose garden. It was not a comfortable journey. We went through the narrow outer doors to the Casualty unit and turned sharp left down a short corridor and left again through the Royal blue inner doors. As we entered the waiting room a familiar figure awaited me. Sister Kathleen Duffy typified what the Providence Hospital was about. She was an Irish catholic who devoted her life to the care of others and was known with respect and affection throughout St. Helens. Although the National Health Service provided the funds, the Catholic nuns' order that had founded the hospital in the late nineteenth century still had control. Nuns and catholic nurses, who came, in the main, from Ireland, staffed the hospital.

Nurse Duffy was an icon. You felt safe in her hands but she couldn't guarantee that you would be free from pain.

"She wore a blue uniform with a white apron. On her head sat a nurse's cap similar in shape to a nun's veil. She stood, hands on hips, beaming. It seemed like God had placed her there to be happy and make others feel the same way.

"Well now Philup. What have yer been doin' to yerself?"

"I fell on a wall."

"What in heavens name were yer doin' on a wall?"

I explained as well as I could as Sister Duffy undid the

bandages at high speed. She slowed with considerable gentleness as she unravelled the last couple of wrappings which revealed blood soaked dressings.

She peeled them off gingerly.

"Oh lad, lad, whatever have yer done?"

She had a kind smile but she didn't mince her words.

"Never mind we'll have you patched up in no time."

Those reassuring words disguised the trauma she was about to put me through. Three nurses swept into action. Antiseptic, catgut, scissors, kidney dishes swirled around me. The nurses put on masks.

I was told to lie back as Sister Duffy's cheerful smile was replaced by the grim expression of concentration.

"Right nurse, hold him."

One of the younger nurses leant over me and pressed herself on to me. At first I didn't mind. I was just becoming aware of sex and she had a marvellous chest. I felt it as she squeezed down on me. She took hold of my arms and pressed and I felt a burning sensation as the angel Duffy turned into a witch from hell as she began inserting twenty stitches. I felt every one.

What made the pain worse was the fact that the weight of my muscle was pulling the two sides apart as quickly as they tried to re-join them. The pleasure of that young woman's breasts disappeared immediately.

I tried not to struggle and didn't cry once. Brave boys didn't cry then. Instead I kept letting out strangled gasps as I tried not to cause a fuss. I always tried not to make a fuss.

Half way through the agony my mum arrived. She couldn't have entered from a worse direction. The door to the treatment room opened directly onto a view of my half stitched leg. She clasped a hand to her mouth as she felt the horror. Mum understood that her maternal duty was to show no reaction and to be brave for me so she smiled but I saw the lie.

"I'm alright. I'm alright mum! Honest I am."

I took hold of her hand as if I were the adult with the strength to reassure her. At least I'd had time to get used to the situation. She had had no warning of how badly hurt I was. We began talking and my mum took over the job of stopping any movements although in practice I kept myself under control very well. I tried to make mum laugh. That was the way I dealt with things. I laughed.

She looked so young, rather like my daughter does now and I was so sorry for causing her such pain. My mum was beautiful and her smile lit up my world. I was so grateful for her bravery. I knew she wanted to cry. I wanted to cry. Neither of us did.

Before I knew it they'd finished.

"Good boy Philup."

"He's a good boy," my mother beamed.

"Yes he's a very brave young man. Always has been. Right Philup. You just rest there now until the doctor comes down to see yer. I just need to have a word with yer mum. Ok?"

I didn't know it but the basis of the conversation was that my injury was very serious and they wanted to keep me in for bed rest. There was a serious danger that the stitches wouldn't hold in my soft skin causing it to tear. Unfortunately they hadn't got a bed available so I was allowed home on the condition that I had complete rest. The next morning, after my parents had left for work, I got dressed and put on the sock that had been on my cut leg the previous day. A nurse had washed it in casualty. I felt something in the foot of my sock as I drew it on. I took it off and put my hand in to remove the offending object. It was a piece of my own body fat. I held it in my hand between forefinger and thumb, looking at it in wonderment. I was not alarmed in any way. In fact an understanding of how unpleasant this was only became apparent to me much later in life. I was engrossed and fascinated and turned it round, examining it from all ends before throwing it onto the coal fire that burned brightly in the hearth. I listened to myself sizzling in the heat. I watched it glow and then fade to ash. I remember thinking that that's what must happen when you die and they burn you.

"One minute you're here and then you're gone."

Part of me was gone. They weren't pleasant thoughts. After a while I broke free from the hypnotic effect of the fire and finished dressing.

Both my mother and father worked full time so I was unsupervised during the day. At thirteen I was never going to rest as the hospital required. I didn't understand the meaning of the word. They would have had to tie me down to get bed rest. They didn't and I suffered grievous consequences that have lasted all my life.

I was a very conscientious young man and I didn't want to have my mum and dad go out to work all day, and then have to care for me when they came home as well as doing the housework. This was not the first time I had suffered a serious injury and I was very aware that I placed a great strain on both my parents.

I resolved to do as much housework as I could to reduce the burden on my parents and to ease my guilt. One morning I began cleaning the bathroom. As I hopped along and sprayed the Vim into the bath I suddenly felt a sharp burning sensation beneath the bandages. I couldn't quite make it out but it was significant enough to stop my movement immediately. I stood there trying to understand what it meant. I was bent double over the bath, in shock, cloth in hand. Then the sensation seemed to stop. I calmed down and bent over to finish the bath when I felt my leg explode. I gasped and my body shook from head to toe.

I was very scared and had no means of summoning help.

I dropped the Vim and cloth and left them lying on the floor. I hopped, in excruciating pain, back to my seat. The warm glow of the fire did not ease my terror. I was alone and didn't know what to do. I was frightened of whatever was happening to me and even more frightened of telling my dad. Had I been naughty again? Had I been stupid? All I'd done was to try and help. I fell into the chair grasping its sides as my head arched backwards and my chest heaved rapidly. I lay there, with my foot raised on a stool, trying to work out what to do. Thankfully the pain eased and eventually, exhausted, I fell asleep. I slept all day and only awoke as my parents opened the front door. They were good people and I couldn't bear to frighten them. I smiled as they came in.

"Everything OK?"

"Yes mum," I lied.

"Oh the fire's gone out. Aren't you cold?"

"I hadn't noticed".

"You've not eaten your sandwiches I left you."

"I wasn't hungry."

I was starving.

"Are you alright? You look very pale."

"I'm tired mum that's all."

"You're bound to be. You've been badly hurt."

She smiled and kissed me. I desperately wanted to cry out; to tell them. As the sleep fell from my eyes the pain began to creep up my leg. It was throbbing but I didn't want to cause a fuss. I didn't want to alarm them. I was desperate not to be a burden.

By eight o'clock I was in bed. By six the next morning I was in casualty.

I had woken up in the early hours and could bear it no longer. I cried out.

"Mum!"

My dad, whose stern manner disguised his caring nature, was there in an instant.

"What's up?"

I could hardly speak. Dad pulled back the bedding. Blood was seeping through to the outer layers of the bandages. We both gasped together.

"Joan!"

"What?"

"I'll have to go and phone for the ambulance."

My dad carried me downstairs paying no attention to my apologies. He placed me strongly and tenderly onto the chair and placed another as a support under my raised leg. He left without saying a word. All my efforts to avoid being a burden had come to nothing. I felt awful but I felt even worse when they took off the bandages.

I spent the next five weeks visiting hospital on a daily basis. Every day they rubbed copper sulphate crystals over the half healed wound that could not be re-stitched. The scar is now an inch wide in some places and I was off school for 9 weeks.

Mum cleaned the bath.

Chapter 3 Back Again

Nine weeks later I walked out of Casualty with a big grin on my face. I had just been discharged and I returned home, in a state of elation, to get myself ready for school and friends. Tuesday woke as a beautiful December day despite the grey drizzle. I was free, free from crutches, from the confines of the house and from the total boredom and social isolation I had endured.

No one warned me that my happiness would be short lived. If they'd warned me it wouldn't have happened. I needed some protection, some advice, but received none.

No one warned me.

No one warned me that my leg was weak. No one said, "Take it easy. Build your strength up. You haven't walked properly for weeks, months.

No one warned me.

Next morning I went to the top of Lugsmore Lane to catch the bus to school. The lane rises up a short but steep gradient onto Prescot Road, which is the major dual carriageway link between St. Helens and Liverpool. The drizzle had now turned into heavy rain. I saw the bus coming and ran across the road in order to catch it. I was a good lad. I had the sense to look both ways before crossing. I checked the traffic. I was safe. I knew I could make it and set off. Before I got half way across my ankle gave way. I fell prostrate over the central white line with traffic hurtling towards me. I got up and tried to get across to the other side. The pain shot up the full length of my leg before returning down once more to my ankle. I was in agony. I hopped across the far carriageway before spreading my hands out onto the wall as I collapsed against it. I looked for help but no one had seen me in the darkness of morning. I knew I had to get to hospital. I hopped and limped to the bus stop using the wall for support. Somehow I managed to climb aboard the bus. Once more I didn't want to cause a fuss. I sat in a seat, bent double as my right hand tried to stop the pulsating sensation in my ankle. Again I didn't cry. I sat there willing the bus into the town centre.

"Threepenny please," I said to the conductress.

"Are you alright?"

"Yes thanks." I banged my ankle. I'll be OK"

She nodded and carried on collecting fares as the bus ploughed through large puddles on its way to town.

Eventually we arrived at the terminus. I waited for everyone to leave before getting off the bus, grabbing each rail as I walked to the rear exit. I had become used to hopping on my left foot but now each time I moved, my right thumped with pain. Pathetically and damply I inched the half a mile to the hospital using walls for support. The rain was beating down and I was now wet through. Water dripped from the brim of my school cap and onto my nose. It ran in rivulets down my cheeks.

As I squelched my way to Casualty no one came to my aid. I staggered through the outer green gates I had left so happily only the day before and hopped 50 yards past the rose beds that offered as little support as the people I had just passed. I entered onto the main corridor that led to Sister Duffy's kindness but it now seemed more out of reach than ever. I felt sick and my head was spinning. I could barely stay upright but somehow made it to the blue inner doors of the treatment room whereupon I collapsed in a dishevelled heap.

My Irish heroine opened the door.

"Oh Philup whatever next?'

A pair of strong arms belonging to a porter swept me up on to a trolley.

I lay there alone and in agony. They examined me, X-rayed me, bandaged me and returned me home in an ambulance. It wasn't one of those posh Princesses that had borne me in so regally ten weeks earlier. It was a basic mini bus used for ferrying outpatients to and from home. I sat upright as my ankle throbbed. I don't remember any painkillers. I never ever had painkillers.

When my parents came home from work that evening they were greeted by the same pair of crutches that I had been using for the previous nine weeks. They stood in the doorway, mouths open in disbelief, as I explained to them what had happened. I left out all the details about my struggle to get to the hospital. There was no point in causing them any further distress. I was off school for another two weeks and as a result of both injuries missed nearly a full term of school.

There has never been a day when I don't think back to the moment my shin hit the wall. Each time I do, my right hand involuntarily grasps my right shin in a vain attempt to stop the bleeding that no longer occurs. Nevertheless the feeling of panic is always real. My leg still hurts and I can't forget.

The injury didn't just affect me physically. From that instant when I first saw the blood trickling down my leg and felt the hot, sharp, tearing pain as my skin separated from the bone, my character changed. No one understood it at the time but my personality was as traumatised as my shin and it would take many years and many more injuries before I began to come to terms with the damage I have suffered.

I have had several serious and unpleasant injuries since then including cuts requiring 200 stitches; dislocated knee caps; ruptured knee ligaments; a dislocated shoulder; a broken scaphoid bone; two broken metatarsals and a displaced base of my spine, but those nine weeks were the worst period of my life.

Until now.

Part 2

Until Now

Chapter 4 The Ladders

There is a saying, "There is no such thing as bad weather only bad clothing". I enjoy all types of weather. I find it relaxing to walk in the rain, invigorating to cycle in the sun.

Spring is full of hope. Everything is fresh and the lengthening days peel the sleep of winter off a weary nature. In summer I enjoy moving slowly dressed in cool linen shirts and trousers. I sit, sometimes for hours, in our garden and watch house martins sweeping over my head in the fading light of evening.

I love the misty mornings of autumn. A mixture of bright orange or burgundy leaves still hang on the trees whilst those that have fallen provide a soft carpet to walk on.

Walking through frostbitten fields lit by the broadening rays of a pink sun as it shines a path to some distant hedge is one of the delights of winter.

I love the brightness of the snow and the comfort of warm clothing denying the crisp chill in the air. It takes me back to childhood. I feel safe, like a baby in a shawl.

The Christmas lights fastened to our garage weatherboard illuminated the dark nights of early winter. I love the Christmas period but in 2008 it nearly killed me.

We had had a fantastic time. Both our mothers and our eldest son, Robert, had spent the whole holiday period with us. Boxing Day had seen Andrew, our youngest, and his wife Kim bring their two little ones Maia and Violet to visit. Sarah, our eldest, with her brood of six had added to the pleasant confusion.

It was a very busy but extremely cheerful time. Two days

later we had spent an entertaining afternoon with Sam, our friend and her family, drinking and playing some card games. Between then and New Year's Eve we returned our mothers to their homes across the Pennines and, on my return, relaxed a little with Robert. All three of us saw in the New Year with a traditional Lancashire hot pot garnished with pickled red cabbage.

Andrew and his family came once more on New Year's Day. Maia was then a delicate, highly intelligent and beautiful two year old, whilst Violet was almost as big as her at eight months. Maia, quiet and reserved, makes me smile. Violet is the more outgoing and makes me laugh. They fill my life with joy. Then, all too soon, it was time for them to leave. As evening drew in the blue Ford Focus powered over the small bridge that separates our house from the main road. It turned left and moved away along the road that runs parallel to our house as two little hands waived their goodbyes.

Linda went inside immediately to get out of the cold but I walked up to the road and stood there, staring at the trail of exhaust fumes clearly visible through the rear lights that shone like fading Christmas lights in the damp evening air. I smiled at images of my grandchildren who were probably already asleep, lulled by the sound of the engine and the warmth of the heater.

Suddenly my gratitude and happiness were overtaken by a deep melancholy as I reflected on the fact that their departure signalled the end of a wonderful Christmas holiday and the descent towards February. I felt a chill and turned to follow Linda into the house, making a note to take down the bright lights that mocked my depression.

"Do you want a cup of tea?" This was Linda's stock response to such situations. It usually solved all problems but not this time. I shook my head.

"I'm going to sort out the garage," I said.

"What, now?" Linda asked as she looked at the clock that was showing 4.00pm.

"Now's as good a time as any, I need to sort some things out. I won't be long" I stood in the doorway trying to smile at her. I felt that doing something useful, if only for ten minutes would lift my mood and stop me moping about. Little did I know that those ten minutes would ruin the entire year.

I walked outside. The darkness of night had closed in. Our white double garage stood before me bathed in orange, green and red lights. I lifted the large, red, metal doors overhead. The mechanism groaned with age and effort, as did I. The fluorescent tubes flickered on and off and back on again as they warmed up. Some of them didn't respond at all and left the garage in half-light.

"I must replace some of these tubes," I thought to myself. That same thought had entered my head, every time I had opened the doors in the darkness of winter, for the last five years but I had never managed to do anything about it. As I entered and surveyed the chaos and confusion that lay before me a dead tube suddenly burst into life. The increased light confirmed my fears that maybe this was a bigger job than I had estimated. It was going to take several hours to clear this mess.

A wiser man would have decided to leave it to another day but my mood would not release me. I had to do something. Undaunted, I began. I was only going to take ten minutes

24

but the garage is large. In front of me and down the entire length of the right wall stood four workbenches that I had rescued from Linda's school. They were sturdy but had been deemed surplus to requirements when the school's laboratories were refurbished. They were full of tools, half closed toolboxes and all kinds of rubbish. I put the tools into the boxes and the boxes onto shelves. It made no impression. I got a black bin bag and filled it with paper. A second bag was filled with broken plant pots, old compost and dead plants. These should have gone on the compost heap but I wasn't walking round there in the failing light and I was desperate to make some headway into the still undisturbed mountain. My initial enthusiasm was beginning to wane but I reasoned, it was better than watching some of the drivel that passed for entertainment on television. I pressed on. A half hour later five full bags waited collection by the dustman. I now started to sweep the floor that could now be seen clearly beneath my feet. I sprinkled some water to stop the dust billowing everywhere. As I swept I noticed some larger lumps of dust. On closer inspection they turned out to be rat droppings. I had seen one or two around the place and suspected that they might have nested in the relative warmth of the garage. This confirmed it. I swept the entire floor very carefully and mopped the section where I found the droppings with disinfectant. "I'll do the rest tomorrow," I thought. "It'll soon be tea-time." I had already spent over an hour there and was beginning to feel the cold.

I placed a set of ladders up against the large shelves that were suspended from the ceiling and ran along the back wall. I turned to look at a number of children's electrically powered cars that were stacked on top of each other. These were substantial vehicles that occupied a considerable corner of the internal space. I intended to free this area by lifting a couple of the smaller ones onto the large shelves that lay above me. I stood there working out the practicalities of moving them on my own. It was a ridiculous idea. Just then the ladders slipped making a terrible clattering noise.

" Whoops," I said to myself.

"I didn't set them at the right angle. It just goes to show how easy it is to make a mistake," I said to myself. "You could do yourself some serious damage falling off one of them."

I moved the ladders to the area where I intended to put the cars.

"Do you want a cup of tea?"

"Yes please love. I'll be in, in a minute. I'm finishing now."

The sound of Linda's voice in the loneliness of that place was most pleasing.

I now wanted to get out of there but decided to finish this last job. I picked up the smallest vehicle. It was a green and yellow tractor designed to carry just one child and I began to climb the ladder. I swung my right arm over, placing the tractor on the shelf. I paused for a second before stretching to push it further on to ensure that it didn't fall off.

Then it happened.

The ladder moved. It slipped in exactly the same way I had just witnessed moments earlier. Evidently in my rush to finish I had not understood the implications of what I had seen. The ladder juddered and stopped. I clung to it for dear life, relieved that it hadn't fallen the full way to the ground as it had previously. My mind raced. For a nano second I thought I was safe but before I could do anything the ladder slipped off the shelf completely, twisting as it fell and hurled me some four or five feet to the left. I ended up facing the door that had just been behind me. The noise of the crash was frightening. As metal ladders hit wood and concrete they also contrived to smash a fluorescent tube. It sounded like a bomb had gone off.

I hit the floor and bounced with a considerable force that propelled me forward so that my legs hit something. My first sensation was of a very sharp pain in my left forearm. For a second I thought I'd burst the skin as I had on my shin when I was thirteen but as quickly as this pain appeared it was replaced by an awful, sickening, massive dull ache below my waist. I knew I was badly injured and realized immediately that I was in danger. I screamed the loudest scream of my life. I shouted Linda's name just once. I knew there would be no point in shouting again. If she hadn't heard that she wouldn't hear anything else. I thought, "If she doesn't come I could be here for hours." I spat out blood from my mouth and saw that I was lying in the rat shit I had just swept up. It was as if I had placed the filth deliberately, as if I had calculated the trajectory of my fall and placed the droppings there to cushion the blow. I spat again and again. I didn't want an infection. I tried to shout but had no strength. As my head descended towards the rat shit I was conscious that a cloud of white dust was falling on me. The poisonous chemicals from the fluorescent tube had found me and were covering me in a white shroud.

I was lying alone on a cold concrete floor in total darkness covered in poison with my head lying in rat shit.

"Is this it?" I thought to myself. "I'm a man of culture. I enjoy music and literature. I have spent my life educating others. I sing in a choir. I have loved a beautiful woman and have a wonderful, loving family.

Is this it?"

I thought I was dying.

I thought to myself "I'm in deep shit" and then half laughed at the realization that I actually was.

Just then I heard Linda shout as she ran towards me.

"Philip, are you alright?"

I thought to myself, "Do I fucking look alright?"

"Yes. Yes. I think so. I think I'm alright"

I knew I wasn't but I hoped I was. Deep down I knew I'd broken something, my pelvis probably. The pain was high in my leg but it travelled down to my ankle. What was worse, I couldn't tell which leg was hurt. Maybe I had broken both. It felt like the worst toothache possible magnified to the size of my legs. As I tried to push my body off the floor, to re-assure Linda and, not least myself, my lower half didn't move. I did not let Linda know this.

"Shall I phone an ambulance?"

"No wait a minute I think I'm just winded."

Of course if I had been winded I wouldn't have been able to speak but that was the only way I could describe it. My legs had been winded. They'd had the stuffing knocked out of them. Then I made one more attempt to move. The pain told me to stop and I had to admit defeat.

"You'd better phone an ambulance."

Linda ran for the phone. I don't know how long she was gone, maybe seconds, but I have never felt so lonely or so frightened. I vaguely remember Linda giving our details to the operator. I tried not to hear her say,

"I think he's broken both his legs."

I could feel my strength ebbing away as my head touched the concrete once more. I no longer cared about the rats. Not for the first time in my life I thought, "I'm in serious trouble." I kept apologizing to Linda.

"You're going to have to do all the running around. I'm so sorry."

She just kept saying, "Don't worry. There's no need to apologize."

I tried to raise myself up but immediately felt nauseous and had to put my head down again. My whole body felt numb, except for my leg which still hurt. It was a very strange experience. I apologized to Linda yet again. I suppose I felt the need to keep talking but I hadn't got anything to say.

"Wow it hurts." My stilted words were set to a backing track of an ambulance's siren.

"It's coming." I said to myself. "I can last another 5 minutes." I didn't let Linda know I was thinking this.

"Soon be OK" I smiled at Linda but I can't remember if she smiled back. She was strangely quiet. I wondered if she was thinking about the insurance money and how she was going to spend it.

"I'm sorry." I whispered again. I was conscious that I sounded a little pathetic.

The siren stopped. Tyres crackled over stones and the garage was illuminated by a soft blue light.

"The ambulance is here."

Linda got up to go and greet them. In her absence I again felt very lonely even though she was only away for seconds. I could hear people talking about me and not to me.

"Evening sir. Now what have you been doing?"

"Fell off ladder. Sorry"

"Where does it hurt?"

"Legs. Awful pain."

I was aware that I was talking in short, sharp sentences as I struggled to get my breath. I realized my body was going into shock.

"OK sir I need you just to take some slow deep breaths."

I had been holding myself up for a while but my arms were getting tired and began to shake uncontrollably.

" Right what's your name?"

"Philip" Sister Duffy's "Philup" suddenly entered my head.

"OK Philip I need you to lie down and rest."

The paramedic guided me down to the floor as something was put under my head. As he examined me he carried on talking, trying to reassure me.

I apologized for the filthy state of the garage. I couldn't stop apologizing.

"I've been in a lot worse than this" he smiled as his hands travelled up and down my body. I'm a qualified first aider so I knew what he's doing. He was feeling for lumps, protrusions, anything that shouldn't be there and anything I hadn't told him about. If he found something I'd not noticed it could be dangerous but luckily the injuries seemed confined to my legs. I did not like being on the receiving end of something I was trained to do to others.

As he finished his examination another blue light appeared in the room and any trace of the night disappeared. Outside two more voices talked about me and not to me then a woman who was obviously in charge spoke.

"Right Philip we need to get your trousers off."

I smiled as I thought "I haven't had a woman say anything like that to me in years."

Before I knew it she was cutting my trousers open with a huge pair of scissors that advanced up my trouser leg heading straight for my testicles. I was just about to shout, "Hang on a minute!" when they veered away towards my waistline.

Suddenly the trousers were off and the medics knelt down comparing my thighs. The man said,

"Mmm, looks like you might have broken your femur mate."

I looked down but couldn't see any difference between the thighs. I tried to work out what it was they were looking at but they looked the same to me. Then I thought to myself, "That's funny I don't feel cold any more," followed by "That's funny, my leg doesn't hurt as much." When I asked why I was told, "We gave you an injection of morphine a couple of minutes ago."

I hadn't noticed.

"We'll have to pull you clear of all this rubbish on the floor Philip. Then we can lift you onto the trolley. OK?"

"OK."

"How are you feeling?"

"Fine." Morphine is wonderful stuff. I could tell that I was badly hurt but the pain had gone.

They pulled me clear and lifted me onto the trolley. Morphine couldn't disguise the pain that this caused. Gloved hands put a mask on me and administered oxygen and then the crew wheeled me out of the garage. There was a strange mix of colours. Orange red and green Christmas lights mixed with the flashing blue of the emergency lights as I headed to the yellow interior of the ambulance. I felt the trolley bang over the one-inch lip of concrete where the garage floor met the outside yard. Worse was to come. The flat concrete ended and transformed into a gravel covered driveway. The trolley's wheels dug in and it jarred and jolted its way to the ambulance. I felt that movement as well. I was dreading being lifted into the ambulance. I imagined swaying in mid air before banging onto the ambulance's floor but instead an electrically operated platform guided my stretcher noisily but gently into the back of the vehicle.

There are no street lights in this remote area of Humberside and the rear of the ambulance shone out like a stage in a theatre. It was quite dramatic. I was dimly aware of a small audience. Our neighbours were standing on the other side of the fence. Their's is the only house within 300 yards of ours. Linda was explaining to them what had happened. I could see the distinctive outline of Robert's head. He had just arrived home from work to be greeted by this mess. I apologized to him. He took hold of my hand. I squeezed his and was conscious of how weak my grip was.

"I think I need to get to hospital."

"I'll bring mum."

"OK."

With that I passed out.

Shock, exhaustion and morphine must have combined to knock me out. I noticed little of the 15 mile journey to Hull Royal Infirmary apart from asking the ambulance man to give me the second shot of morphine he had said was available if needed. They stopped the ambulance because the driver was the only one qualified to administer it. She opened the rear door. Cars slowed warily before passing, their pulsing blue outlines reflected in one of the side windows.

Finally we arrived at Hull Royal Infirmary. I was dimly aware of being wheeled into casualty and lying there waiting to be seen. After a few minutes Linda and Robert arrived from the car park. "Hello!" I beamed as if I hadn't seen them in weeks. Then I apologized once more.

The smiling faces of two very young and very pretty radiographers dragged a portable X-ray machine around me. I couldn't always see the activity as nurses and doctors and other unspecified categories of staff swirled about me but I could hear it. People whom I did not know smiled at me and then disappeared to be replaced by others. I seemed to be smiling continuously-probably the effect of the morphine. I knew my leg was badly hurt and my body was in pain but I no longer felt it. Everything seemed a little distant, a little removed. I began to worry about all the smiles.

"It's not natural. Perhaps they're hiding something."

Then a young man in a white coat spoke to me. He seemed as young as the radiographers but was nowhere near as pretty.

"Hello Mr. Howard. The x-rays show that you have a fracture of your left thigh-bone."

I smiled.

"OK"

It didn't occur to me that this was serious. I had no understanding of what was to happen nor did I care. As far as I was concerned it was just another addition to the catalogue of injuries I had suffered. The doctors would fix it and I'd be on my way.

Then something really serious happened. Another doctor asked if he could cut my t-shirt off. I consented but as he lifted the bottom of the shirt I realized that this was impossible. This shirt was a sacred garment. Some years ago my home town rugby league team annihilated our arch enemies Wigan by seventy-five points to nil. It was a wonderful, once in a lifetime, ridiculous day. To commemorate it the club produced black t-shirts with the score and the scorers etched on it in gold letters. There was no way that I would let this be cut.

"I shall keep this all my life. I even want it with me in my coffin."

Then I thought, "Actually that might not be that far off."

The doctor laughed as Robert and Linda held me up whilst I took it off. Linda smiled at me. She also had one of these shirts and understood perfectly. I was so grateful to both of them but the effort of taking it off exhausted me and once more I passed out.

Chapter 5 Emergency Ward 9

I was vaguely aware of being in a lift. I couldn't work out where I was going and couldn't gather myself to talk to the staff. I passed light after light, mounted in the ceiling. Doors opened and shut and the noise of movement echoed in my head.

"One two lift!" Hands transferred me onto a bed but I couldn't work out to whom they belonged. Suddenly Linda appeared. She looked tired.

"I'm sorry." I smiled at her and waved to Robert. My wave consisted of a slight movement of my right hand devoid of energy.

"I'll come and see you tomorrow."

"Wh..Where am I?"

"In the ward. You're safe."

"What's happening?"

"Ssh, go to sleep. I'll see you in the morning."

They said their goodbyes but I was asleep before they had gone through the ward doors.

xxxx

"Tea or coffee dear?"

My eyes dragged themselves open. A ward assistant was standing at the foot of the bed. Staff in all kinds of uniform were busying about.

"Can I have some water please?"

"There's a water jug by your side." I looked round at my unfamiliar surroundings. The woman, dressed in purple covered by a white plastic apron sensed my uncertainty and poured me a glass.

I drank it down in one and gasped with pleasure.

"Tea or coffee?"

"What time is it?"

"Seven o'clock."

"Tea or coffee?"

"Where am I?"

"Ward 9."

She hesitated and added, "Hull Royal Infirmary."

I nodded as I began to realize that all this was real. I was not dreaming. I ran my hand over the limited hair that I still possess.

"Tea or coffee?"

I realized she has asked me this several times. I was very groggy.

"I'm sorry, coffee please."

I always have coffee in a morning. It's tea in the afternoon. I've no idea why.

"It's OK dear. Come in last night did you?"

"Yes. I think so"

I did not know if the night had passed. Did the clock indicate seven in the morning or evening?

"It's all very confusing but you'll get used to it, by the time you leave".

She smiled but it sounded like she'd said this a thousand

times to other patients who have been subdued by painkillers. As she put my drink on my cabinet a shriek from the behind me pierced the air. The man in the bed, next door shouted,

"Oh Jesus!"

The orderly smiled.

"She's started early today."

"Fucking arse hole!"

"Language Bill!"

The bald headed man apologized but did not mean it. The woman cried again.

"Nurse, I want a cup of tea."

"Coming Agnes!"

"Nurse!"

"Oh for fuck's sake!"

The man hid beneath his bedding. The orderly turned to me and confided, "This used to be a lovely ward when it was a man's ward. They don't cause a fuss but women…" She shook her head in disgust as she went round the partition to give Agnes a drink. This was all too much for me. I couldn't absorb all this information, amusing as it might have been. Fortunately, the painkillers brought me peace once more.

I became aware of an Asian man standing at the bottom of my bed smiling. Others accompanied him but he was obviously the man in charge. I thought immediately of my cup of coffee but it had long since gone.

"Mr. Howard?"

I tried to speak but was too dry. A nurse poured me a glass and everyone waited for me whilst I drank it.

"You slept well?" he asked holding one page of my notes in his left hand. He was short and slim and immaculately dressed in a navy blue suit, white shirt and red tie. I never look immaculate no matter how hard I try and I definitely didn't look good at that moment. I hated him already but I was impressed by his style. I nodded. He introduced himself but as soon as he said his name I had forgotten it.

"I am in charge of your case. Tomorrow we shall operate. You have broken your femur and we need to pin it. How is the pain?"

"OK."

"Good. I'll see you tomorrow."

I thought to myself, "I bet I don't. I bet I'm unconscious. I bloody hope I'm unconscious."

Then I felt a twinge of fear. Suddenly after talking about the pain I started to feel some. How can any pain be OK? I realized that it was all in my mind and I needed to take control of myself.

"After all it's not as if I'm going to die. Am I?"

I felt overpowered by the situation I was in. What exactly were they going to do tomorrow? What did pinning involve? I imagined that they would attach a plate to the outside of my bone and screw them onto the sides. I found out later that this view was way off the mark but for the moment it didn't matter. Before I could worry myself further, the painkillers took over once more and I passed out.

I woke up. I tried to work out how long I had been in hospital. I thought I had been lying flat on my back for two days but was not certain. The ward was on the eleventh floor. I looked out of the windows to my left. All I could see was a depressingly grey January sky.

I would like to describe the people who occupied the four-bed bay with me but I can't remember any of them. I must have been unconscious for most of the time and hardly remember a thing about the first three days due to a combination of morphine and painkillers. Linda says that she came to see me and I lay there asleep, only waking up as she got up to leave.

At eleven o'clock staff came to take me to theatre. I have endured many surgical procedures and have never been bothered by any of them. I have always just got on with it but as I left the ward I was filled with a sudden, awful sense of foreboding. I was really frightened.

"Perhaps I'm getting old," I thought to myself.

"Perhaps the drugs are playing with my mind," I reassured myself.

They disturbed my bedding when they lifted me onto the theatre trolley. I saw for the first time the extent of my injury. My left thigh was twice the size of the right and was black and blue.

"Perhaps I'm really badly hurt," I thought to myself.

'Oh Jesus !"

"It's a good one," the nurse smiled cheerily.

'Don't worry we'll have you back in no time."

I glanced at the clock and noted that it was 11.30am as I

left the ward.

The nurse chatted pleasantly as the trolley's rubber tyres squeaked along the corridor but I can't remember anything about what she said. A man in a green gown and mask received me in an ante-room. He smiled. Everybody smiled. As he washed me in iodine I tried to say hello.

I awoke. A nurse was taking my pulse and blood pressure.

"It's OK Philip. Relax. You've had an operation and you're back in the ward now. Everything is OK"

"What time is it?"

I couldn't make out her face but I knew she was looking at her fob watch.

"It's ten to five."

I tried to work out the hours but she did it for me.

"You've been in theatre for over five hours.

"What day is it?"

"Wednesday"

"How long have I been here?"

"You were brought in yesterday."

I passed out.

I woke again. Linda was sat watching me.

"What time is it?" My conversations could not have been described as stimulating.

"It's five to eight. I have to go soon."

I got the feeling that she was annoyed with me. Perhaps she was just very tired. Maybe I was just hypersensitive, feeling guilty about the mess I'd created.

"How long have you been here?"

"An hour."

"Oh."

I meant to say that I was sorry but the message didn't get to my lips.

I woke up. It was dark. I turned to Linda but she wasn't there. I had a foul taste in my mouth and I needed a drink. I fumbled in the darkness for my light switch so that I could see my nurse call unit. I didn't need it. As soon as the light went on, a nurse appeared by my side. Her skin was as dark as the night but her smile lit the room or at least my bed. I was pleased to see her. This was the first real eye-to-eye contact I seemed to have had with anyone since I landed in the rat shit.

"I need some water please." I whispered, aware that others must be asleep. In truth I didn't even know if there was anyone in my bay. I watched this angel of light as she poured me a drink. She lifted my head gently and brought the water to my lips. I was in love. The sensation of her touch was only just less gratifying than the beautiful freshness of the water as it caressed the back of my throat. I felt it go all the way down. Nurse held my head the whole time I drank.

"Would you like some more?"

I was enchanted and wanted to say yes to anything she offered but as she stood there smiling at me my eyes were forced shut once more. I never saw this vision of loveliness again.

"Tea or coffee?"

This time I have been awake for over an hour. It was the beginning of a complete loss of my sleep pattern. This loss would cause me much anguish later but for now I could start to look around me. I watched the staff and began to talk to other patients. Being in hospital was nothing new to me. I have been a patient many times. In truth I quite enjoy being in hospital. Someone looking after me in the softness of a bed light shining in the middle of the night reminds me of my childhood. I remember my mum giving me some medicine to ease a rasping cough. Her sweet words and soft smile always made me feel safe as did the warmth of the cocoon of blankets wrapped round me.

"How many injuries have I had?" I asked myself. I tried to count them but my concentration span was too limited to get through the whole list. Was it twenty, thirty or even forty? I lost count at two. I tried to cheer myself up.

"This is no different to all the other times. I'll deal with this just like I've dealt with all the other injuries I have had. In no time at all I'll be alright"

I could not have been more wrong.

For the present I concerned myself with the immediate situation. I nodded at the other patients, drank my coffee and began to accustom myself to the ward routine. Next morning nurses came round with bowls of water so that those confined to bed could wash themselves. I tried to take off my vest but it was difficult due to the fact that it was soaking wet with sweat. My bedding was also wet. I felt very, very hot. I told the nurse who looked most concerned when she took my temperature. Within minutes two electric fans were blasting cold air at me from cabinets on both sides. It dawned on me that I was breathing through an oxygen mask and saline fluid was being fed into my arm through a drip. Things seemed to happen to me when I wasn't looking.

"The operation went well Mr. Howard." I heard him say as I woke up. I needed a drink again and kept them waiting once more but the whole team that surrounded me was very patient if a little intimidating.

"We are a little concerned that your temperature is very high. We need to avoid an infection." This sounded off an alarm in my head as I thought of the rat droppings but I simply nodded weakly. I felt an overpowering need to shut my eyes. The consultant, smiled kindly.

"We are concerned about your skin colour. You have a ghost like quality about you.

"I'm always pale."

They smiled. The night before Ann and Adam had come from work.

"You look surprisingly well," said Ann. "We thought you'd look much worse."

I thought, "Shit I know I'm pale but they thought I looked well compared to what I normally look like and this guy who doesn't know me at all thinks I look really ill. God I must look really crap on a day-to-day basis. I must look even worse than this."

All through my life people have commented on how pale I am. It's something to do with the Ehlers Danlos syndrome. Because the skin is thin the bones underneath affect its colour. I have a "bony" pallor. Once, when I was working in the Health Service a senior nurse took me into a room and took some blood before I had a chance to consent or object. As always it proved OK. I am not normally anaemic.

I have an image in my head that at some time in the distant future I am being visited by my tearful relatives as I lie in my coffin. I am wearing a grey suit, white shirt and red/orange tie. The undertakers have skilfully touched my face up with blusher. I picture the surprise on my relatives' face as collectively they think, "God he looks better dead than he did alive."

The doctor and his entourage left. I was really grateful for their effort even if I didn't show it.

"Tea or coffee?"

It was morning. I vaguely remembered eating a passable breakfast. Perhaps I'll pass it tomorrow. I smiled but I am aware that I have not used the toilet since, what day is it?

The nurses busied themselves. Blood pressures and temperatures were checked and wash bowls cleared. It was all very efficient and impressive. They changed my bedding and as I moved I was conscious that I was soaking wet again. I felt even hotter than the previous day and the nurse taking my temperature stared at the thermometer.

"How do you feel Philip?"

When people call me Philip I instinctively feel bad. Only my mother, boss and wife call me Philip. It usually means I'm about to be told off. She stood there waiting for my reply, her arm outstretched with thermometer still in hand.

"Not good actually."

"Mmm."

She placed the oxygen mask back over my head.

"You need to keep this on. It will help you breathe"

"Why am I so hot?"

"You've had a nail hammered down the centre of your femur and it's secured by two nuts and bolts at the bottom and two at the top. Infections can occur when the body tries to reject these alien objects. The infection is making your respiratory system work harder, hence the increasing temperature." Then she added, "Your body has been through a significant trauma. You may have difficulty fighting the infection in your weakened state. You must rest."

I dutifully fell asleep.

A young woman whom I thought I recognised from somewhere was standing by my bed.

"I'm a phlebotomist. I've come to take your blood." I immediately thought of a famous sketch from the 1960's entitled "The Blood Donor". In it Tony Hancock exclaims when told that they need a pint, "A pint! That's an armful!"

"I've come to take your blood."

"But I need it." I replied.

She looked at me and smiled uncertainly. Perhaps she'd heard it before. I chuckled to myself as she stuck the needle in my vein and drew out the sample. I was surprised at my ability to alternate between unconsciousness and sharp wit.

"You used to teach me."

"Did I?"

"Yes at Wilberforce College."

"I thought I recognized you."

I don't think she believed me.

"Sociology goes well with phlebotomy," I replied.

"I enjoyed the lessons and I enjoy this so…"

I was asleep before she had finished.

I felt a gentle rocking motion at the same time as I heard her voice. She was slim, blonde and quite pretty. Her name badge said "Michelle".

I couldn't stop falling asleep but was able to wake quite quickly.

"We need to get you out of bed and up and about," she said.

"I thought you said you wouldn't start until Friday?"

"It is Friday."

"Oh."

I tried to work out where the time had gone but the task was too intellectually demanding. She and her assistant, a young man, peeled back the bed covers gently. My left thigh looked like it belonged to a Samoan rugby player. It was huge, even bigger than before.

I gasped.

"It's OK"

"Why is it so big?"

"You've had a very serious operation".

I didn't know if I found this explanation re-assuring or not.

"It's also quite a brutal one. They hammer the nail down the centre of your bone. There's no finesse about it. All they do is hit the nail, then take an X-ray to see that it's in the right place before they hit it again and so on."

"Oh."

I was grateful for her explanation but was left speechless.

"Don't worry it'll go down and it'll go down all the quicker if we get you moving."

I obeyed her every word. She took hold of my leg with a grace and a strength that belied her slight build. Michelle held my ankle and as I slid to the edge of the bed she let it drop slowly to the floor. I hadn't sat up properly for three days. Then whilst I was sat there getting myself ready, this little girl commanded me to stand. I obeyed unquestioningly, full of trepidation. Their hands clasped my arms and steadied me as her assistant slipped a Zimmer frame into my hands. I grabbed the bar without hesitation but thought

"It's a Zimmer frame, bloody hell; if my students could see this…"

The physiotherapists walked me to the edge of the bed and I ventured into the middle of the ward. I now knew what Christopher Columbus must have felt like, stuck in the middle of an ocean far from safety. If they had left me I'd have been lost. Michelle told me to turn and I did. I was aware of a number of faces, patients and nurses watching me. I hadn't really noticed my fellow patients but I knew they had changed since I came in. I could sense that they were willing me to make it as I moved back towards safety.

I sat on the edge of my bed and she lifted my leg back up onto it.

"Well done Philip"

I was so grateful for her praise. It was the first time I'd felt that I was fighting back.

"I'll see you tomorrow." I nodded and as she left I noticed the clock on the wall. It was 9.15am. I sat there thinking about the scale of my achievement. I was pleased but suddenly felt very tired.

"Tea or coffee?"

An eye opened and looked at the clock. It was 12.30pm. The walk must have exhausted me. I fell asleep without answering her.

I awoke.

I checked the clock in the dimness of the night lights but I couldn't make it out.

"Why are the night lights on?" I asked myself.

I fumbled for my glasses and then fumbled with improved vision for my mobile and pressed a button. It lit up to reveal that it was 5.30 am but I didn't know what day it was. I could hear nurses at their station busying themselves. They were chatting and laughing.

"They weren't this busy yesterday," I thought to myself, not certain as to when yesterday actually was. Uniforms rubbed against curtains drawn around the next bed to me and there was a flurry of activity.

"One two three lift."

Someone, singular or plural grunted and gasped and then, suddenly all was quiet again. I wondered what could have happened to the man in the bed next to me. It was very early in the morning to be admitted to the ward. His accident must have happened around two or three in the morning. Was he a drunk driver?

"Probably a bloody boy racer," I muttered to myself, angry that my disturbed sleep had just been disturbed.

"Serves him bloody right," I said to myself with righteous indignation before I returned to sleep. In the morning I discovered that Dennis was an 83 year old ex policeman who fell over his cat when he went to the toilet and he too had broken his femur.

"Tea or coffee?"

"Coffee please."

"You didn't drink it yesterday did you?"

"No."

"You didn't eat your breakfast either."

I smiled uncertainly.

"Do you want breakfast?"

"Yes please."

I didn't feel very hungry but I made myself eat most of it. We washed and shaved and the nurses changed my bedclothes, which were still wringing wet in the morning. At nine, two physiotherapists arrived. Katherine was all smiles with a seductive Irish lilt that captivated me immediately. She was Sister Duffy re-incarnate but better looking.

"Right Philup, we need to get you up. How are yer?"

"I'm fine thanks."

Plainly I was not but this was the most alert I had been since I arrived three, or was it four days ago?

"What day is it?"

"Sunday."

"I didn't know you worked Sundays." She smiled as she busied herself in preparation.

"We work all the time. We never go home." She smiled. I smiled.

"Now Philup. So far you've walked to the edge of the bed with Michelle?"

"Yes."

"Well today let's see if you can go further but not too much mind?"

"No."

She lowered my leg to the floor and I stood up to meet the Zimmer. Katherine and her assistant, the same young man who had accompanied Michelle stood to my side and rear as I began my steps. I got to the end of the bed and before I knew it, I was venturing out into the uncharted depths of the middle of the ward.

"Take it steady now," said Katherine. "How do yer feel?"

I told her that I felt fine and continued onwards to the other side of the ward. I was surprised at my powers of recovery and for a brief moment felt almost superhuman. I was so

51

pleased with myself.

"Well we don't want to overdo it, so turn back round now."
I obeyed but turning round was more difficult than I had
anticipated. I was slow and awkward and it took a lot of
effort. I turned round like a cumbersome Spanish galleon
and then headed for home. Just as I started to enjoy my
moment of triumph the consequences of dragging a leg
twice its normal girth began to take hold. I stopped dead,
gasping for breath. My head bowed forward as strong
hands grabbed me on either side. My head was swimming
and I couldn't focus. I sensed that other staff had come to
my aid but couldn't see them. I heard the noise of an easy
chair being dragged towards me and was only too pleased
to be pushed down into it. My legs could not support me at
all. I passed out for a moment and was brought round by
her soft dulcet tones.

"Now come on Philup. Can you hear me now?"

Her voice was sweet and gentle but in complete control. I
obeyed and woke up.

"You did a bit too much, now?"

"Yes."

"Well it was still good. You did very well."

After a minute or two they helped me into bed. I lost a
whole day. I didn't notice visiting time and I didn't
remember teatime. I lay in my bed trying to work things
out. I was completely disorientated. Time flew whilst I
slept and passed very slowly when I was awake.

It was mid-morning. I must have fallen asleep again. I
began to talk with the other patients. Ali came in yesterday.
He's English with Somalian parents. He was born over

here and talked with a southern accent, probably London. Once you get past Watford they all sound the same to me. He was tall, lean and muscular but it didn't stop his falling off a stool whilst trying to adjust an aerial. He landed awkwardly and broke both his tibia and fibula. I just managed to hear the doctor saying, "Do you lift heavy weights at work?"

Ali nodded a "yes" and the doctor said,

"Well you'll have to find another job I'm afraid," and abruptly left. Ali was left shocked and bewildered. To the doctor it was just another procedure; to Ali it meant the disappearance of his livelihood. He was a big young man with an innocent's face. He looked at me and shook his head. I nodded in support but could do nothing. I had problems of my own.

"Tea or coffee?"

"What time is it?"

" It's lunch-time." I ate a really good meal. In fact I devoured it. I have no complaints about hospital food although I am easy to please. I'll eat anything and I do think people are too fussy. I always enjoyed school dinners and was always up for seconds. Now I had a second helping of pudding. I love apple crumble and was really hungry.

"Such hunger must be a sign of recovery," I thought to myself but they kept taking my temperature and each time looked with concern at the thermometer. Both fans were still busy at my side. I stared at them, hypnotized by the whirring sound of the blades when it dawned on me that they had removed the oxygen mask and I was no longer on a drip. I hadn't noticed their removal.

I looked at the clock. It was half past one. It would soon be time for afternoon visitors. I knew that Andrew, my youngest offspring was coming to see me and I was really looking forward to it. I was definitely feeling brighter. I chatted to nurses and patients. I read for a bit then I listened to some Classic FM on my mobile phone. The newspaper lady came round. I bought a paper and managed to read it for the first time but I couldn't manage the serious stuff so I limited myself to the sports pages, which described Saturday's events confirming it was now Sunday.

My head fell back on the pillow. I sighed and looked out at the sky, which hadn't changed colour since I came in. It would be nice to walk to the window to look at the view. 'I bet you can see a magnificent view of the Humber Bridge from here,' I thought to myself. I was reminded of another Tony Hancock radio sketch from the 1960's. The show begins in total silence. All you can hear is heavy breathing, followed by sighing and tutting and more sighing. Finally Hancock says "God I hate Sundays," and the audience roars.

I sighed and looked at the clock, which was further down the ward. It was a quarter to two.

"My God!" I exclaimed and woke up Dennis. I apologized. I couldn't believe that time had gone so slowly. I sighed and thought of Hancock. He was right. "I hate Sundays to."

Finally visiting time arrived and people began drifting in. We all nodded politely to each other. I closed my eyes for a second.

"Hello Dad."

Andrew is a lovely lad. All my kids are lovely but he has always been the baby of the family. Now he was standing over me looking strong and protective. I realized how weak I was. We hugged. There is something very re-assuring about him. I saw him differently from this moment on. He was taking control, organizing things. He agreed to get me clothes; bring me fruit; phone friends. I stared weakly in admiration. This was no baby.

Andrew also did it all with a very dry sense of humour that his mother could not muster because she was so exhausted. I realized how much I love him. The time that dragged so slowly before visiting had now flown by. Before I knew it he had left and I was fast asleep. All the energy I felt during his visit lasted no more than half an hour. Laughing and smiling had exhausted me.

I awoke. A young doctor was standing at the foot of the bed reading my notes carefully. He looked at me and smiled seriously.

"Mr. Howard. We have a slight problem."

I love that word "we".

"Your haemoglobin level is very low. It should be between fourteen and seventeen units."

I didn't catch what he said the units were but I understood when he said, "Your blood test shows that your blood count is low, very low."

"That's bad?"

"It's not good but I wouldn't worry. You've had some heavy internal bleeding from the break. It's common when you break the femur. We'll just keep an eye on it. A couple of years ago we'd have given you a blood transfusion when your blood count went below 13 units but we try to avoid that," he said in a matter of fact way.

"We try to avoid it now because we're short of blood and we've found that people can manage on a low count whilst they are not doing much. As well as that a blood transfusion is not without its own risks so we're monitoring you for now. If it goes below eight we'll have to do a transfusion immediately. We start to worry when it gets below eight."

"What is it now?"

"Eight."

I thanked the doctor. I wasn't certain that I liked modern democratic medicine. Did I want to know that I may be in serious shit or would I rather carry on in sweet ignorant bliss until the consequences hit me?

Next day I was taken to the X-Ray Department.

"We need to check the position of the nail, to make sure it's seated properly in the bone," said a nurse I had not seen before. She smiled a very young, authoritative smile and suddenly I felt very old and weak. The people who were in charge of me were younger than my daughter.

A porter came to collect me in a wheelchair. As we passed the ward office a voice says, "Hello Phil!" I looked at another young and smiling face that belonged to the ward clerk. "You used to teach me at Wilberforce College. Do you remember me?"

"Yes," I lied. I couldn't remember what I had for breakfast.

Actually I did know her but I couldn't recall her name. It seemed a long time since she was in my class. It seemed a long time since I was in work yet it was only a fortnight. We exchanged pleasantries and then I was on my way again. This was the second ex student I had encountered. "You're popular," said the porter. We chatted aimlessly as we entered the lift and rolled to the X-ray department. As we spoke a strange feeling was creeping over me. This was the first time I had been out of the ward and I had a sense of being overpowered by my surroundings. I was on the 'outside', away from the comforts of the ward, away from the safety of my bed, under the control of the porter and the drugs. I had not even seen out of the window. Before I knew it I was being parked in a corridor. The porter left me with the words "Somebody will be out to see you in a minute." I was alone, unable to move and I felt very hot and very tired. My head began to drop but I was stirred by the arrival of a radiographer. She was someone else who was as young and vibrant as I felt tired and weak. She looked at my notes.

"Oh so you're Phil Howard!"

I looked at her bewildered. I definitely didn't recall teaching her and couldn't believe that my name had been recognized yet again. Were there any more people from my past lurking in these corridors? On reflection I decided that there must be. I taught people in a college, which produced educated, trained and skilful people. Many of them will be working in places like this hospital. I couldn't decide whether being recognized was a good feeling or not. I supposed many teachers who have dealt with hundreds of young people in their working life have had this kind of experience. At least mine have been positive, so far.

Seeing all these ex-students brought on a feeling of déjà-vu. It was not the first time I had had a "visitation". On previous occasions I have imagined being in an old folks' home when my carer says something like,

"Do you remember me? You taught me at Wilberforce College. I got an E."

There is an evil pause.

"I should have got a C."

The latex glove slaps on to her hand as she prepares to insert a suppository up my backside.

"Now it's my turn."

Stirred from my thoughts I suddenly realized that the radiographer was waiting for me to reply.

What did she say?

"Oh yes I am Phil Howard. Why?"

"Oh nothing. We've seen your X-rays that's all."

"What about them?"

"Oh nothing, they are just pretty pictures."

I wanted to know what she meant but I was whisked in and out of the X-ray room before I had the chance to pursue an enquiry. She disappeared and I returned to the ward none the wiser.

"What did she mean?"

This was very important to me but by the time I got back in bed exhaustion had crept over me. Before I had a chance to answer my own question I was asleep.

I had a dream. I was in the mortuary on a slab. They were about to carry out a post-mortem. Just as they leaned over my head the doctor says,

"He used to teach me."

Bloody hell! Not another one! Will I go to the Pearly gates and be met by St. Peter saying, "Hello Phil do you remember me. You used to teach me!"

I'm terrified of meeting God.

That afternoon Dennis was taken to theatre for an operation to repair his leg but returned quickly. They had been unable to operate due to the fact that he was on Warfarin to thin his blood. They decided at the last minute that an operation would have been too risky so he had to wait until his blood thickened. This was the second time they had not been able to operate. When he recovered from the anaesthetic this old man was in tears. Ali and I tried to console him but it was difficult to use gentle words effectively when you had to shout them at the recipient from the confines of his bed. Nevertheless he did respond to our kindness and was soon sat up smiling at us.

At about two in the morning another doctor came and took blood. I thought to myself, "If they keep taking blood at this rate I will need a transfusion."

In all my times as a patient in hospital I don't ever remember being visited so many times by so many people. All was not well.

"Good morning Mr. Howard."

Several people were gathered at the bottom of my bed. It was the consultant's ward round.

"Is it morning?"

I tried to work it out. I thought I was getting better. I had certainly felt better apart from the temperature and the fact that my bedding is wet every morning.

I tried to work out what day it was. Was it Monday? That meant I'd been there for nearly a week.

"Mr. Howard, how are you?"

"OK." In truth I was. I felt little pain. The tablets were seeing to that. I was being waited on hand and foot, and leg. I hadn't seen the outside world for a week but it didn't seem to have bothered me too much. I could see the sky. Even if I could have seen the outside world I couldn't have functioned in it. I was in my own little cocoon. I was safe.

"Your temperature is still high but I am pleased that it has come down a little. We'll keep the fans on you and we'll give you some antibiotics just in case. Those last words woke me up.

"Just in case?"

"Just in case your body has had a reaction to the insertion of a nail in your bone. We'll be monitoring you closely but there is no need to worry. We just want to make certain everything is all right. I am more confident now that your recovery will proceed"

A thought did occur. He said he was "more confident that your recovery will now proceed". That means he wasn't that confident before. I closed my eyes and tried not to think too much. I was still very weak and had to place my trust in these people I did not know. He turned to his aides and said something I couldn't hear. He then smiled and took his leave. I went to sleep.

Someone was shaking me gently. My left eye could see that it was my physiotherapist. Physical exercise did not stop despite my temperature problem. My walking on one leg had improved considerably. By the middle of the second week I had acquired a pair of crutches and was walking further everyday. I felt well apart from the fact that I was so hot and I couldn't stay awake.

Perhaps all was not well.

Chapter 6 Suppositories

After my physiotherapy session I fell asleep once more only to be woken by a staff nurse. This time, however she had not come to take my blood pressure or my temperature.

"Hello Philip. Can you remember when you last went to the toilet?

"I haven't since I've been here."

"Have you opened your bowels since your accident?"

"No".

She pulled the same face as she did when she took my temperature. It was a question I had been waiting for and I knew what was coming.

"Right well we need to do something about that. I'll be back soon to give you a suppository OK?"

"OK."

I shrivelled into my bedding.

I had been half expecting it. The same thing happened in 1980 when I ruptured my ligaments in my left knee. I had been bed ridden for over a week and had not moved. I don't remember doing any physiotherapy at all. I realized that I was off colour when the nurse collected my plate after lunch. She looked at it with concern as she walked out. I had hardly eaten a thing. At first they gave me some laxatives that didn't work. The next day they gave me a suppository. Still nothing happened. In the evening my cousin who was a staff nurse in the same hospital, came to visit me. She joked with two of her friends who were working nights on my ward. They had just qualified which meant that they would have been about twenty one. They looked like young girls to me but they didn't appear so about four hours later when I woke up as the combination of laxative and enema took effect in catastrophic manner. I tried to shout "Nurse!" as I grabbed the water jug to be sick in. I was concious that my voice sounded weak and tremulous. These two young girls acted with great speed and professionalism. Neither of them looked more than seven stones in weight but they wrapped their arms round my back and lifted me whilst sliding a bedpan underneath me at the same time. I looked down in horror at what was happening. I could only think of one thing as the shit hit the pan; "Mr. Whippy!"

The sun was shining through the window of the side ward when I woke up. I could see the male staff nurse changing the bedding on the other bed. He looked up and smiled. "How are you?"

"OK," I managed.

"What time is it?"

"It's a quarter past eleven. We thought we'd let you sleep. The night nurse's report said you had a massive bowel action and had passed out. Do want something to eat?"

I could only nod. I was shattered but the thought of the previous night linked to breakfast didn't put me off. I was starving. Those two young nurses must have sorted me out and cleaned me up as I lay there unconscious. I have absolutely no recollection of it whatsoever. I can only thank them on these pages as I never saw them again.

So the prospect of another suppository was not something I was looking forward to as this young slip of a staff nurse approached me with a kidney dish and bedpan wrapped in a smile. She was very sweet and matter of fact as her gloved and lubricated finger entered my rectum. It was done very efficiently and quickly. At the end all I could say was "Thank you."

What else does one say?

Before they stuck me on the bedpan I made certain I had everything I needed. My experience had taught me that I would be unable to reach for anything over the next half hour.

The nurse stood at the bottom of the bed as she prepared to exit through the drawn curtains.

"Have you got everything you need?"

I went through my list in my head; phone, book, notepad, newspaper, pen, water. I had everything I needed, or so I thought. It was only as she disappeared out of earshot that I remembered the last item on my list. As the sound of her footsteps trailed away and out of earshot I thought to myself, 'toilet paper'!

Chapter 7 Dennis

Dennis had only been with Ali and me for four days but in that time we had formed a little band of brothers. It was a very strange mix of age and ethnicity that worked wonderfully well in adversity. We supported each other totally and never had a cross word. Ali and I had also got to know Dennis's wife Tina. She was tiny in comparison to Dennis but was obviously the one in charge. Tina was always immaculately dressed when she arrived for visiting. When visiting time ended they held each other in a loving embrace and she gave him a warm squeeze of the hand before separating from him. They were a lovely couple who obviously worshipped each other.

On Wednesday of my second week in hospital Dennis went down to theatre once more for another attempt at an operation.

We waved him off with smiles and laughter wishing him good luck and told him that if he wasn't back in time for lunch he was not to worry because we would eat his share. He laughed softly due to the effect of his pre-med and half waved as the trolley took him out of the ward.

His bed still lay empty at tea time. Ali kept looking at me and shaking his head. We felt so helpless. Time dragged on until sleep erased our fears only for them to return next morning. For some reason I had Dennis's home phone number.

"Do you think we should ring?" I asked.

Ali hesitated. After a few minutes we agreed to ring. Tina's voice answered.

She thanked us for our concern and said she was really

touched by it.

She told me that they had again been unable to operate due to the inability of Dennis's blood to clot as a result of the Warfarin.

He had suffered a heart attack due to the stress on his body and had been taken to intensive care instead of being returned to our ward.

Tina confirmed that our friend Dennis whom we had only known for a couple of days had died in the night. I didn't know what to say and I could see Ali sat as upright as he could manage with his mouth open. I spoke some gentle words as best I could and wished her well and then left her to her grief.

Being confined to that small area had had a strange effect on our emotions. We had formed a close bond which had now shattered. Ali and I hardly spoke for the rest of the day. There was nothing to say.

Chapter 8 On The Mend

Despite our sadness the brutal fact was that we could do nothing except hasten our own recoveries as much as possible. The suppository had worked well and, coincidentally or not, my temperature had dropped to normal. I no longer found myself in soaked bedding in the morning. They had also stopped taking blood samples and I was now beginning to feel stronger although my real condition was masked by three types of painkillers and the fact that I was being waited on hand and foot. Nevertheless I was starting to take far more note of my surroundings than I had done before. Ten days had gone by and I was walking round the ward on crutches instead of using a Zimmer. I was even able to go to the toilet escorted by a nurse although it took a great effort to drag my heavily swollen thigh around and it was even more difficult to balance myself before sitting down on a toilet seat. It is a good life skill to be able to enjoy small victories and I took an achievement such as this as a significant marker on my route to recovery despite the exhaustion I felt on my return to bed.

I was so busy working on these small gains that I did not appreciate how badly hurt I had been and I don't think my friends and family realized it either. When I returned from one visit to the toilet my friend Steve was sat by my bed waiting for me. He'd nipped out of work in his lunch hour. He watched my painfully slow progress intently as I moved towards my bed. I sat down and sighed with the effort.

"Bloody hell," he exclaimed, "I didn't realize it was as bad as that. That's horrendous. It's so swollen". The same afternoon I was talking to a nurse who had appeared on the ward for the first time. I had explained to her how the accident had occurred and she said, "You are so lucky. You could have broken your back!" I didn't share her view that I had been lucky but both she and Steve had made me realize that I had been and still was in a serious condition.

I was now beginning to reflect on my situation which was probably a sign of recovery and I realized that I had had a narrow escape. Not only could I have broken my back as the nurse suggested, I could have killed myself. This thought made me even more determined to recover. You can't waste your life when it's been given back to you.

Whilst thinking these profound thoughts I fell asleep.

I woke up with a start. Linda was sat with me and the ward lights were on. The sky was dark and ladened with snow. She had finished work, driven fifteen miles home in filthy conditions before returning to visit me. Linda would then have to drive back again after visiting time which meant that she would not get home until at least 9.30pm. This was very exhausting for her but at that moment I had no real understanding of what she was going through.

"You look tired."

I meant it in a loving, caring way. I was concerned about her and whilst tact has never been my strong point I was hardly in a position to exercise subtlety.

"Thanks very much. I haven't come here to be insulted." I didn't understand why she was upset and my apparent indifference upset here even more.

"I am tired. I'm running round all over the place and the kids have been awful."

Linda teaches in a really tough inner-city school. Her life

was stressful enough without this. I understood without any real understanding. I couldn't help her and I knew that I was a drain on her.

She calmed herself and we held hands but it was the first sign of a fracture, not only in my leg but in our relationship. I had been in hospital for nearly two weeks and she was exhausted. So was I. This was not a good time in our lives but the next day things took a turn for the better. The consultant came to see me. My temperature had dropped to almost normal. I was eating well and my blood count had been rising steadily over the last few days.

"As soon as physiotherapy and occupational therapy say you can go home, we will discharge you."

"How long will it take to heal?"

In my naivety I believed that it would take about six weeks.

"You must prepare yourself for the fact that a full recovery will take at least six months although you will be active before then."

I was aware that my jaw had dropped. I was not upset about the length of time it was going to take, rather it was the realization once more that I must be badly hurt. Little things kept happening to show me that my understanding of my situation was completely at odds with the reality. He smiled kindly. "Don't worry Mr. Howard, you will be OK. It's just going to take a long time that's all. With that he and his team departed, smiling.

I fell asleep.

Chapter 9 The Young Doctor

I woke up, disturbed my movement at the side of my bed. A dark haired young woman was standing by me. She flashes a smile of beautiful white teeth.

"Mr Howard?"

I quickly become alert and slowly and feebly sit up.

"Yes?"

"Hello. My name is Sandra. I'm a student attached to the team that is caring for you. I have to do a life history for my studies as yours is an unusual case. Would you mind? It shouldn't take too long".

"I'm not going anywhere." I smiled. "It will help pass the time."

She drew up a chair.

"You have Ehlers Danlos Syndrome?"

"Yes".

"Who told you?"

I explained that I had been misdiagnosed as a haemophiliac as a child and had only been confirmed as suffering from EDS when I was nineteen.

"Yes I've looked on the internet. It says that misdiagnosis is quite common. Do you mind if I examine you?"

She carried out a brief check.

"You look perfectly OK. Your blood pressure is fine and your pulse is strong. What problems do you have?"

I showed her my legs.

"Oh you have a lot of scarring."

She touched my knees and pulled gently on the skin.

"Does that hurt?"

It's very unpleasant.

"Mmm. You have multiple scars on your shins as well."

I related the story behind the big scar on the right side of my right shin.

"Mmm, and what was this scar caused by?

She was pointing to a one inch scar on the left side of my right shin.

"That was Christmas 1964."

"How do you remember the dates?"

"I remember every one."

"Really?"

"Do you think you have been emotionally scarred as well as physically?"

For a moment I was silent. The thought of emotional damage had never occurred to me but I had to admit that it was unusual for me to remember the details of every injury I have ever received. Perhaps she was right; I had been more affected than I liked to believe. She must have seen the concern on my face and she quickly took me out of my distress.

"What happened?"

She had touched a nerve. This was the only injury I recall when somebody deliberately hurt me. As Christmas 1964 approached it looked like I was about to see a whole year pass without a visit to hospital but it was not to be. I was playing a game of football at dinner time. I was in goal when a boy who was supposed to be my friend chased a ball that was heading towards me. I dashed out and got there first kicking the ball clear only to feel the full force of his boot on my shin. He had decided that if he couldn't get the ball he'd get me instead. I went flying and landed in a crumpled heap on the floor. He laughed as he trotted back down the pitch, oblivious to the agony I was in.

Miraculously I managed to stand up and was amazed to find that my leg was not cut. After a good rubbing it felt better and I continued with the game. I thought no more about it. The next morning passed uneventfully until break time when I spent fifteen minutes chasing my friend round the changing rooms at break neck speed until the bell sounded for a return to lessons.

We had Latin with "Ned" Naish , a kindly young man who stood at least six foot five in height. Ten minutes into the lesson the left side of my right shin exploded in pain.

I tried to pull up my trouser leg but the swelling from the now emerging bruise would not allow it. I stood up shakily.

"Sir!" I cried looking down at my shin.

Mr. Naish reacted instantly. He could see that the bruise was larger than my shin. Without hesitation he hoisted me onto his shoulder in a fireman's lift and carried me to the office. Once more I was transported to hospital in one of those cream limousines and before I knew it nurses who were about four years older than me were carefully wrapping me up in bed.

I was in love.

I was also in agony.

I spent a week in bed and did not get out once. Then one morning, without warning, I was lifted onto a trolley and taken to theatre where they cut my shin and inserted a tube to drain off the congealing blood. They had had to wait for a week to ensure that I did not continue to bleed when they cut me. I was then taken back to the ward. Four days later Mr. Boyd, my form tutor, arrived with two boys bearing gifts paid for by my fellow students and the staff. They had been informed that I would be in hospital over Christmas. I hadn't the courage to inform him that, whilst that had been the original plan, I was to be discharged the next day! It wasn't my fault.

Everything had been arranged between my parents and the hospital. I had a great if sore Christmas.

"I can see you've had lots and lots of cuts. Are there any other injuries not involving cuts?"

"I broke my scaphoid and I've dislocated my kneecaps several times."

She was writing note after note.

"And I sprained my ankle twice and I've broken my foot."

"Gosh."

"Oh and I got hit by a lorry."

"What?!"

"I was knocked off my push-bike."

"How did it happen?"

"Well I used to coach an under 13s Rugby league team.

We'd just finished training on a Saturday morning. As the kids left I told all of them to be careful on their bikes. They are ever so giddy when they leave."

Sandra nodded as she wrote.

"Anyway I sent them on their way, locked up and left. I was cycling down Holderness High Road, a major dual carriageway. Do you know it?"

She nodded without lifting her eyes from her notes.

"A large white truck drew up alongside. I remember thinking 'That's new. You can tell. The tyres are unmarked.' Then I thought, 'bloody hell those tyres are close.' I looked forward and tried to shout into his mirror hoping he would see me but as I did so there was an almighty bang. Next thing I know I'm flying backwards and I landed on the floor!"

I looked at her for a reaction. She was shaking her head as she wrote.

"It was funny but I didn't feel a thing until I got home. I was covered in road dirt so I went for a shower. It wasn't until I saw the cuts to my left leg that it began to hurt. I had ten stitches in three cuts."

"You went to hospital?"

"Well as it happens Linda used to be a nurse so she put steri-strips on. It's the same as stitches. I got £2000 in compensation!" I smiled.

"Do you always laugh at your injuries?"

"There's nothing else to do."

"I was just wondering whether they had affected you

personally, emotionally? It's not normal to have so much violence against your body is it?"

Her question took me aback. I had never looked at it like that. My attitude, if I even had an attitude had always been to get on with it. I had never thought about the effects that continued accidents might have had on me.

It was now time for her to go. I had not even got half way through the whole list of injuries.

"Thank you. It's been very interesting. I hope your recovery proceeds well."

We shook hands and she took her leave. Sandra did not know it but she had started a process in me that would change my life. I was beginning to examine my behaviour in an attempt to put a stop to the never-ending stream of injuries and now I would have to consider their effect on my character.

It was only a beginning however. I had to concentrate on getting better, a process that was going to take much longer than anticipated.

Chapter 10 Going Home

Michelle, my first physiotherapist, materialized at the foot of the bed.

"Hello. The consultant came to see you yesterday."

Yesterday? I don't remember where the day went. I seem to flit between absolute clarity and prolonged sleep.

"We need to get you prepared for going home."

She and her assistant walked with me to the double doors that lead to a rear staircase.

"I want to see how you handle the stairs."

I already knew how to climb and descend on crutches. I had had so many opportunities in my life to practice. This was the sixth injury I had had requiring my use of crutches for a sustained period. I was well practices and unsurprisingly I passed the test with ease.

"You have very good upper body strength."

I nodded as I completed the descent.

"I'm happy for you to go home. We'll give you another run out tomorrow but you're steady enough."

I was surprised and although I didn't show it I was quite frightened and uncertain. Suddenly I felt very vulnerable. I got back into bed and once more fell asleep.

"Mr. Howard?"

This was a voice I had not heard before. I raised my head from under the blanket.

"Hello I'm Janice from Occupational Therapy."

"What time is it?"

"One o'clock."

'Bloody hell,' I thought to myself, 'I've missed lunch again. Then I noticed the plate on my tray and I remembered or at least I thought I remembered. Yes I did eat something. I shook my head in resignation.

"I need to go over some things with you about going home."

I had forgotten for a second that she was there.

"We need to make certain you can manage."

I nodded. She went through a check list.

"Will there be anyone at home during the day?"

"I don't know. Linda and I have not discussed my coming home."

This was happening too quickly for me.

"She's a teacher."

"Well if she works we'll have to get a home help in to feed you and help you get washed and dressed. We'll need to arrange for somebody to come and fix some grabs in and around your home."

"Am I entitled to all this?"

"Oh yes Philip."

She spoke the next words with an earnest tone that shook me to the core. Her eyes looked into me as she said,

"You've been very badly hurt. It's going to take a long time for you to recover and your wife won't be able to help you on her own."

This was the final confirmation of how bad my injury was. Finally, it dawned on me that I wasn't simply going to limp back into action in a few weeks like I had done before when I ruptured my knee ligaments or inverted the base of my spine. Dislocating my left shoulder or breaking my right foot did not compare to this injury. A sprained left ankle as well as countless cuts requiring ten stitches or more had not seen me as exhausted as I was now. All those had been bad enough but it was now obvious if it hadn't been blindingly so before that this was the worst injury I had ever had, not withstanding the fact that I was considerably older and would not heal as quickly as I had done in the past.

I looked at her face as she spoke in such matter of fact tones and without warning burst into uncontrollable sobs. It wasn't the type of crying that makes your chest heave. I didn't wail in self-pity. It was the sincerest form of crying I have ever done. The tears just flooded down my cheeks in silence. I couldn't stop them.

I was trying to avoid placing demands on Linda and I had never felt so alone. I cried and cried in front of this stranger who sat there talking gently. Despite my outburst she got all the information she needed and got up to leave. She placed the chair back against the wall and turned as she got to the bottom of the bed.

"You WILL get better."

She smiled kindly and then left. It was the first time I had had an emotional reaction to my circumstances. Ironically it was probably another sign that I had begun the long process of recovery but it didn't feel like progress at the time. I was exhausted and fell asleep seconds after she left.

Next day had a surprise for me. Ali was taken to theatre to have his leg pinned. I did not find out why or how he had ended up in Hull but in this confined environment where neither of us could move without assistance, we had become very close. We had helped each other through moments when family and nurses could not. We had survived together. I waved him off and wished him well.

Then a nurse came and told me that I was to be transferred to another ward because they had other patients coming in. As I was no longer a high dependency patient (I didn't know I was a high dependency patient) I was to be transferred to an Ear Nose and Throat ward which had some spare capacity. Within an hour I had been transferred, possessions and all and I never saw Ali again. I can only hope that his operation went well.

These were strange times when intense friendships rose and fell in a moment.

I did not like this new ward. I felt uncomfortable from the very first moment I arrived. Other patients walked about, their noses stuffed with post-operative swabs. They nodded half blinded and spoke rarely. I lay and watched. It was also much quieter than my previous ward. Men entered, had their pre-op followed by their operations and left a day later. I was quite isolated. I also had the feeling, perhaps unfairly that I was an inconvenience, an alien brought in from another world with different needs. Perhaps I was a symbol of the fact that management thought that the ward had spare capacity. It certainly didn't mean that the staff didn't work hard for they never stopped. Perhaps I was being over-sensitive. I was vulnerable. One thing I didn't need was to be thrown out of my comfort zone which was precisely what had just happened.

Chapter 11 Discharged

Three days had passed and I had not been seen by any of the medical staff. Had I been forgotten in this outpost?

I asked the staff nurse who promptly checked with ward 9 as to when I was to be seen again. Within an hour the consultant came to see me confirming my thoughts. Was I being paranoid? It could simply have been that, as I was no longer high dependency, I didn't need so many visits but still I didn't like that ward. Some of the staff were very nice, others less so. I wanted to go home and yet when the consultant said I could, I panicked. I didn't feel strong enough. I had too many unanswered questions. How would I cope? Would Linda stop off work and look after me? What if I fell in the middle of the day? What if I was lonely? What if somebody knocked on the door? What if there was a fire?

I didn't like it one little bit. Thoughts and fears raced through my mind. I had been desperate to leave that ward but now, it was the last thing I wanted.

"Stop panicking. This is good. You're on the mend. They know what they are doing. You'll be fine. Anyway they've said that you won't be discharged until physiotherapy and occupational therapy say you can go. You'll be fine."

The Physiotherapists had already given me the all-clear. I then had the strange experience of being watched by an occupational therapist whilst I washed my bottom at the sink. She wanted to see how well balanced I was. I couldn't help wondering if they would ever have had a man watching a woman wash her bottom; very unnerving.

As a result an over-efficient staff nurse took all this as the signal for me to be discharged. They told me to phone my wife. I phoned her on her mobile. Although she was in class she answered.

"Linda, I can come home."

"What? When?"

"Now. As soon as you can get here."

I could the sound of children's voices.

"It's very inconvenient," she snapped.

"What do you mean?"

"I'm teaching."

I was taken aback that she was not overjoyed at the fact that I could come home but I was too exhausted, too concerned with my own recovery to be able to understand her problems.

It appeared that my discharge was the last thing that Linda wanted. I was confused and upset. It was all too quick. It felt that after all the care and attention I had received I was about to be shoved out with a boot on my backside to the less than willing arms of my wife. I knew she was under pressure but I wished she could have found another word, any word other than "inconvenient". I switched off the phone and buried myself in my bedding. There was no-one else in the ward. I was alone both physically and emotionally. Not for the first time in this awful, awful period in my life, I dissolved into tears.

I was crying a lot, often without apparent reason. Although I was brought up to show my feelings and have done the same with my own children, I was embarrassed by it. I have rarely cried. The last time I cried openly was in 1985

81

when my granddad died.

I felt reasonably well but the painkillers must have been deluding me. The crying was a sign of my physical and emotional exhaustion. Throughout my life I have never given in to my medical problems. All through my childhood, cuts, bruises and broken bones did not stop me from playing rugby and football in an attempt to live a normal life. Mr. Lillee, my primary school Head, described me to my parents as "the toughest little boy he had ever met" but maybe this was one fight too many. Maybe I needed to lie down and hide. Maybe it was time to give in. I had had enough. I just wanted to feel safe. I was sick of being a "brave little boy." It had caused me nothing but pain and anguish for more than fifty years. Feeling so vulnerable was definitely a new experience for me. I thought that I would have been happy at being discharged but I was full of apprehension. I was down and almost out.

At 2.00pm Linda arrived. School allowed her out early and covered her lessons. I knew there would be no problem despite her fears. Before I knew it I was sat in a wheelchair with all my possessions sat precariously on my lap in two plastic bags.

As we were about to leave another occupational therapist arrived.

"Oh I've just come to take you down to the kitchens to see if you can cope at home!"

I smiled. She smiled. We stood there uncertainly.

"Oh well I'm not going to stop anyone going home. Good luck!"

Her appearance confirmed the fact that I didn't like this ward. It was not geared up to my and I suspect, others' needs. Orthopaedics was an inconvenient add-on there. I was trapped between the uncertainness of the therapy assistant and my need to go home. I did not know what to do. Linda made my mind up for me and pushed the chair towards the doors. I exited the ward and proceeded towards a home that had no grabs fitted and no home help arranged. I would not realize how difficult this would make my life until much later.

I felt totally unprepared for my new life. It had come too quickly and I had not been assessed properly. As we descended in the lift all I could think about was the missing wall grabs they had said I needed. I wanted to return to my bed but said nothing to Linda. I felt frightened and I knew I was an "inconvenience". A tired panic enveloped me. It was too much. The heavy doors parted and   I was confronted by a herd of people trying to get in. They hesitated in unison and let me exit the lift. Noise hit me as I glided helplessly through the throng. I had been isolated from the outside for only a fortnight but I was completely unprepared for my return. As I tried to adjust to the sudden change in the pace of life the freezing cold bit me even though we were still inside the building. At the main entrance sliding doors opened and devoured us. Stinking cigarette smoke drifted from gaunt faces as they peered from worn out dressing gowns. In the car park puddles of water flowed into overworked drains. Across the road people stood at the bus stop hunched against the cold. Half melted snow still lingered on rooftops that lay beneath a grey sky. Our car was grey. The people were grey as were their shabby damp clothes. My mood was grey. I have never felt so ill and desperate in all my life.

Linda's hair brushed my cheek as she bent to apply the squeaking handbrake. For a moment I had a sense of pleasure as her scent drifted across my nostrils. Her hair was soft and warm against the bitterness. She fumbled with the car keys as I tried to get out of the chair under my own steam. She could see the state I was in and her anxiety only made her fumble more. Eventually I got in and watched as she returned the wheelchair across the car park before re-emerging out of the crowd.

The door banged, the seat belt clicked and the indicator pulsed. Before I knew it we were on our way. I was shivering violently and I think Linda was quite alarmed but soon the effects of the heater kicked in and sleep shortened the journey.

I awoke as we arrived home and after a little hesitancy, I negotiated the two steps into the front entrance. I stopped for a moment. It was good to be home. The Christmas decorations had gone as had the tree. The removal of these is something I normally take the lead in but I had forgotten about Christmas. It was January 18th. The festivities seemed an age away.

The house looked lovely. Linda had made a big effort or perhaps, with my absence, it had never got that untidy! The large settee dominated the dining room. I was trying to work out why it was there instead of the lounge but as I entered the lounge it became obvious. One of the Grandchildren's bunk beds was in the place where the settee used to be.

"God you have been busy."

The beds were made by a friend and were very solid pieces of work. To take them apart and re-assemble them would have taken a considerable effort.

"I bet it took you ages."

"Sarah helped me to take it apart and carry it down."

I was so grateful to Linda.

I sat down in the easy chair at the side of the bed. Linda slid the poof under my broken leg. Immediately I realized that this would not work. The seat was too long and I couldn't get comfortable at all. I spent the next three months in the bed. Thank goodness it was so well made.

Chapter 12 Recovery Begins – I Think

`I said before that I hate the descent from New Year into dreary February. Enduring a broken femur does not brighten this period one jot. In the morning I was woken by Linda as she brought me a cup of coffee before leaving for work. I had hoped that she might stay at home for at least a day but she didn't want to. She was a curious mix of independent feminist and mother hen.

"Are you not stopping off work to look after him?" my mother had asked.

My mum was 80 years of age and lived over 120 miles away. She was bothered about me and was looking to Linda for reassurance. "Am I bloody hell" was not reassurance. I think words like "He'll be OK mum, don't worry," would have been more soothing. "Sarah (our daughter) is nearby and will pop in to see him. I'll be home at four O'clock and in reality he's not going to be going anywhere is he? I'll ring him at lunch-time and check he's OK and so will Robert. He's not even going to go to the toilet yet. He's got a bottle if he needs a wee."

She was very efficient but not very tactful. She gave me the impression sometimes that she was angry with me. Linda can be very loving but also very hard. She takes pride in having a reputation at work for being very scary and this aspect of her character is the last thing I needed at that moment in time. I knew she was busy and under pressure but at the end of the day it was only a job and I was in real trouble.

In the actual event my mother's fears were unfounded. I had a small set of free-standing shelves at my side. The four legs were blue and the three shelves yellow. On the middle shelf I had a bag of sandwiches, a writing pad, a book and the television controls.

On the top shelf stood a flask of boiled water, tea bags and a cup. Next to them in a plastic container were my painkillers, Paracetamol and Tremadol. To the left of my shelves and within easy reach but tucked away from view sat a plastic, four litre milk bottle now posing as a urine bottle. Four litres proved essential. The only time I seemed to be awake was when I needed a pee. My whole life was centred on this small number of objects.

The first day passed without incident. I managed to watch "Homes under the Hammer and "Animal Park" in between bouts of sleep. Before I knew it Linda was back, all sweetness and light. She kissed me and then immediately removed the urine bottle and emptied it in the toilet. I think she preferred teaching to nursing. She looked tired and I tried not to be a nuisance but I couldn't get anything for myself. After cooking tea Linda got me a bowl and I had a full body wash at the table. It would be three months before I could get into the bath.

The next day my friend John brought me some DVDs to pass the time. One of them was the complete series of "The Office" which I enjoyed thoroughly. The other was not as good a choice. "Searching For Private Ryan" is a very powerful and moving film that pulls no punches. How the hell anyone could go to war is beyond me. It was perhaps not that good a film to watch when you felt like you've been driven over by a Sherman tank. Nevertheless simple kindnesses like this were so important to my morale.

I slept through the first week. Nothing happened and I was too tired to be bored. At the weekend Sarah brought her 5 children to visit me. I had not seen her for nearly three weeks. She lives in rural isolation some miles outside Hull which makes evening visits difficult. Her husband doesn't get home from work until after six. Weekend visits were also awkward because he works Saturdays in the shop and Sunday is the only day they have together as a family. I understood her difficulties but wondered whether these were the real reasons she didn't come to see me.

Sarah has my medical condition and has suffered several injuries herself. Was she afraid that I am her future and didn't want to see it?

"They're here." shouted Linda. Everyone had disembarked and were in the house before I had got out of bed. I met them in the kitchen. Sarah was laughing and smiling as she talked with her mother. As I entered the kitchen they all fell silent. She looked at my swollen leg and then gave me a knowing look as if to say "You really did it to yourself this time." Without speaking she moved towards me as her arms opened into an embrace. She held me with the gentleness of a mother. I was touched and overwhelmed by her gentleness and her concern. As she pulled me to her and rested my head on her shoulder I supported myself on my crutches and without warning, unleashed a flood of tears.

"Poorly leg?"

Mimi was two years old. I nodded.

"Poorly leg." I replied.

"Not poorly?" She pointed to the other. I smiled and the tears stopped as I looked into her earnest blue eyes.

"Not poorly"

Mimi stared in silence. I released a finger from my crutch handle and she took hold of it.

"Poorly leg." She whispered.

"Yes very poorly but I'm getting better."

We stood together, my finger in her hand, in gentle silence.

"Would you like a cup of tea?"

It is Linda's solution to everything. It broke the tension.

The next fortnight passed awkwardly and slowly. This period was punctuated by three events. One of them was not without humour, if it were not quite so pathetic but the other two were quite disturbing.

The first unfortunate occasion involved my return to hospital for an out-patients appointment some ten days after discharge. I had been looking forward to it enormously as I had hardly seen the outside world for a month. The furthest distance I had travelled had been a twenty five feet limp to the downstairs toilet.

Amazingly I was washed and dressed by 9.00 am. This was a complete contrast to my non-activity of the previous fortnight. I didn't actually feel very well but I resolved to make the most of this exciting trip to the hospital. When the knock came I jumped up immediately. I smiled embarrassingly at the ambulance man as if he were my best friend. He guided me slowly to the ambulance that was parked at the end of our long drive. This was a precarious journey. I had to negotiate a yard covered in loose stone before making my way along a fifty-yard long driveway of muddy potholes. My concentration was so intense I hardly noticed the freezing January chill.

I held on to the sides of the platform lift as it guided me into the vehicle. The walk had taken a lot out of me and by the time I strapped myself into the seat I was exhausted. Worse still I had to sit with my leg down for the whole journey. My ankle joined the thigh above in swelling painfully and my shoe became so uncomfortable that I had to take it off. A journey that I had looked forward to for a week had become a nightmare within ten minutes.

I had no choice but to deal with it so I simply gritted my teeth and prayed for it to end. The ambulance picked up other patients from a series of detours that meant I had to sit there for over an hour. Finally we arrived at the outpatients department and I couldn't wait to get out. I had felt bad enough when I left hospital for the first time but this was incomparably worse.

If I thought that getting out of the ambulance would make me feel better I was seriously deluded. I had been isolated in the ward and then my home for a month and was groggy from the effects of the painkillers. My leg was more badly bruised than normal because of the Ehlers Danlos syndrome. I needed to lie down and sleep. My lips dried up and I broke into a severe sweat. As I stood in a queue at reception for ten minutes people and walls swirled around me. Finally I slumped into a seat. I desperately needed Linda to be with me but she had gone to work. I don't think she had a clue about how bad I felt. I was so weak and shouldn't have been alone.

I needed a drink but didn't feel strong enough to get one from the WRVS shop. It was only thirty feet away but I was daunted by the crowd and it was agonizingly out of reach.

I closed my eyes, hoping it would all go away but the drugs made my head swim. I probably looked like some semiconscious tramp sat on a park bench with drooping eyelids and dribbling lips. It was not my best moment.

Someone was calling my name but I could not respond. Then I woke from my sleep and rose towards her smiling face. They took x-rays and then returned me to the same park bench.

"Mr. Howard?

A nurse was gently shaking me.

I got up as quickly as I could, embarrassed by the smiling faces and followed her into the consulting room. I recognised the young registrar from one of the ward visits.

"Hello Mr. Howard. This is just a routine examination to check that the nail we inserted is settled well. I'm pleased to tell you that it is and I'm quite happy with the situation. It's of course too early to talk about the healing process. We'll look at that on your next visit in six weeks."

"Will I be able to go to Egypt? We've booked a cruise."

He paused for a moment. "When is it?"

"April."

He paused again. "That's about ten weeks? Yes I should think so. Yes."

Relieved I exited back into the waiting room. I texted Linda the good news whilst I waited for an ambulance. I was so relieved. This holiday had been booked for six months and was our biggest and most expensive ever. We were both excited by it. We knew we'd have to make plans to deal with my weakened state but I felt happy that I was on the road to recovery. The dark sleepy mood that brought me into hospital had gone and I quite enjoyed the journey home despite the increased throbbing in my leg. I was relieved to get home and after a cup of tea and a cake I fell fast asleep exhausted but weakly triumphant. I had passed my first test.

The second of the three events involved an orange. One evening shortly after my visit to hospital I tucked into a large juicy one with relish. Less than half an hour later I was convulsed in pain feeling terribly dizzy.

"I'm going to be sick!" I shouted. Linda was horrified and helpless as she watched the panic in me. I scrambled out of bed in a frantic slow-motion dragging my thigh on crutches. It was still twice its normal size and felt very heavy as I swayed drunkenly from side to side through the kitchen

I threw myself into the downstairs toilet possessed by an overwhelming need to empty my bowels and proceeded to do so with the utmost force. It was like, what I imagine to be, an attack of deadly dysentery.

"Sick! Sick!

I tried to scream but didn't have the strength. Linda's hand appeared round the door holding a papier-mâché vomit bowl given to us by the hospital. I could hear her wretch. It was almost funny but I had no time to laugh. I grabbed it and filled it to the rim immediately, with such force that it hurt both my chest and leg. The lack of control over my body was really frightening. Serious cramps in my chest caused great pain but I couldn't stop being sick. It felt like it was never going to stop but just as I was about to ask for another bowl, that we didn't have, it did.

Linda's hand appeared round the door holding a plastic bag. Without speaking I knew what she wanted me to do. I wrapped the bowl in the bag, tied it tightly and keeping it horizontal to avoid spillage handed it back. As I wiped my mouth with tissue the outside door opened and I heard the sound of the wheelie bin opening and closing. I flushed the toilet and opened the window hoping to get rid of the stench before sorting myself out.

"I hope the neighbours can't smell that," was the only thought in my head.

"Are you alright?" Linda asked.

"Yes thanks. I'll be out in a minute."

It was a good five minutes before I felt steady enough to stand. When I opened the door Linda was stood waiting for me concerned but unsmiling and faintly nauseated. It was obvious how difficult it was for her.

"Are you OK?"

I nodded weakly.

"Can I have some water?"

My strength didn't last to the word "please."

The return journey to bed was much calmer and slower than the previous one to the toilet. Linda gave me a drink and I managed to say "Ta". I took two sips before collapsing back into bed.

The whole episode was reminiscent of that night in hospital when the two nurses helped me. Thankfully Linda never saw that.

I woke up as daylight began to find its way into my room.

My mind was trying to work out what time it was when Linda opened the door. She was dressed and ready to go to work. She placed my sandwiches and a flask on the shelf before giving me a quick kiss. I wondered what my breath smelt like and before I realized it she had gone. It was obvious that she needed to escape. So did I.

I lay there wondering what could have made me so poorly. The only conclusion I could come to was that the lining of my stomach must have been affected by the painkillers and had reacted to the acid in the orange. I didn't eat oranges for months and I have never taken Tremadol since.

The third incident is funny at first glance. Only when you examine what happened more closely does it become clear how ill I was. The drugs had sedated me and nulled any pain. In this they served a useful purpose. The downside was that I slept most of the day and night. In the first couple of weeks I must have only been conscious for a couple of hours a day. It didn't matter whether Linda stayed at home or went to work. I was simply existing and I would have been no company whatsoever.

By mid February I had begun to stay awake more. I must have been getting used to the tablets and I was also beginning to take fewer of them as the injury settled down. I took shorter naps every day but still found myself waking in the early hours of the morning before falling asleep again as dawn approached. As a result I lost my sleeping pattern completely.

One cold February night I woke up not knowing whether it was late night or early morning and for some reason I sat bolt upright in bed. The atmosphere in the room seemed alien and hostile. The house was totally silent and the room was very, very cold. I felt an overpowering sense of darkness and menace.

I wanted to talk to someone but Linda was asleep and I knew that I couldn't disturb her. I switched on my table lamp and wrapped the duvet over my head. I swung my legs out and my feet searched for slippers on the freezing floor. They found my right one easily but the left had to be gently forced over my swollen foot. I did not know why I had got out of bed or where I thought I was going. I just felt I had to move. Before I realized it I had stood up and began searching for something but I didn't know what I was searching for.

I felt an overwhelming need to get out of the harsh environment of that cold room. I think I was looking for something, anything to comfort me; to make me feel better than I did; a painting to admire, a comedy programme on television to make me laugh or a good book to enjoy. It could have been something as simple as a bottle of beer, anything to give me a lift. I knew I couldn't have a beer in combination with the tablets and I hadn't got the concentration to read a Mickey Mouse comic let alone a book. It was also impossible to watch television as I didn't want to risk waking Linda who was sleeping above me. Before I knew it I found myself in the kitchen. I opened cupboards and drawers searching desperately but to no avail. I was beginning to feel tired and desperate and was resigned to returning to bed dissatisfied when I saw it, lying on a shelf in a cupboard.

It was a three-pack packet of Smarties.

Linda had bought them for our grandchildren who were visiting the next day. There was but a fleeting moment of guilt-inspired hesitation before I ate the lot. I gulped them down and yet managed to savour every one. I was like a drug addict who'd found the key to the medicine cupboard.

I stood there resting on my crutches, my lust sated, when the realization of what I had done set in. I had stolen the children's chocolates. Quickly I grabbed the tops to the tubes and put them back on. Then I put the tubes side by side in the ripped packet and placed it back in the cupboard with the tear to the rear so that it could not be seen at first glance. Somehow I must have believed I would get away with it. There was no logic to this act. It was madness to think I could get away with it but I was so desperately, stupidly, in need of comfort.

I returned to bed and thought no more about it until mid morning when a little voice said, "Granddad have you pinched our Smarties?" My mind suddenly cleared and I remembered the awful truth of my guilt. I could do nothing but apologize. I turned over and hid under the duvet pretending to be asleep.

Linda's face must have been a picture. She would have smiled gleefully to her grandchildren saying something like, "Close your eyes. I've got a surprise for you." I can see her standing there, in total disbelief, holding three weightless packets of Smarties in front of three expectant children.

It was laughable and pathetic.

I'm sorry. Truly I'm sorry but I must have felt pretty bad. I don't normally pinch sweets off children.

xxxx

Saturday the February 23rd was a day of significance. It was the day I went out of the house on a routine shopping trip for the first time since the accident. Linda and I went to Tescos in Withernsea, a small, run down seaside town about six miles from our home. It has a large white lighthouse that has not seen the sea in decades.

It was also a significant journey because the purpose of the trip was to get some passport photographs taken. We were beginning to make preparations for our much anticipated holiday to Egypt. There was a sense of optimism as Linda drove us to the store.

We did the weekly shopping and I managed to last the course but by the time I entered the photograph booth I had had enough. Linda guided me to the seat and I sat down very tentatively. The stool provided no support and of course there were no hand grabs. I could not adjust my position and had to crunch myself down in order to fit in between the guiding arrows that set the photograph. Lights flashed as I try not to grimace.

"Right. That'll have to do."

Linda's hands popped through the curtain to help me out. I was now desperate to get home. And waiting for the photograph seemed to take an age.

"Why don't you go back to the car and I'll get these?"

Gratefully I accepted her offer. Although the snow had gone it was still very cold and the ground was wet. The biting wind cut me in two. The outing had been very important for me but it now needed to end. I was desperate to get home. My hands fumbled with the keys and I dropped them. Bending down to pick them up was a huge effort and I flopped unceremoniously onto the seat.

"Are you driving then?"

I had fallen asleep in an instant and awoke to Linda's smile. I was, for some reason beyond my understanding, sat in the driver's seat. Linda helped me round to the other side before loading the boot with our supplies. She dropped coldly into her driving position.

"Take a look at those handsome!" She thrust the photographs into my hand.

I gasped in horror.

"I look like a live person lying on a mortuary slab with its eyes open."

Death warmed up did not begin to describe it. The eyes were black, the cheeks hollow; the complexion white and dull. The lips were thin and devoid of blood.

"God! I'd frighten the vultures!"

The photograph didn't lie. I looked absolutely terrible but I couldn't be bothered to get another set.

Every time a customs officer looks at my photograph they always take a second look as if to say that no-one could look that bad. I still feel I have to explain to them,

"I was ill when that was taken".

I hope they'll feel sorry for me, horrified that anyone could look so bad but they never say a word. There must be an enormous amount of ugly people in the world. As I held the photographs a thought entered my head.

"I won't be going to Egypt."

I looked awful.

I dismissed the thought however and said nothing to Linda.

I knew how much she was looking forward to the trip. I had been looking forward to it as well. The idea of not going was impossible to countenance so I put the pictures in my wallet and tucked it into my inside pocket. It was a case "of least seen, most forgotten." I could not forget it.

Over the next few weeks I kept talking positively to Linda as we busied ourselves with preparations. We laughed when my new passport arrived and we saw how awful the photograph was but the feeling was growing in me that I wouldn't be ready. From the moment I saw the image I knew that I would not be physically capable of a ten-day cruise down the Nile. I dreaded the prospect of telling Linda and hoped that she had begun to think the same thoughts as well.

Chapter 13 Recovery continued – I think

Towards the middle of March I was able to walk to the toilet without supervision and the bottle beneath the bed had been discarded. Andrew bought me a cup with a lid on so that I could make my own cup of tea and carry it safely back to the bed I was still residing in. What joy! What freedom!

It was now obvious to everyone at work that I was going to be off for a considerable period and I had been buoyed by the number of well wisher cards I had received. Several students had sent me emails wishing me a speedy recovery. It was very gratifying to receive these but they made me realize how distant everything had become. Most of the time I had been too busy dealing with immediate issues, like finding the most efficient way of getting a cup of tea, to realize how socially isolated I was becoming.

Six weeks had passed since my first visit to out-patients and I was now to return for a check on my progress. I had not been out of the house apart from the visit to Tescos so I was looking forward to it but I had a mixture of emotions swirling inside me. On the one hand I was feeling much stronger and more confident. My swollen leg had reduced considerably and I was not afraid of the journey as I had been on the previous visit but I couldn't help feeling some trepidation.

Two people had told my friend, John, that recovery from a broken femur could be a precarious journey. I was concerned about what the doctor would say particularly as people with Ehlers Danlos syndrome often take longer to heal their wounds.

The day did not begin well. The ambulance driver was the

same one who had called for me before. I stepped out of the house but was a little too over confident. I stepped down onto the first step and turned to lock the door. Then I attempted to step down backwards and lost track of where I was. My crutches missed the step and I began to fall backwards only to be saved from disaster by the secure hands of the ambulance driver who was safeguarding my rear.

I laughed but it could have been quite nasty. I understood instantly as to why the occupational therapist had talked about having grab rails fitted. I should have written a letter of complaint about the speedy discharge but I had too many other things to worry about. I should not have been discharged in the manner that I was. I was put on a ward aimed at caring for patients with different needs and the staff did not understand mine.

If it hadn't been for the vigilance of that driver I could have been in serious trouble yet again.

For a moment it knocked my fragile confidence but I was determined to press on.

I had not thought to ask Linda to come with me but it was now blatantly obvious that I needed support. It was too much to deal with by myself. I was also frightened of what the doctor was going to say when I asked him about Egypt. I was scared and tense and unbelievably hot. My leg began to throb as I sat in the waiting room with my leg down for almost an hour. Finally my name was called. As I walked from the waiting room to the open door of the consulting room I could see my X-rays being downloaded. The Consultant was very pleasant and very re-assuring. By his side sat two young women who were obviously medical students. One of them was Sandra, the young woman who had interviewed me on the ward. He explained to them the nature of my injury and that I had Ehlers Danlos syndrome.

"This medical condition has added significant complications to the injury because of the extra bruising involved. It will have a significant impact on the timing of recovery."

I didn't know that I had extra bruising. Nobody had said anything about added complications although I had wondered. The doctor turned to me.

"You lost a lot of blood due to haemorrhages from the break and have serious internal bruising but please be re-assured that despite this everything is OK It will take a long time to completely heal OK?"

The two students stared at me intensely and studiously. It was quite unnerving but in the end it was all very pleasant. The consultant smiled. He had assuaged my fears. I thanked him and left. I was half way to the ambulance reception and about to order my return vehicle when I realized that I had completely forgotten to ask about Egypt. I turned back and stood hesitantly at the consulting room door. The consultant was talking to his students about my case.

"Yes yes come in." he smiled.

"What can I do for you?"

"My wife and I were planning to go to Egypt for a holiday at Easter.

"When is Easter?"

"It's the middle of April".

His smile vaporised. The students watched. I knew what he was going to say and I didn't want to hear it. He sucked in a long breath like a builder does before telling you that the job will cost a fortune.

"Er no." he said softly, hiding his eyes in the computer screen.

"I don't think that's a good idea Mr. Howard. You won't be capable of such a journey. You're not strong enough. I think that you would find it too taxing. My advice is that you should not go. You must understand that any breaking of a limb is a serious injury but breaking the femur is very serious indeed. You lost a lot of blood and you are still very weak. My advice is that you should not even consider this."

He smiled sympathetically. I had never really believed that I would make it but nevertheless it was still a shock.

"Will you tell my wife?" I joked. The students laughed but a tiny part of me was serious. It was a huge disappointment and I was crushed with guilt. I don't remember much of the journey home. The ambulance bumped and twisted over the sleeping policeman that guard the suburban estates but I suffered no discomfort. I just kept thinking about Linda's reaction. I phrased and re-phrased the words but when she came home I just said,

"Sorry love but Egypt is off."

It was the best I could do.

Linda just blinked. I think she was too tired for histrionics.

"Oh well never mind. I didn't think we would."

"I'm sorry."

"There's no point in being sorry. It's just the way it is."

After tea Linda phoned the insurance company and requested a claim form. She deals with adversity by getting on with things. Being busy allows her to mask her real feelings probably in much the same way that jokes protect me. The insurance claim was fully met without a fuss and we got all our money back within three weeks. Three years later we still haven't made it to Egypt.

During this time I discovered a new interest. The number of people who do jigsaws is surprisingly high. It seems like it's a secret pleasure that people don't talk about. It's very relaxing and unlike reading it keeps you busy without disturbing your emotions. It suited my mood perfectly.

I became lost in the world of a 1940's street party celebrating the end of the Second World War or maps of the Lake District. I sat, rather uncomfortably, at an angle with my leg sticking out to the side of the table. One morning I sat engrossed as I neared the completion of a particularly challenging picture. I was aware of my growing hunger but couldn't break away thinking, "I'll get my breakfast soon". I was not yet dressed and hadn't done my exercises. I resolved to sort these omissions out after breakfast but still continued at my desk.

Finally hunger forced me to stop. I went into the kitchen intent on a bowl of cornflakes. I was amazed to see the kitchen clock indicating a quarter past one! I had been so involved that I had lost the entire morning! Then I thought,

"Maybe I gained an entire morning."

I was pleased with this positive thought. It was an indication that I was getting better. The jig-saws proved to be a great therapy.

I was bored with the endless nonsense on daytime television. I am sure that chat shows that serve only to advertise someone's new book or CD are designed to drive people back to work in order to avoid the mindless drivel. I have just watched an episode of "It's me or the dog" in which a large black dog was shown humping the leg of the expert trainer.

"He's having his evil way with me!" she laughed.

The dog was in effect masturbating on her! I couldn't help wondering,

"What would happen if I did that to her? She wouldn't laugh then."

Then she said,

"I've been humped by a few dogs in my time."

It was priceless but I couldn't stand it any more.

The days were getting lighter and so was my mood. My physiotherapist, also called Michelle, came once a week and I was walking further on each visit. By the end of March I had managed to get to the end of our drive. It had been a long hard struggle.

April was pleasantly warm and sunny. Greenery was returning to the fields that surround our house and I was feeling much better. Every day I went for a walk down the lane, increasing my distance by one telegraph pole each time. They stood about a hundred yards apart which meant that my daily journey increased by two hundred yards. I was able to put my foot down with pressure but was still using crutches.

April 16 was a mixed day. It was the day I was given

permission to start driving. I drove three miles to the nearest village to collect a paper I wouldn't normally read and I bought a cream scone from the bakery as a reward. When I got home I sat at the table looking at it before eating. It was the first thing I had been able to get for myself in 14 weeks. The scone was filled with cream and strawberries and the taste slid down the back of my throat. It was almost worth breaking a leg for!

Unfortunately April 16th was also the day I had been booked to do a 5 minute amateur comedy routine in Beverley, some miles away but reluctantly I cancelled the show. This was the second time my attempt to launch a comedy career had stalled. A few years earlier I had enjoyed some success with a couple of amateur performances in the locality. Then I had an absolutely terrible night with an audience that had the intelligence and sense of humour of a dead dog.

Soon after this experience I moved out of the family home because Linda and I were having marital difficulties. Shortly after I had returned in anticipation of happier days, my dad died. All these factors combined to knock my confidence and self belief.

I had been ready to give it another go and had booked the April appearance in December but it was not to be. Even if I had been fit enough to drive that distance I don't think I would have been capable of dealing with an audience.

I have subsequently written a comedy routine about being accident prone. There's nothing like a bit of trauma to make people laugh so long as they are not the ones suffering it! Sadly it lies in a drawer in my desk along with the rest of my comedic dreams. After this disappointment I decided to concentrate on getting my strength back. Perhaps fate was telling me, in a rather perverse way that going to the likes of Halifax to face a potentially hostile audience before returning at 1.00 in the morning was not for me.

The rest of the month passed fairly peacefully and pleasantly. I was now walking well on crutches. I even managed a week-end rugby trip to Cardiff with John. It was a big occasion. I was surrounded by thousands of people and walked considerable distances. I was very pleased with my strength and stamina. For the first time a return to normal living entered my consciousness including a return to work.

I had not enjoyed work for a long time but I knew that going back would be a significant indicator of my blossoming recovery. I began to look forward to the month of May with considerable anticipation.

Unfortunately it didn't deliver.

Chapter 14 A Not So Merry Month of May

My visit to the hospital in May proved very disturbing.

"Mr. Howard, please sit down."

The consultant had been nothing but pleasant and charming since the day I first staggered across him but I could tell that something was wrong.

"Just let me look at the latest scan."

He examined the results on the screen. From my angle I couldn't even see the break line. Everything looked good to me but then he delivered a hammer blow,

"Unfortunately there has been no change since your last visit. 63% of the bone had healed when I last saw you but no further progress has been made." He looked over his glasses at me giving time for this news to set in. He outlined the geography of the break. I could now see a long crack down my bone.

"You had a spiral fracture of your femur." His blue Parker fountain pen traced it down the image. For a minute I thought "I like fountain pens. They are so much better than biros."

"There are gaps here, here and here."

I was forced to concentrate. I had not been told that it was a spiral fracture. I watched with both interest and alarm as the beautiful pen continued its ugly journey. It was a surprisingly long one. All this would have been very interesting if it hadn't for the fact that he was talking about **my** leg. He continued to look at the screen. The silence was becoming disconcerting.

"I need to discuss your case with a colleague who is a specialist in non-healing bones."

My mind started to whirl. Slow healing would have been one thing. People with Ehlers Danlos syndrome do take longer to heal and slow healing at my age was to be expected but he said non-healing

"Non-healing?"

"At the moment yes; please don't worry. I shall consult with my colleague and we shall formulate a plan."

I tried my best not to look worried.

"You should come back in three weeks."

"The list is full," said the nurse efficiently.

"We'll have to have him back. We'll have to make room. This can't be left."

The words sounded like a bell in my ear.

"Can't be left? Have to have him back?"

I said nothing as a glimmer of panic began to edge out mere worry. I was on my own and desperately needed Linda's support. I knew that she would have asked the right questions. I was too busy trying to stay calm.

"In the meantime we'll provide you with a bone stimulator. It's an ultrasound device. There's some evidence that it promotes healing. We'll see how that goes."

I nearly made a joke about the fact that my bone had not been stimulated in months but the situation was not funny.

"Some evidence that it works" sounded a little like clutching for straws.

I thought "Well does it or doesn't it?" but couldn't say anything

The doctor sensed my apprehension.

"Don't worry I'm confident that you won't need another operation."

I nodded dumbly, grateful for the fact that I might not need something I didn't know I might need!

It would have been useful to have asked "What operation?" but I was too stunned. I didn't say another word.

I was hoping the doctor's confidence was not misplaced but as I got up to go he grabbed my hand and shook it warmly. I left not feeling confident at all. The handshake seemed to be re-assuring him rather than me. I spent the next hour being supplied with the bone stimulator. I was shown how to use it by a diminutive technician with blonde hair and a kind voice.

"Oh dear it's not healing is it? Oh well, let's hope this will do the trick."

"Some evidence" combined with, "Let's hope" did not inspire confidence.

"Didn't you ask what kind of operation?" Linda asked impatiently.

"No I didn't. There's so much going on and I was really alarmed. I didn't think to ask."

Linda sighed but she used to be a nurse and knew what questions to ask. No matter how nice and caring health professionals may be the fact is that the patient is always in a vulnerable position surrounded by people in an enclosed space. That is very difficult to deal with by yourself especially when you are not well. No-one should go on such a vital journey alone. I was simply not strong enough to deal with my problems by myself. I was alarmed at the news that, after nearly six months, my leg had not made the required progress and I faced the prospect that I could be laid up again for another considerable period that might involve further surgery.

Patients need protection from even the kindest of doctors.

I returned three weeks later and had a scan instead of an x-ray. I could tell that things were not good as I walked towards the open door of the consulting room. The man who held all my hopes in his hands was hunched over looking at my results on the screen. He seemed ill at ease and he did not turn to greet me in the same way he had done before. He was examining the screen intently. I sat down in apprehension.

"Riiiight Mr. Howard. I have your scan here." He turned towards me and said, "I'm afraid there appears to have been little improvement. There has been some but not enough. I think you need to go back to work and use your leg as much as possible. This will make the bone work more and generate growth."

"Am I strong enough?"

"Yes," he said. "Yes. I think it will help and we will see you in six weeks."

"Right. Er what about the operation?" There was a long pause.

"I hope we will avoid that."

I tried to work out whether that was better than "I'm confident you won't need an operation". I came to the conclusion that it was worse.

"Can I ask what the operation would entail?

The doctor looked at me and smiled sympathetically. He put his pen down, turned and faced me.

"We would need to take the bolts out of your bone and remove the nail. Then we would put a drill down the bone and scarify the hole. It stimulates growth. Then we'd put another nail in." He paused. "Believe me we want to avoid that at all costs. You'll have a very tough time and you've already been through a lot. I know that all this waiting is annoying but there is some improvement, not much, a tiny bit but as long as we are getting some then we'll have to keep waiting." He smiled kindly. "OK?"

I nodded. I didn't know whether to be relieved or not.

"So we'll see you again in six weeks. In the meantime you should go back to work and use your leg as much as possible."

I nodded. I don't know what shocked me the most; the prospect of that operation or the sudden return to work. Then they delivered another surprise. They took the crutches off me. I felt naked!

"How long will it be then?" Linda asked.

"I don't know."

"You don't know? Didn't they give any kind of idea of likely time-scale?

"No. It's all a lot to take in you know."

She paused thoughtfully.

"When's your next appointment?"

"August."

"Right I'll come with you."

I was so relieved that she was going to come with me at last. I had felt so vulnerable, weak and tired and I looked forward to her support with some happiness. I was less happy about returning to work. I had been out of any work routine for over six months. I knew that the boss did not want or expect me to return. He had been very helpful in getting me details of early retirement options. In fairness I had had quite a bit of time off over the previous six years and I think he felt that it was time.

The boss informed me via the personnel officer that the college was not happy about my return if my leg was only partially healed. They wrote to the consultant and asked for a report. He confirmed that a return to work would aid my recovery but the college was still not happy claiming that they were concerned about health and safety. The example was given of a student running down a corridor and bumping into me but this had never happened in thirty years of teaching. My occupational consultant who was assisting in the planning of my return to work argued that this was simply a matter of timetable planning. My return to work should be organised so that I could avoid crowds. I was not certain that this was possible but I was more concerned that the real reason was that the college didn't want me back at all. This was further emphasised when the boss re-organised the department and appointed a new head who taught the same subject as me. As a result the department would be seriously overstaffed when I returned.

This made me more resolved to return. I had worked at that

college for over twenty years and was not going to be shunted out even if I did want to finish. I had held talks with the Principal before about retiring early. I had been struggling for a while on two counts.

Further Education had changed for the worse. Many students were there simply because of the unemployment situation rather than any commitment to learning. As a result teaching had become much more difficult About five years previously I had had six months off work with depression. I simply couldn't face it any more. Somehow I recovered and returned but it wasn't the same and I was now working simply to build up my pension contributions.

There was another problem however. Sufferers from Ehlers Danlos syndrome get tired easily. The looseness of the ligaments make the joints ache and the body sags. Linda took a photograph of me once. It showed me on my return home from work. I was sat in a chair still wrapped in my overcoat with a cup of tea in my hand. I was fast asleep. I had come home and sat down into an immediate sleep. It looked funny but in reality it was not. It was telling me that I had had enough. A chiropodist once told me, "Your feet work twice as hard as other people just to do normal things." That applies to my whole body. As I approached my sixtieth year I knew I had reached the end of my working life. I was exhausted and ready to go.

The boss was doing his best to ease me out. I could understand his point of view. The situation was very uncertain and no-one could guarantee that I would avoid further absences There had been several difficulties in finding a temporary replacement to teach my classes and he didn't want a repetition of the problems the college had had in maintaining an adequate service.

114

It was a very unsatisfactory situation but I had to look after myself. I just wanted to get well and to be seen to have recovered. I felt that a failure to return to work would have meant that my medical problems would have beaten me for the first time. I saw that as the beginning of a slippery slope into a vulnerable old age. I simply couldn't afford to let that happen. I was to return to a job I hated in order to get well so that I could leave when I decided. It wasn't the best logic. In hindsight I should have just left but I wasn't in the best position to apply perfect logic.

I had to have an extension of my sick note whilst the wrangling continued. I wrote directly to the college telling them that if my car insurance was willing to let me drive because the doctor said I was fit then they had no case. I informed them that I would be returning the following week, working three mornings a week as recommended by my consultant. Reluctantly, the college agreed.

This was a good time to go back to work. It was quiet in college as the end of year exams were in full swing. I would be able to potter around for the last weeks of term and get used to a normal life again before going on holiday. By the time students returned in September I expected to be fully fit and ready to go.

I was wrong.

Initially my return to work went well. Three mornings a week allowed me to settle back into a work routine and my strength returned more quickly than I anticipated. I was very pleased. None of the problems I had imagined happened. In fact meeting people again was very pleasant but I learned an important lesson however. Relationships at work are shallow and temporary. Two of the teachers aides,

Sue and Julie came to visit me as did Neil, one of the teachers. Lots of people sent a card which I really appreciated but they very quickly returned to their own lives. Generally speaking work does not deliver meaningful human relationships. Only a few people really matter. All those staff nights out and the occasional weekends away come to nothing in the end.

My recuperation continued over the summer holidays. My strength was returning quickly and I went walking considerable distances each day. We spent a week in Majorca in early August and I found the sunshine and daily swimming in the sea very beneficial. We enjoyed a day in Alcudia; a beautiful medieval walled town that also has a fantastic market. We walked round for a couple of very pleasant hours before I became happily exhausted.

I felt fitter than I had done in several years and returned to work in late August full of confidence. I had a light timetable due to the fact that we had an extra member of staff but despite this and my feeling of well-being I struggled with teaching from the first day. I had lost completely what enthusiasm I still had. Linda was still off for a further week and with her support, as promised, I entered the consulting room hoping for good news. I had done everything that was possible to enhance my chances of recovery.

The news was devastating however. No further progress had been made. The results of yet another scan showed that there was still a crack in the bone. The possibility of another operation appeared again. I was sent reeling by this. I had been expecting to be told that everything was OK The consultant apologized as if my lack of healing was his fault. He sat with us and explained the situation.

116

"We desperately want to avoid another operation. It will be very difficult for you. We have been waiting and accepting the tiniest of improvements but no progress has been made since the last visit. Whilst we want to avoid an operation we can't keep hanging on for ever. I think we have to set a limit. I want you to come back in six weeks. If no further progress has been made then we will operate."

I nodded as if everything was OK but it clearly wasn't. Linda fidgeted in her seat.

"How long will it take for his leg to heal if he has the operation?"

The doctor was uncomfortable with his inability to say anything with confidence.

"The operation should provide the stimulus for the leg to fully recover but we are totally dependent on Philip's body. Healing always takes longer when you are older and no-one knows what impact the Ehlers Danlos is having on this process. We will have to wait and see."

"What will happen if you don't operate?"

There was a noticeable tension.

"I don't know. It may heal but he could be seriously incapacitated if it doesn't."

Then he turned to me.

"We are not considering failure yet. Keep on doing all the exercises you have been doing and use the bone stimulator."

There were no further questions to be asked.

"My batteries are flat."

I pointed to the bone stimulator but I could have been referring to me.

"The technician will sort you out."

I looked at the nurse who had just spoken. She smiled silently. It was obvious we were both upset. I looked meekly at Linda.

She smiled.

I dithered.

Linda took my hand and we left.

I went across the waiting room to the technician's office.

"Oh dear is it still not healed?" she enquired sympathetically. "It's taken a long time hasn't it? We don't normally have to re-issue these batteries."

I explained the situation to her. She nodded and sighed.

"Oh dear," she muttered once more.

"Well let's just hope this works. Fingers crossed eh?"

She smiled.

Everyone was smiling.

Except me.

I didn't feel like going back to work where I would have been involved in a staff training day to prepare for the new term but the new term was the last thing on my mind. I sat in the cafe of Marks and Spencers as Linda got our drinks. I watched her sorting everything out. I was so pleased to have her with me. She can be so strong. I smiled in gratitude as she sat down to enjoy her drink. "You'll have to go by yourself next time."

"Why?"

"I'll be back at work and I don't want to take time off. I need to get my new job sorted out."

I was as stunned as I had been elated when she said that she would come with me on today's visit. I knew her job was important to her. She had just been promoted in what was a significant recognition of her contribution to the school. I was very pleased for her but her statement was a blow to me. I had taken it for granted that she would be with me and was counting on her support, particularly if they were going to say that I would need a second operation. The next visit would probably be the occasion when I needed more help than ever. I was very upset.

Her timing was awful. She could have kept quiet whilst I dealt with the current disappointing news and told me later but she had managed to blow all my admiration and thanks away in an instant. I felt terrible. I faced another serious operation. I had the prospect of several more months of uncertain recovery and was concerned about my employment situation. I felt the walls of the cafe closing in on me, the smell of coffee nauseating and the heat overpowering.

"Are you OK?"

"Yes" I lied.

"You don't look good."

"How do you want me to look?" was what I thought but I shook my head gently, resigned to defeat.

"You'll have to ask Robert to go with you."

I didn't want to ask Robert. He's a fantastic son but I

wanted my wife to come with me.

"I really appreciated your presence today. I can't tell you how much I valued your support". I looked her in the eye and said, "I need you to be with me" but my mixture of praise and pleading was to no avail however. I had to accept her decision. There was no point in having Linda with me for support if being there was not her priority. She would have been no help at all. I needed someone with me who was committed to being with me.

The next time I went to hospital I went alone.

I tried to understand. Linda had been under a lot of pressure looking after me for the last 8 months and the atmosphere in the clinic would be tinged with yet more worry. It would not be the most pleasant of experiences. She was also worried about her new job and wanted it to go well from the very beginning. Yet again I was an inconvenience.

I accepted her position without creating a fuss but was nonplussed some months later when our daughter Sarah asked Linda to accompany her to hospital for a pregnancy scan. She had no hesitation in taking time off work for that. I know that such a visit would be a much more pleasant experience than sitting in an orthopaedic clinic waiting for some potentially bad news but it did serve to remind me of my position in the scheme of things. I've always said that I was ranked behind the kids, the grandchildren and next door's dead cat. It now felt that I ranked below her job as well.

I returned to work and pretended I was coping but I was feeling more and more alienated everyday. I wanted to leave but hadn't yet found the energy to take the necessary steps to liberate myself. I was too busy existing.

Six weeks later the sliding doors parted and I smiled at the receptionist. I had to wait for an hour. For some reason they could not locate my notes. This only served to exacerbate my nervousness. Finally I was ushered in to the now familiar consultation room. Surprisingly I was seen by a junior doctor whom I had never seen before. The consultant was not there.

The young man took a long time to read my notes. It was reassuring that he was taking his time but disconcerting that he did not appear familiar with my case. It felt like the whole medical team had changed. After what felt like an age he turned to me.

"Right Mr. Howard. What do you think about another operation?"

"I don't understand. I don't know what to think. I haven't got the evidence."

I explained to him what the consultant had said at my previous visit and he pondered again. I did not need this uncertainty. I needed to be told what was going to happen so that I could prepare myself. I didn't want a discussion about my feelings. If the bone had not healed my feelings didn't come into the matter. If I needed an operation then I had to have it. You don't discuss with a mechanic whether your brakes need replacing. If they are worn then you replace them.

"Right, there doesn't appear to be any improvement." He looked at me. "I feel that an operation is necessary."

I had wanted a straight answer and he'd just given me one. I didn't know whether to thank him or kill him. I sat there trying to absorb the bluntness of his words.

"However I think that you should see the consultant just to make sure. I think you should come back in three weeks."

I was now very concerned.

"If my leg is not healing, should I continue at work?"

"Oh yes I think you should continue. Activity is good for your leg."

I left feeling that I had seen a junior who was uncertain about his judgement. I did not feel this was good enough. I didn't want special treatment but mine was not a simple case. I should have been seen by somebody senior. I sat drinking a coffee in the hospital cafeteria as I was unwilling and unable to go back to work.

I was confused. I had thought that this visit would have been the defining one. Now I had to wait again. It felt as if someone had taken their eye off the ball and I was yet again left in limbo. The morning had been a massive anti-climax and I was emotionally drained and not to say a little angry. I was angry at this cock up, angry with my absent wife but most of all I was angry with my bloody leg. I had had so many injuries and spent a considerable portion of my life in hospitals. I had always dealt with it but now I felt weaker than ever and useless. I sat drinking my coffee as people busied themselves round me leading hectic lives whilst mine was on hold.

"What did they say?" she asked.

I thought to myself, "If you wanted to know you should have come," but I didn't say that. I just gave her the bare facts.

"Didn't you complain?"

Again I bit my tongue. What I was actually thinking was, "No I didn't. That's why I should have had someone with me. It was too much to handle." I was too fed up to argue with anyone.

I went back to work and continued as normally as I could. When interviewed by the personnel officer to see how my return to work was progressing I just told her that I was fine.

"Have you been discharged?"

"Er no, not yet."

"Is there a problem that we need to know about?

"Not that I can think of," I lied. "They just want to check on my progress."

I didn't see the point in saying anything. Strictly speaking there was nothing to say. I decided to wait until I knew for certain what was going to happen. It was not as if I was going to be re-admitted as an emergency. Any operation would have to be planned and the college would have been given plenty of time to make alternative arrangements.

There was so much doubt about what was going to happen and I was still clinging to the hope that I might not need another operation. There were too many worries already. I didn't want work breathing down my neck before anything had been finalised. I didn't lie. I just didn't tell the whole truth.

Eventually the appointment day arrived. I turned up prepared for the worst.

"Well I'm pleased to tell you that an improvement has

occurred. It's not fully healed but I feel that continuing as you are doing will now see a full recovery." The head man beamed at me. He seemed as relieved as I should have been. I smiled but was confused.

"I thought I was coming in to be told I'd need another operation. Are you saying that everything is now OK?"

"Well I wouldn't say OK but there is a definite improvement. I think that you should come and see me next May."

"Why has it changed?"

"Who can say? Your body just decided to start getting better again. The truth is we don't know. What I can tell you is that there is about 85 percent healing. I am happy now that you will fully recover."

I didn't know what to say. I simply shook his hand, thanked him and left. For nearly a year I had been doing nothing else but trying to recover from a serious injury and now suddenly the battle was won. I didn't go back to work. Instead I went home and on the way I bought a creamed scone with strawberries in it. I was happy but it would have been nice to have celebrated with someone.

xxxx

I was able to meet the physical demands of work because I had been given a light workload. Due to the over-staffing however I had a mixed bag of a timetable and was teaching subjects I had little knowledge of. In the end the demands of new courses and the behaviour of some of the students proved too much for me.

One particular group caused me no end of problems. Apart from one or two students, they had no wish to work and no

124

commitment to their studies. Those students gave me the worst experience in one lesson that I have ever had in twenty five years of teaching. I finished that first lesson soaked in sweat.

I don't blame them personally. They were refugees from unemployment and for some of them from low income families, the £30 a week that they received from the Educational Maintenance Allowance was a great help. Having sympathy for them was no help to me however. I had to survive as well and I was too old to be dealing with this level of stress especially when management hadn't got a clue as to what was happening in the classroom.

I could not take any more. It was a mockery of education and I didn't want to be a part of it.

When the college offered redundancies I took the opportunity to go. I decided that my time was up but in truth I think I was done before the accident. You can only maintain the energy required to deal with a crowd of young people for so long. When I decided to become a teacher I did not realize how demanding the job could be. Most people haven't got a clue. They all think they know what a teacher does because they've been in a class room. They know nothing. As the year progressed it was clear to me that it was time to seek pastures new.

The accident made me realize that life can end at any time. You should not waste it. When the Principal asked for voluntary redundancies I agreed immediately. I have always thought that you should never give your job away as it is not yours to give. Accepting a redundancy means that someone else would be denied a job. I was comforted however by the fact that someone had already been appointed in my place. Strictly speaking there had been no job loss at all and by July I had left.

Now that I have retired I realize how thoroughly exhausted I had been for a number of years. Anyone who suffers with Ehlers Danlos syndrome tires easily and I am no exception. Generally speaking however I am quite well and have always exercised to keep myself fit. It was this fitness which allowed me to overcome the problems caused by my medical condition but it was now time for a rest. After all my body had been through I felt that I deserved it.

Part 3

A Catalogue of Accidents

Chapter 15 The List

During my enforced idleness I began to think about my conversation with Sandra the student doctor. The cut on the right side of my right shin and the breaking of my left femur were both traumatic injuries that acted as landmarks in my life.

As well as these however I have had numerous accidents. Many of them have resulted in serious injuries including several cuts, broken bones and dislocated joints. A couple of them have been near escapes from death.

I drew up a list, as best as I can remember, of everything that has happened to me. I then began to recall the details of several incidents. This cataloguing was a step towards real change in my life. I had always dealt with each accident as they happened. Now I began to put them all together. Mine has not been a normal life. I was so busy dealing with it I hadn't realized.

THE LIST OF INJURIES

1)   1950 - My birth. Even this was an accident.

2)   180 stitches throughout my life in a variety of cuts of various sizes including:

i)   1950-1952 - 10 stitches forehead.

ii)   1950-1961 - Several unidentifiable cuts to both knees.

iii)   1961-1967 - stitches lower right knee.

iv)   1963 - 17 stitches right side of right shin.

v)   1964 - 11 stitches left side of left shin.

vi)   1964 - 5 stitches lower left side of left shin

vii)   1965 - 13 stitches left side of right shin.

viii)   1966 - 7 stitches right forearm

ix)   1972 - 5 stitches lower middle right shin.

x)   1990 - 22 stitches both legs during the removal of
            varicose veins.

xi)   2002 - 3 stitches right heel.

3)   1962 - Sprained and dislocated right ankle.

4)   1964 - Severe bruising to right shin requiring bed
            rest and an operation to drain it.

5)   1964 -79 Seven dislocations of both knee caps.

6)   1966 -86 Several broken metatarsals in both
            feet.

7)   1968 - Serious bruising to chest after bicycle
            collision with lamppost.

8)   1975 - Inverted base of spine.

9)   1977 - Broken scaphoid bone.

10)   1979 - Ruptured ligaments in left knee.

11)   1987 - Broken metatarsal right foot

12)   1991 - Knocked off bicycle by lorry. Cut knee
            and wrenched back and chest.

13)   2002 - Dislocated right shoulder.

14)   2008 - Broken left femur.

15)   2010 - Dislocated thumbs.

17)   2011 - Attacked by a dog

18)   2012 - Broken metatarsal and sprained ankle.

19)   2013 - Ruptured right bicep.

Chapter 16 Taylor Park

My childhood saw a continuous flow of injuries. It must have seemed to my parents that they would never stop. I had not managed to tell Sandra about every single one during her interview.

In the summer holidays of 1961 my friends and I played daily in Taylor Park. There was a large shelter at the top of the hill. I loved it there and I still have fond memories of my youth spent playing football and cricket all summer long. In fact I spent most of my childhood there.

I was 11. It was a lovely sunny Sunday morning. I know it was Sunday because when I came back home, my mother and father were still in bed. Dad only allowed a lie in on Sundays.

I was playing cowboys and Indians with a friend of mine. I was in the shelter being shot at by that famous Indian brave Ian Bott who was a couple of years older than me.

I could see him lurking behind the stone wall that ran some ten feet behind the shelter and bordered a small wood. I was concentrating on him as I stealthily walked along the highly polished, slatted benches that ran along the whole length of the shelter unaware that someone had broken the slats and lifted them off leaving a jagged gap just wide enough for a child's foot to fall through. I wasn't being stupid. I wasn't clumsy. It wasn't my fault at all. I was just a little boy trying to outwit a "red Indian".

I saw Ian's head suddenly appear from behind the protection of the wall. As I took aim he disappeared from view as my body dropped and my head jolted back. I felt

131

pain as my shin crashed against the jagged edges of the remaining slats. I knew instantly that I was cut. I lifted myself out of the hole as the blood began to trickle down my shin from just under my kneecap. I screamed in pain and ran crying and wailing out of the shelter. Ian could not see my leg from behind the wall. He just saw and heard my tears. In alarm he kept shouting "Philip what's wrong. What's wrong?" I thought "Can't you see?" He couldn't and I didn't stop to explain. I left his voice trailing behind me.

I ran and cried all the way home. I kept looking down at my shin hoping to find that the accident hadn't happened but each time I looked I saw that the sock was getting bloodier and wetter. I approached an old guy walking his dog. He was a man we used to see every Sunday. He was always friendly but I never got to know who he was. I sped past his glasses and comfortable tweed jacket leaving his voice trailing behind as I had Ian's. All I wanted to do was to get home and yet I also feared my father's reaction when I arrived. I had no choice. I needed to be cared for, to feel safe.

I barged through the back gate, the handle banging metallically against the brick wall.

I plunged through the back door and raced, screaming up the stairs. I met my dad at the bedroom door. He stood there in his pyjamas wondering what the hell was going on and then he saw my leg. "Joan get up." he snapped. "We have to get Philip to hospital."

I had ten stitches inserted. Two weeks later I was back in action but even then I began to think about the number of injuries I was getting. I remember thinking that this time I hadn't done anything wrong. Other injuries had been the result of playing football or doing some other forbidden activity. This time I had just been playing cowboys and Indians. This was a reasonable harmless activity. I hadn't been a silly boy. Some one else had wrecked the seat and I had simply fallen through the hole. The question that wasn't asked, however, and would remain unasked for the next forty five years was "Why me?" I had a medical problem it was true. My skin broke easily but why was it me who fell and not any of the others? If Ian had fallen through the hole he would have banged himself, rubbed his knee and carried on but Ian didn't fall through the hole. I did. The one person in the entire park in the entire town who could not afford to fall through that hole did so. Whenever there was a chance of something going wrong it always seemed to involve me.

Not long after my recovery had been completed I sprained and dislocated my ankle. I was playing outside the house. It was an Edwardian mid-terrace with a low wall fronting a small garden. It was a very small garden, so small you could jump over it if you stood on the wall or so I thought.

The previous day my father had told us off for doing precisely that.

"Don't be silly. You'll hurt yourselves!"

That was yesterday and dad wasn't here today. I jumped off the sandstone coping stones that sat on top of the wall. I launched myself, right foot first, from a height of about three feet. Halfway across I realized that I would never be a long jump champion. In a flash it dawned on me that I would not make it. I stretched as far forward as I could but to no avail and came crashing down. My foot landed on the bevelled top of the edging stones and my ankle went over, catapulting me towards the front steps. My brother and his friend were doubled over in laughter. I was in too much pain to cry out to them to shut up. I hated their laughter. I just lay there and thought "Oh no not again." I stood up. The pain was excruciating as I hobbled into the front room. I could hear my brother and his friends playing outside as I raised my foot onto the couch. I intended to lie there until mum came home. She'd fix it. All it needed was a bandage and a cuddle. I knew that if my dad saw me I'd be in trouble. I was in too much pain to have trouble.

"Philip."

"Philip!"

My dad was shaking me.

"What have you done? Victor says you fell and hurt your ankle."

I rose from my sleep trying to find a lie in the remnants of my dreams.

"I fell over and hurt my ankle."

"Did you jump off the wall?"

"No! I just turned quickly and fell."

"Victor says you jumped off the wall."

"No!"

I looked him in the eye. I had learned that that meant telling through the truth and I had to lie convincingly. I needed help and sympathy, not a telling off.

"OK. Let's have a look at your foot."

He took off my slipper and sock.

"Joan!"

My mum came in and her hand went to her mouth. I looked at her then I looked at my foot. My toes peeped out from the swelling. I don't remember how we got there. I certainly don't remember an ambulance. My parents didn't have a car nor the money for a taxi and I was in no state to go on the bus. The only thing I remember was Nurse Duffy coming in to the treatment room and announcing that it wasn't broken but very badly sprained. Then she said something very strange.

"Now Philup did you fall over or did you jump off the wall? We need to know because it'll affect how we bandage it."

I remember thinking that she was trying to trick me and that my dad had put her up to it to see whether I had been telling the truth.

"I fell over." I said making certain I looked her in the eye.

"OK well we'll put it in a plaster cast anyway".

I thought, "It won't make a difference will it?

I saw her give my dad a knowing smile and was convinced that I was right. I hoped I was right. I didn't want to be crippled but I was too frightened to tell the truth. I spent the next three weeks or so in a cast worrying about whether my lie had resulted in incorrect treatment that would cripple me for ever.

Again the link between injury and being a naughty boy had been confirmed. I got hurt because I was a silly, naughty boy. If the pain I endured throughout my childhood was any measure, I must have been a very naughty boy indeed.

Chapter 17 A Brief Respite

The list shows that the injuries stopped for a short while. In the early seventies I had got married, started a family and had a developing career in the Health Service. All seemed well but it was merely a lull.

February 1978 was a very cold month. We had had a couple of days of heavy snowfall which had remained and turned into thick ice. For some reason this did not stop my running the full mile to the railway station as I did most mornings. I seemed to be perpetually late for my train. Every morning I was in a rush but extremely fit as a result. On one of these icy mornings the penny finally dropped. I was about a quarter of a mile from the station when I said to myself,

"This is bloody stupid. You could break your leg or your neck running like this on the ice. You of all people should take care. Don't be stupid."

I stopped running and began to tread more carefully.

"If you are late for work then you're late. Loads of people will be late today. Stop running" I instructed myself.

I took three sensible steps on the ice, half turned to check the traffic before crossing the road and fell flat on my face. My body twisted as I fell and I slapped the floor with my hand rather like judo contestants slap the mat in order to break their fall. Despite the sudden shock and disorientation I couldn't help noticing a young woman passing in her car. She looked on helplessly, her mouth hanging open in alarm as she drove by indicating the severity of my fall. I felt no pain however. At first I thought I'd just bruised my hand. I hadn't just slapped the floor however; I had belted it with considerable force. As well as breaking my fall I had broken my scaphoid bone which is located in the main body of the hand below the thumb.

I began to feel an awful dull ache as I sat on the train but it didn't stop me falling asleep as I did every morning. I left Liverpool's Lime Street station and walked another mile to my workplace.

It was becoming increasingly obvious that my hand had something wrong with it but it was not until a further hour of pain had passed that I happened to mention my predicament to one of the nurse managers. He responded by placing my hands together side by side. It was only when I saw the comparison that I realized I'd done some serious damage. My right hand was swollen enormously in comparison to the left. Amazingly I had not noticed how swollen it was until he did that. I couldn't believe the difference. It was so obvious. I went immediately to the Accident and Emergency department at the Royal Liverpool Hospital where it was confirmed that I'd broken the bone. I was shocked when the doctor gave me a sick note for 3 months.

"I don't need that do I? I'm a clerical worker."

"Yes you must rest. It needs time to heal."

I took the sick note in disbelief and followed the nurse through to the appliances section where I waited to have a plaster put on my arm.

"I've been told to stop off work." I said to the technician as he wrapped the wet bandages round my hand and arm.

"The doctor's put me off for 3 months."

"You'll be off for a lot longer than that," said the

technician.

"The scaphoid is only a little bone but your thumb moves on it. It's very slow to heal because it's at the extreme of your body and yet does such an important job. It doesn't get the nutrients as much as other bones. You'll be off for months."

Now the prospect of being off work didn't bother me at all. I was disillusioned with my job and totally bored and was, in the event, soon to leave but I did not seek to be off work at any time. Nevertheless I was criticised for being off work so long. Questions were asked by both my managers and my colleagues and some unpleasant criticisms were made. Today I don't think this would be acceptable. I think it constituted harassment. Not only that but it is a fact that if you turn up to work when you have been certified as sick then you are not insured. If I had suffered a complication as a result of using it when I was supposed to be resting would my employers have helped me out? I don't think so. In the event I was off for sixteen weeks and didn't return to work until May.

I don't know if they still put people off for that long but this injury caused me a lot of problems with my employers. What was most annoying however was that the accident happened, not because I was being reckless, but just at the point when I decided to be cautious and sensible.

I have to watch myself constantly and monitor my activities but it is possible to be too careful. A generalized anxiety about my safety was creeping into my thought processes. It was highly likely that this had begun to add to my problems instead of reducing them. It seemed that I was destined to suffer accidents and injuries for the rest of my life no matter what steps I took to avoid them. It seemed like there was no escape.

****

Would you like a heavy breather Madam?

It was Sunday May 18th 1980. I know the exact date for two reasons. Firstly May 18th is my wife's birthday. Secondly I had started university in 1979 as a mature student and was approaching my first year exams held at the beginning of June.

We had had a very pleasant day and had celebrated Linda's 27th birthday with a walk in the park and a pub lunch. The kids had enjoyed feeding the ducks in the pond and had fallen asleep as soon as their heads touched their pillows.

Linda had gone out for the evening and I was sat at my desk revising. Our bedroom was at the front of the house and I was sat against the window positioned as far away from the door as I possibly could be. Sarah and Robert were fast asleep in the next room. As I sat there engrossed in my work, the phone rang downstairs in the hall.

When we first moved into the house we had decided not to cover its lovely tiled floor with a fitted carpet. Unfortunately the blue, brown and white mosaics now acted as an echo chamber and amplified the shrill tones of the phone some five fold.

Anxious not to let it wake the children I shot up from my work, dashed quietly across the bedroom and landing and hurried down the stairs towards the offending instrument.

Unfortunately I had spent some of the afternoon making shelves for the front room. I had not finished and had left all my stuff out in the hall in order to complete the work the next day.

As I hurled myself down the stairs in the fading light I did not see the piece of wood that sat on a chair. I hit it with my flexed left knee and immediately fell to the floor in agony. I could not get my breath but still felt the need to stop the phone ringing. I crawled along the tiles to the cause of my pain, pulled it to me by the cord and lifted the receiver. It was Linda's friend Rita.

"Hello, Linda?"

I could not reply.

"Hello?"

"Aaagh" I groaned.

"Hello?"

"Aaaaghh." I repeated.

"Who is this?"

"Aaaarghhhhh." I continued with heavy breath.

"Linda?"

"No it'ssssss meeeee." I said it all in slow motion.

"Are you alright?"

"Noooooo. IIIIII'veeeee bangedddddd myy knneeeeee."

"Oh dear. Is Linda there?"

"No. She's gone out to her mum's." I replied. I was now getting my breath back but was still lying on the floor.

"When will she get back?"

"Oh not long Aaaargh."

"Could you ask her to ring me?"

"Yes."

"Hope your leg is OK. Bye"

Rita is probably the only woman in history to have phoned her own heavy breather!

I put the phone down and lay there in the fading light clutching my knee hoping the pain would go. I could now see the half formed shelf, chair and tools. How could I have missed them? They blocked the entire exit from the stairs. After about ten minutes I got up. I could just about walk. I cleared my self-made obstacles to the side in order to create a safe passage but I was in too much pain to put things away. I climbed the stairs very slowly leading with my right leg. I put the fact that I couldn't bend my left knee to the fact that I had bruised it. It took me an age to return to my desk and just as I was in the act of sitting down Linda came in. I got up and repeated the journey that I had just made and limped down the stairs. My leg was beginning to throb. I smiled at Linda and offered to make a cup of tea.

"No I'll do it. You go and finish your work. I'll bring you a cup up."

So I turned to climb the stairs once more. As I turned the remaining strand of ligament that had not been cut by the sharp edge of the wood severed and I fell down the stairs in a heap, screaming as I did so. I made more noise than the phone had ever done. Fortunately the children slept on but my sleep would be severely disturbed for weeks.

My brother was called to take me to hospital where a Jones dressing was applied. This consisted of cotton wool wrapped round the entire length of my leg. This was then wrapped in crepe bandages. Another layer of cotton wool

141

was applied covered by yet more bandaging. I was issued with crutches and told to come back the following morning for X-ray.

By the time I got home I was in agony. The doctor had not allowed for the fact that sufferers from Ehlers Danlos syndrome bruise more readily than normal. My knee was throbbing as the bandaging constricted the swelling of my knee. I couldn't stand it and persuaded Linda, against her better judgement, to take the bandaging off.

She was right to hesitate. When the knee was released it ballooned in front of our eyes and a dark head to the swelling curved round my knee in ominous fashion. All three of us gasped together. Linda phoned Casualty and was told to re-apply the dressing and bring me back in. I managed to sit down on the back seat of Victor's car with my leg extended fully. When we arrived at the hospital I stood up out of the car. My leg was getting heavier by the minute and my knee pulsed as I moved. Every swing of my crutches took my breath away and it seemed to take an age to get through the casualty doors. The doctor took one look, tutted and I was admitted immediately.

I had ruptured a ligament in my knee and had to have surgery to fix it. The reason I had so much difficulty was because the doctor was unaware that EDS resulted in excessive swelling. I was more damaged than other patients and the swelling placed abnormal pressure on the bandages. I spent a fortnight in hospital and was only able to take my exams in September. I passed them easily having had little else to do but revise.

Laughing cleaners

In 1986 I re-established the rugby league team at David

Lister High school. Out of hours sports had always been a part of the job for many teachers. In the 1980s however, a series of industrial disputes occurred over working conditions and wages. In addition to strike action, teachers withdrew themselves from unpaid weekend and evening activities such as sports and art clubs and drama groups. After the strike many never went back to these activities. I fully agreed with and supported this action. The problem was that it was assumed that teachers would do this kind of thing and when teachers wanted recognition for the quality of the work they did and the commitment they showed, they were told to get stuffed.

I was still a very new and enthusiastic teacher when the strikes ended and I found myself volunteering to run a rugby team. I thought it was an important part of the job and helped the kids develop a pride in their school and each other. It also helped build strong relationships between pupils and teachers.

We had a good season in that first year and were preparing for a cup match towards the end of the season. It was a lovely April evening, one when the sun is in your face and the temperature is rising heralding the coming of summer. It stopped being such a lovely evening however when I went over on my right foot. One of the boys said later that someone had pushed me but I don't recall that. I simply remember the hot, tearing sensation as I fell over. I clutched my foot and rubbed it thinking it was just a bit of a twinge. I got up and continued, ignoring the pain that refused to go away. After training I waited for the boys to shower and change.

The boys left and I locked up. As I turned away from the door I felt a second stabbing sensation in my foot. It made me stop short. I shook my foot hoping that that would somehow sort it. I walked between a set of classrooms on my left and nicely manicured lawns on the right. It was all very pleasant but such thoughts disappeared as the pain became more intense and it became impossible to walk. My foot had swollen rapidly when I took my boot off and removed the restraint on the injury. Putting on my shoe as a replacement had merely served as an attempt to put the restraint back on but my foot would have none of it.

I stumbled to a stop and knelt on the floor clutching my foot. Some cleaners in one of the classrooms laughed as they thought I was messing about as I passed their window but when I didn't move it became clear that I was in some difficulty. They came out just as Penny, one of the teachers arrived. She had seen me walking in her direction and was able to tell immediately that something was wrong. Within minutes I was in her car on my way to my second home.

I emerged several hours later with a pot on my foot. This time there was no mention of a sick note. I had a day off work to rest and then returned. I tried to walk the short distance to work. I managed to walk a few hundred yards before the pain in my hip became unbearable. I had been walking at an angle due to the height of the surgical shoe that was wrapped round the pot. As a result of walking at this angle I had trapped a nerve. I found myself sat on a garden wall contemplating the fact that I couldn't make it to school and couldn't get back home when a member of staff stopped and gave me a lift.

I managed to do the first 2 lessons but by break time I was exhausted. If ever I should have been given a sick note it was for this. The plaster was beginning to cut into my foot which was turning a mixture of black blue and red . Once again a doctor had not understood the extra damage sustained by sufferers from Ehlers Danlos syndrome. Within an hour I was back in casualty with my plaster removed and my leg raised.

I was fitted with a larger plaster and told to go home and rest for a fortnight. I couldn't help contrasting this with my time off sick when I broke my scaphoid. This looked much worse. I know the scaphoid is a very difficult bone to heal but it seemed to me that the doctor who saw me about my broken foot was simply unaware of the likelihood of excessive bruising in someone with EDS. Not for the first time I had suffered increased problems due to the lack of knowledge regarding my medical condition.

Chapter 18 A Lifestyle of Calamity

Not all my accidents have resulted in injury although they have placed me in harms way.

The lack of injury did not make them any less traumatic.

It was a dark, dark night

In early 1968 I was a spectator at a rugby match between my home town St. Helens and near neighbours, Widnes. Two friends and I cycled the nine miles to the ground, watched the game and then cycled back home. Games between these rival clubs are always very intense affairs but I can't remember the score. In fact it's surprising I remember anything from that night. On the return journey we decided to cycle on the wide pavement in order to avoid the line of traffic. Cars stood bumper to bumper for the entire mile of road that lay between the ground and the first set of traffic lights. We were three fit and strong young lads hurtling along at great speed with me in the rear. Bushes and garden walls whooshed by in the darkness.

Suddenly I saw a man walking his dog on my left. He was dressed in a black coat and a black hat. Even the dog was black and yet I saw them both in the darkness. He had stopped to let us pass and was stood with his back against a garden wall holding the dog's leash tightly both for our and its protection.

I was a considerate and well brought up young man. I knew that I shouldn't have been on the pavement and moved out to my right to give him room. I made full use of the wide pavement and as I swept past him I began to shout "Thank you," but I didn't finish the sentence. Despite the darkness of the night I had seen them both clearly. What I hadn't seen was the lamp post!

It stood some thirty feet in height, was approximately twenty inches in circumference and consisted of several tons of concrete. It was bathed in "thousands" of megawatts of light and I didn't see it! Luckily I didn't catch it straight on. Instead I hit it with my right handle bar in such a way that I flew off at an angle to the left. My eyebrows brushed the concrete tower and I was almost able to smell it. I landed, after a perfect swallow dive, on my chest, at the feet of this man and his dog. I scared the living daylights out of all three of us.

"Are you alright lad?" he enquired as I got up off the floor and checked my bike.

"Yeh. Sorry."

I turned and saw a woman in a passing car mouthing to a fellow passenger "Oh he looks a mess."

As I re-mounted my bike I thought to myself, "I've just hit a concrete lamppost at twenty miles an hour. What's your excuse?" With that I was up and away again. I caught my friends up just as we entered the main road to our estate. They had no idea that something untoward had occurred to me. The only signs of a problem were revealed when I walked into my mum and dad's chip shop, which was bathed in bright light.

"Oh Philip whatever has happened to you?"

"What?"

"Your chest. Look at it."

My brand new white tee-shirt had a hole in it the size of a saucepan and my chest was scratched and bloodied.

"Oh." I looked down in surprise.

"I fell off my bike."

With that I went out again and put my bike away.

I went upstairs, had a bath, binned my shirt and thought no more about it.

This accident illustrates something important about how I had learned to deal with the enormous number of injuries I was suffering. To me it was just another accident. It was nothing unusual. I just got on with it. It wasn't a case of "Oh how awful!" It was more, "I was lucky that time. I didn't need stitches."

Downright or Upright?

I left school in 1969 and began work as a trainee hospital manager. The training included spending a week in as many hospital departments as was practicable. Alongside my studies I worked in a mortuary, kitchen, pharmacy portering, laundry, transport, switchboard and in the bin yard. During my time on the bins I worked alongside Joe, a jovial man in his fifties. Standing at 5' 6" he possessed a full head of pure white hair. His ruddy complexion combined with a pot-belly to suggest that he enjoyed a pint or two. I had spent two days laughing my way round the back alleyways of the hospital but on Wednesday Joe turned to me with a serious expression on his face.

"Do you want to drive my truck?"

For some reason Joe was very proud of his bin wagon. I couldn't see why. It was the ugliest, dirtiest and most weird looking contraption I had ever set my eyes on and must have been at least thirty years old. It was a flat bed truck, big enough to carry three domestic sized bins. At the front was housed the electric motor which stood some three to four feet in height and acted as a back rest for the driver who stood on a dead man's brake pedal which was located in the footplate. This meant that you had to take your foot off the pedal in order to operate the brake instead of pressing down on the pedal as you do in a car.

A lever extended forward to the driver's right. This lever steered the vehicle.

"It's simple," said Joe, unaware of the fact that I had never driven anything in my life before.

"It's downright to turn right and uplift to turn left." As he said the latter he cupped his hand as if supporting an imaginary woman's breast. I nodded enthusiastically and with Joe stood balancing on the flat bed behind me we set off down the long slow gradient towards the rear of the hospital. The road accommodated one vehicle at a time. It was flanked on the left by a high stone wall and to the right lay a manicured lawn with flower beds lovingly tended to by the hospital's gardening department.

I stood on the dead man's pedal that took the brake off and allowed the truck to accelerate quickly over the wet road surface. It gathered pace quickly and I became aware that the road and the wall turned right at a sharp angle ahead of me. Instinctively I pressed on the brake pedal that only served to release the brake even more. This and the gradient combined to send the bin cart hurtling towards the wall. I pressed and pressed but nothing would slow it down inducing panic into my brain.

I couldn't remember how to steer.

"Downright" had been Joe's instructions or was it "Upright"?

I remembered, "Uplift" but could it have been "Downlift"?

"No!" I reasoned, as the wall was now some mere twenty yards away. "There's no such word!" Then for some inexplicable reason I pulled the lever up and sent the truck swerving towards the wall on the left. Realising my mistake I pushed forcibly down on the lever and the truck lurched rightwards at full speed round the bend with me still pressing as hard as I could on the non-existent break.

I hung on to the lever for grim death and to my horror saw that a lorry was parked across my path. There was no way I could get past. As the writing on the side of the lorry got bigger and bigger I finally remembered to take my foot off the brake pedal. The truck slithered to a halt on the wet surface. I could smell the paintwork as my nose touched the side of the trailer. There was an eerie calm. I opened my eyes. The writing on the side of the lorry was now so close that it had gone out of focus again. The lorry driver and his mate were standing at the side of me, mouths gaping. I smiled hesitantly and turned to check that Joe was unhurt but he wasn't there. I looked down the roadway and saw legs and arms reaching up from a tubby little body that had just crushed a week's planting by the gardeners. Joe looked like a dead cow lying in a field waiting for collection. Suddenly he stirred, his red face almost purple as he staggered to his feet.

"What the…? What the fuck?"

Without waiting for a reply he gestured to me to get off which I did without hesitation. Joe turned the truck around and headed back to the depot for a cup of tea leaving the driver and his mate still silent and open-mouthed. I walked back in shame and embarrassment and never drove the trucks again.

Ffffffff.......!!!!!!!

I had worked in the Health Service for ten years as a manager but decided to leave in 1979. I was bored with the job and I had not joined in order to implement the cuts to a Government service that were being planned in the office in which I worked.

Obviously our personal finances were a big concern and unfortunately I made a big miscalculation which has affected us ever since. I thought that we would have to move to a cheaper house in order to survive on a student grant despite being twice advised by a neighbour that if I reduced the mortgage my grant would also reduce in proportion. In those days they paid your mortgage if you were a mature student!

Unfortunately the advice didn't sink in and we bought a much cheaper property that needed renovating, in a poorer part of town.

Doing the house up proved too much for me. I had neither the time nor sufficient skills to complete the job. In the end I got a friend to install the central heating. He had just finished a training scheme as a fitter. He didn't do a bad job but it took ages and heaped further pressure on us. Now this person had a slight stammer and I am not making fun of someone who had a speech problem It was the way the whole situation fitted together that made it so dramatic and to some, funny.

One evening I was hammering down floorboards in the front bedroom when I heard a muffled cry from the back bedroom where my friend was busy soldering pipes in the loft. I stopped but heard nothing and so continued with my work.

Again I heard a muffled cry.

"FFfffff!!"

"Hello?"

"FFfffff!!"

"Yes!"

"FFfffff Phil!"

"Yes!"

Suddenly his slim figure fell from the loft to the landing.

"Are you OK?"

My friend stumbled to his feet. He was covered in dust and two white eyes stared out from his filthy blackened face.

"FFffPhil!!"he repeated.

"What's up?" I said.

"FFfffff fire!"

"What?"

"FFfffffucking FFfffffire! The house is on ffffire!"

"I've set the house on fffire! Get the ffffire brigade. QQQuick!"

I looked up through the hole in the loft and could see clearly a warm red glow against the brickwork. He had managed to ignite straw left by nesting birds.

The fire brigade arrived in minutes. They stood on the central heating pipes that lay beneath the absent floorboards and flattened some of them. They cut a six foot hole in my ceiling and flooded my loft. I said

"Thanks!"

A neighbour had phoned Linda. By the time she arrived with her mum there were two fire engines and twenty neighbours stood outside watching smoke (caused by the firemen hosing out the flames) billowing out from the eaves of her new home. It looked far worse than it actually was but it ensured we made a grand entrance to the street. Luckily the central heating still worked!

Trapped in the lift

There have been other incidents that have had their amusing side and have not always involved an injury. I seem skilled at getting myself into a pickle despite my best efforts. One day in 2007 the building officer at work announced that a new teaching block had been handed over to the college. He encouraged staff to have a look round the new facility. I was teaching a second year Advanced level class who were doing revision exercises in preparation for a January exam.

They were all busily engaged so I decided to take 5 minutes to have a quick look at the new building. I was very impressed with the place and reflected on how working conditions at the college were steadily improving.

As the former head of Special Needs I decided to descend from the first to ground floor in the new lift. A lift had been installed in the main block when the college first opened and had improved access for disabled people beyond measure. The only problem with it was that it was narrow, resulting in the fact that wheelchairs could not turn round. Disabled students could enter the lift easily enough but had to exit in reverse, a somewhat nerve-wracking experience, particularly if you could not turn your head.

I wished to see what improvements had been made to disabled access. The new lift was pleasingly spacious. The controls were large and light push-button affairs. The door was glass so it did not feel claustrophobic and anyone walking by could tell if someone was in difficulty for whatever reason.

It had one major draw back however. When it got to the bottom I couldn't open the door. Evidently you could get in by pushing the button outside but once in you needed a swipe card to get out. It was supposed to deter casual users and ensure that only disabled people who had been issued with a card, used it.

My first reaction was a brief sense of panic and claustrophobia. It was an awful feeling and I told myself not to succumb to it. I began to work things out. I tried the alarm but it hadn't been connected. They obviously weren't expecting anyone to be using the lift yet. I banged on the door but there was no-one in the building and kicking the door didn't seem to help either. I was trapped. After about fifteen minutes my students began leaving the teaching block from whence I had just come. They were only forty yards away but were not looking. Even if they had looked they wouldn't have seen me through the different layers of glass. I was trapped behind the doors of the lift, encapsulated in the doors of the stairwell and entombed by the doors that led to the outside. I stared in disbelief and wondered if they were complaining about me as they walked by. I hammered on the door and shouted as loudly as I possibly could but to no avail. As the light began to fade my concern grew.

Another fifteen minutes passed. Staff began walking by on their way to their cars.

None knew of my predicament and no matter how loudly I shouted or how hard I hit the doors not a single person heard me. It began to dawn on me that I could spend the whole night there. I remember thinking "What if I need a wee?" I looked at the cables and wondered about the danger. If I did need a wee would I electrocute myself up a stream of urine? I did not want my body to be found the next morning with my hand attached to the ashes of my penis accompanied by a rather strange expression on my face!

I found out later that had I returned to my point of entry the door would have opened. The thought did occur to me but I rejected it as a stupid way to design a lift. Why would I want to go back upstairs when I had just come down? I wanted to get out at the point I had chosen to so I dismissed it as a silly idea. I was also concerned that the light was fading quickly and the lift travelled very slowly. I didn't want the caretaker to come and lock the front doors whilst I was on my way back up. He would not have seen me so I decided to stay put.

It had now gone dark. Surely I would be seen? I moved about as much as I could hoping to trigger the sensors that would switch on the lights but nothing happened. As luck would have it, the foreman builder came in to pick up his tools. He stood in amazement looking at me before he pressed the pad on the outside. The door opened immediately.

"How long have you been here?"

"Over an hour."

"Bloody hell."

He escorted me out.

"You need to report that mate," he said after we discussed the reasons why it had not opened.

The mode of entrance was subsequently altered. Telling people about it produced mirth around the college. I was the butt of good humoured comments for weeks. Looking back I can see the funny side as I can with lots of my accidents but at the time it wasn't funny at all. I'm glad that people had a laugh at my expense but why was it me who had to be the one to find out that the lift had a stupid mode of operation? It added to the belief amongst others that I was accident prone and somewhat clumsy, a bit of a clown. It also served to ensure that my self esteem sank even lower. No matter what I did I seemed to be an accident waiting to happen. I have been burdened with labels such as these all my life but I hadn't done anything except try to get out a lift!

Trapped in the toilet.

In fact this is not the only time I have been trapped at work. Many years earlier something similar occurred. I was working in a different block; one that didn't have a lift although this didn't stop me having problems. I had finished work and left the staff room. As I got to the end of the corridor I decided to go to the toilet. Whilst sat there I suddenly felt very tired as I usually did when I sat down at home. I'm pretty good at taking power naps. They normally last for about ten minutes. It's to do with muscle tension caused by lax ligaments. The muscles hold my joints together but this causes fatigue. I regularly need ten minutes during the day.

I woke up from my nap still sat on the toilet. I thought to myself "It's awfully dark." I knew that the lights went out automatically and came on when anybody moved. It helped with security when the building was empty. Sure enough the lights came on when I moved to the sink to wash my hands so I thought no more about it.

As I stepped into the dark corridor I thought to myself "It's awfully quiet". I walked to the main doors and lights came on. I pulled at the doors and thought "They're awfully locked."

As in the lift a decade later my first reaction was a sense of panic which I allowed to last for only a very brief moment. "Telephone!" I exclaimed to the empty space. I went back to the staff room and phoned the caretaker. As I waited, hoping he would answer I noticed that the clock was showing a time of 5.45pm. I had been asleep on the toilet for over an hour and had not heard anyone leaving. I presume the caretaker had checked the toilets but I hadn't heard that either. No wonder my bottom felt a little sore! He would have seen that the lights were off and concluded that no-one was in.

The caretaker's perplexed voice answered.

"Hello? Who's that?"

"It's Phil."

"Phil who?"

"Phil Howard. I'm in A block."

"What the fuck are you doing there?"

"I was asleep."

There was a pause followed by restrained hissing, like a kettle about to boil. "You effing wanker!"

What was I supposed to say?

I'm sure Malcolm wanted to make me pay for my apparent stupidity because it took him 25 minutes to cover the hundred yards to the door that would give me my freedom. I wanted to see the funny side of it but he did not smile at all. The police officer who was accompanying him did. He thought it was really funny but I suppose Malcolm was not amused because a call-out by the police cost his budget £100! Evidently not only had I set off the college lights but the silent alarms that registered at the local police station. Blue lights had arrived at the same time as Malcolm had received my phone call so he had not been able to cancel the police call-out. He was not amused.

These incidents were all apparently very amusing and I laughed about them along with everyone else but there were other emotions lurking beneath the surface which I hadn't dealt with. I wanted the accidents and mishaps to stop. Malcolm asked a very pertinent question in his annoyance.

"Why you? Why is it always you?"

Although he didn't realize it this was a very important question. It did always seem to be me. At one point I even managed to receive surgical treatment when I didn't need it.

Titus Underpantitis

In the early 1990s some small lumps appeared in my lower legs which caused a dull ache along their whole length. I had developed varicose veins.

Evidently it is not uncommon in people with EDS. The laxity in their body tissue means that lower leg valves can collapse. I was suffering discomfort in the whole leg however. When I went for my pre-op examination the young registrar couldn't work out what was happening. He had scanned both legs with ultrasound. Even I could tell that there was a marked difference between the sound in the thighs and the lower leg.

He repeated the scan several times, each time pressing harder to the point that he was beginning to hurt me. Then the consultant walked in.

"I don't understand," said a perplexed registrar. The veins in the lower leg are clearly not competent but the result I am getting in the thigh does not fit with the patient's description of his symptoms."

"Why?"

"The sound suggests that all the veins are fully competent but the patient is complaining of a dull ache in his upper thigh and groin."

The consultant listened and agreed with his junior.

"There is an inconsistency. You are correct. Sometimes we get anomalies. We'll operate on the whole leg anyway just to be sure." The younger man nodded and gave way to the wisdom of his senior man who obviously knew more than he did. That afternoon they operated and I thought my discomfort had gone. For a week or two I wore very sexy full length surgical tights to give my new blood routes some support. I was fine when I sat down with my legs raised but if I got up the pain became quite severe until I started to move. Evidently the contraction of muscles was forcing blood through my legs. After a while the pain subsided and eventually disappeared in my lower leg but the dull ache in my upper thigh and groin returned. I was dismayed to say the least. The operation had not cured it. It was only when I weighed myself that I realized what the problem was. I had put on weight and the elastic in my underpants was tight in the groin! I had gained a stone in weight over the previous 18 months but was still wearing the same size clothes. I had naturally assumed that the discomfort was to do with the varicose veins when it was actually caused by tight underpants! It was a very similar feeling! I must be the only person to have had an operation because his underpants were too tight! All I can say to the taxpayer who funded this on the NHS is that I'm sorry. I won't do it again!After a visit to Marks and Spencer the pain disappeared.

I had a reputation as a bit of a clown, someone, perhaps, who couldn't quite look after himself. I wanted these incidents to stop but as my life progressed they didn't and what was even more worrying was I had no idea how to stop them. The fact that my medical condition was linked to all of them had not occurred to me at all. It is clear now that the reason it was, "Always me" was that I was living my life in a permanent state of stress. I was so concerned to avoid situations leading to an accident that I kept walking into them. My whole life had become one recurring accident.

"Oh Phil you're just an accident waiting to happen." People laughed at my apparent clumsiness or apparent stupidity.

I was living a lifestyle of calamity. I wanted it to stop but I couldn't find a way to make it happen.

Everyone laughed.

I laughed. It was my only protection.

It wasn't funny.

Part 4

Relationships

Chapter 19 Starting To Think

Breaking my femur and the subsequent difficulties I had in healing shook me to the core. It was clearly obvious that I was at risk and vulnerable in a way that I had never understood or admitted to before. The conversation with Sandra had set me thinking. She was right. I began to see that the accidents had not only affected me physically. They had left their emotional imprint on me as well. I had blocked out the pain I had endured as a child in order to survive. I knew that I couldn't continue living my life in the way that I had done for the previous fifty-eight years. My life had to change fundamentally.

Doing this is not easy and to be successful I had to plan a strategy. This involved several steps. Firstly I had to understand how the medical problems I had, had affected my life. I needed to look at the relationships I had with my closest relatives and friends and I needed to understand how such a life history had affected me as an individual. Linked with this I needed to find out why I had had so many accidents. Of course I had a medical problem. My skin bruised or cut easily and my major joints dislocated regularly. The question I wanted answering was this; why was I having so many accidents in the first place? That wasn't simply down to the condition of my skin or ligaments. That was down to the way I was living my life. I hoped that it would be possible to avoid accidents in the first place. I had to understand how my personality had been affected by my accidents and if my personality was contributing to their occurrence.

Finally if I was going to change my life successfully I had to construct a plan that would guide me in changing how I saw myself and those around me. I also needed to change how others saw me. In short I needed to turn my whole world upside down and inside out.

I knew that if I failed in this task I might soon be dead.

I began the first part in earnest whilst I was still lying in my hospital bed recovering from my broken femur. I needed to overcome the boredom but equally something was compelling me to write. I kept a diary for each day in hospital; a simple recording task of what was happening to me but very soon I began writing notes about the people around me.

At the same time two colleagues brought in a work booklet from the psychology department at college examining why people have accidents. It was done to cheer me up which it did but it also struck a chord with what I was already thinking. The booklet basically examined two views of why some people have more accidents than others. It examined whether people who have lots of accidents are clumsy and therefore accident-prone or whether there were other, less obvious reasons that might result in a more sympathetic view of the individual concerned.

Whilst in hospital I had received many cards from people wishing me well. Many of them had comments on such as "Oh no not you again?" They reinforced the first view that it was my fault that I had hurt myself yet again and that the accident was "just typical of silly old Phil."

Labelling people as accident-prone puts the blame on them. The accidents are their fault. The alternative view placed the blame outside the individual and looked at whether they were in a life situation that they were uncomfortable with and found difficult to handle.

163

I immediately rejected the first explanation and gravitated towards the second. For years I had been misdiagnosed, labelled as clumsy, even sometimes, downright stupid. I knew I was none of these things but couldn't understand why I had had so many accidents. Suddenly as I read the second half of the booklet a light began to shine at the end of a tunnel. It was a tiny light and the exit seemed many miles away but I began to feel that perhaps the accidents were not my fault. I was not stupid, naughty or clumsy. Maybe I had serious problems that were not my fault.

Without realising it I had begun a journey to understand my circumstances, to confront my difficulties and ultimately to defeat them.

Then just before they left one of my friends commented on how I looked much better than they had expected but I actually felt dreadful. I thought to myself, "Why am I smiling and telling jokes? I am on a saline drip. I have two fans blowing cooling air on me in an attempt to control my rising temperature and the medical team are taking blood samples every day to check for infection. Why can't I stay quiet and act as ill as I feel?" I was masking my feelings as Sandra had suggested.

Maybe I had never come to terms with being the person I was. I had wanted to be someone else with a different skin. To doctors, my accidents presented a series of injuries and problems that had to be treated one by one as they occurred. They dealt with the physical symptoms as they presented themselves but it was clear to me that I had to look at more than just the physical results of repeated injuries. My personality and my relationships with others had been affected by my medical status. It dawned on me how unhappy I was. I had never realized it.

164

There were a multitude of interlinked problems to be unravelled. Suddenly that tunnel exit seemed a long way off. I began unpicking my relationships with every person close to me including myself. I wanted to know who I was and how my experiences had affected my view of myself and others. I felt that if I could do this I could start to understand why the accidents happened and plan a way to prevent any more occurring in the future.

Chapter 20 Dad

It is only normal that my mum and dad both had important affects on my development. My mum was always trying to ease the pain of injury or reduce the impact of the many conflicts I had with my dad. She soothed things as best she could. I could always look to her for sympathy but my relationship with my dad always seems to have been strained and volatile. Only now do I realize how frightened he was and how I misunderstood him.

Every child has problems with their parents. That is simply a normal part of growing up but my medical problems were at the root of many of the conflicts I had with my dad and they gave us plenty of ammunition for arguments.

My father was the third eldest of seven children. By all accounts he had quite a happy childhood, cared for by two loving parents but when he was ten his father died and everything changed. His mother led a hard life of constant work in order to make ends meet and grief-stricken, withdrew into herself.

She had to combine taking in washing, peeling hundreds of potatoes by hand every day for a chip shop with looking after six children. The reason seven had become six was that one of the twin girls, Betty, had been transferred to the care of an auntie. My grandmother who had been pregnant with the girls at the time of her husband's death simply couldn't cope. What was particularly tragic for them was that my grandparents had longed for a girl having had five boys. Granddad never saw them.

Of all the children it seemed that my dad was the one who struggled the most to deal with his loss.

Once, my mother said to me, "I don't think your dad ever got over his father's death." Jack and Joe were older and were very soon drafted into the armed forces. They would have been away anyway and were able to find distractions to help them deal with their loss. The other children were very young and for them the sense of loss was probably less marked.

At ten years of age dad followed his father round everywhere. My granddad once warned him to be careful because if he put his nose any closer to the piece of wood he was planing he'd take it off.

"Your dad lost his father at a very vulnerable age and never came to terms with it."

When he was old enough he was conscripted into the British army serving in Palestine. Whilst on sentry duty the soldier stood next to him was shot dead when an Israeli terror gang launched an attack on the British base.

As a result of all these factors a sensitive lovely young man became an angry and damaged adult. Nobody would have talked to him about his grief. It wasn't the done thing then. As I write these words and remember him I get a sense of his loneliness.

Like all males of his generation, no-one ever said anything loving to him and he would have learned patterns of behaviour that most young men would have followed. As a result he cared for his family in the best way he could, he provided for us. He never stopped working, whether at paid work or in the home. He was constantly decorating and improving houses as we moved from one house to the other in a constant upgrade.

On one occasion my mother happened to mention to my

dad that the kitchen was badly designed.

"If they moved that door to here we could have three walls with work surfaces on instead of three walls each with one door in. Then I could have cupboards all the way round."

Dad was off work the next day. When my mother came back home from her work he'd already knocked a door out of one wall and put a frame in and was near to completing the bricking up of another.

She had only talked about her desires in passing and had not meant him to act on it but that is how he saw his role. He provided a good home to the best of his abilities. Working hard was how he was able to show his love.

When I was about eight, dad became quite ill for a short while. He had developed a triple headed boil on his neck that meant he could not turn his head because of the pain. That did not stop him from going to work on a building site however. He would have had to bend and twist all day and must have felt awful but a working class family couldn't live on sick pay.

My dad never failed us but he was not an easy person to live with. He came across as an angry person and could be very intimidating sometimes. He never showed me any affection and I don't remember ever being cuddled by him. I spent most of my childhood in fear of him. He seemed to get very angry when I hurt myself. He couldn't understand why I wanted to play rugby and cricket and football. He did not follow sport at all so he couldn't understand my passion for it but when that passion was combined with a constant risk of serious injury at any moment he couldn't deal with it.

When I was about eight, I came home from school sporting

a big black bruise on my knee.

"How did you get that?" asked mother.

I had no explanation. I was frightened of what my dad would say when he came home so I sat at the dining table from about 4pm until 6 in order to hide the evidence of yet further apparent stupidity on my part.

He finally came home and we sat to tea. He hadn't noticed anything. For a brief while it seemed that I would get away with it. I planned to go to my room straight after tea and then to bed. With any luck he might not notice but then I made the mistake of asking for some salt.

"It's in the kitchen."

"Can you get it for me mum?"

"No go and get it yourself."

I hesitated, my eyes pleading with her to protect me but I had not made her privy to my plans. She was immovable.

"Go and get it."

I stood up and turned quickly in the direction of the kitchen but the game was up.

"What's that?" he said as my legs moved out from the table revealing their guilty secret.

"It's a bruise."

"How did you get it?"

"I don't know."

My defensive manner probably seemed like arrogance. I was stiff and upright but it wasn't arrogance. It was fear. I stood looking him in the eye waiting for my destruction, trying not to cry.

I can't remember what happened next. What I do recall is the fear I felt. I was under enormous stress. I was injured. I shouldn't have been frightened. I should have felt comforted and protected but I didn't.

Things changed suddenly when I was thirteen. I was stood in the doorway of the dining room that formed part of our chip shop. I was talking to my dad as he cut pieces of fish with a large carving knife in preparation for opening time. My brother wanted to come through and so he lifted me under the armpits and moved me to the left. I brushed the smooth bevel- edged wooden arm of an easy chair with my left shin.

"I'm cut.......!"

"Don't joke!" My father chided. "You'll upset your mum."

"I'm cut I'm cut!" I shouted as I pulled my trouser leg up. A piece of my skin fell on the floor and was quickly scooped up with the knife by my dad and thrown onto the coal fire that burned behind him. I was dimly aware of my skin burning as mum applied bandages and Victor apologized. Dad went to get the van and took me to hospital. This was the first time I was given a local anaesthetic and didn't feel the eleven stitches being inserted.

My dad had seen the accident and hadn't believed I was hurt. It was the first time he had actually seen me have an accident since I was a baby. The fact that the cut required as many as eleven stitches made it even more shocking. He simply couldn't believe the ease with which I had been damaged. He was upset and horrified and resolved to do something.

He took me to see our family GP Dr. Marsden. My father was asking for some sort of guard for my shins, a type of football shin pad. Marsden smiled at my father and said,

"He's just a young energetic lad who is a bit accident prone."

My father nearly hit the roof. I could tell he was seething but fortunately he kept calm and reasoned it out with the doctor.

"Look at his legs," he said. "He's had loads of cuts. How many stitches has he had? I saw him get cut and it was from nothing. I couldn't believe how easily he cut. He needs protection."

I remember his next words.

"I insist!"

He left Marsden with no choice. A month later I was fitted with shin guards.

I remember thinking as we drove home "You actually care then!" I was surprised. I had just seen my dad fighting my corner and winning and I realized something most profound the significance of which took many years to understand.

He wasn't angry.

He was frightened.

Both my parents were dealing with a medical issue that was misdiagnosed until I was 19. Life must have been very difficult for them and it ruined my relationship with my dad and sadly, I only came to understand him after his death.

Dad died in 2001 after having spent six months in a nursing home. We knew he was deteriorating but his death was still a shock. I had never considered that my dad would be anything less than indestructible. Eventually he was taken into hospital. Even then it did not occur to me that these were his final days. I was under the delusion that he'd get better.

I had been to see him over the weekend and had thought he was showing signs of improvement. I travelled some 150 miles back to Hull. Linda and I decided to go to the cinema. We never saw the film. I can't even remember the title. The call came as the title came up on screen. I do remember the couple behind tutting as Linda whispered into the mouthpiece. I had every sympathy with them. It annoys me when people use their mobile phones inappropriately but I was helpless. I didn't want to find out to whom Linda was speaking and I didn't want to hear the stifled complaints from behind either.

"C'mon." Linda grabbed my hand and I followed her without question. I've often wondered what those people thought when we left. Were they angry or relieved that we had gone? Did our sudden departure tell them that something serious, something earth-shattering, had happened in my life? Did they care? Whenever I think of my dad's final hours I think of them and wonder whether they enjoyed the film.

It was snowing when we got outside in the early March air. It began slowly at first and then got heavier and heavier as we travelled along the M62. By the time we reached Saddleworth Moor I began to worry that we might not make it as the snow was beginning to lie on the road surface. A plaque proudly boasts somewhere that it is the highest motorway point in England. It is probably the bleakest as well. Millions of white stars were driving horizontally into the headlights like they used to do in the opening credits of a Doctor Who programme. Despite my fears that we wouldn't get through we were getting closer. I imagined a local radio station informing its listeners that the police had advised people to travel only if it was absolutely necessary.

This was. Linda had told me when we got in the car that they didn't expect my dad to survive the night. We began to descend into the West Lancashire plain passing Manchester and then heading towards Liverpool. The snow had stopped by now but conditions were still treacherous. I was trying not to drive too fast. I should have let Linda drive but I needed something to do. I couldn't just sit and wait. Eventually we arrived in the hospital car park. I was busy trying to find money for the ticket when Linda grabbed my arm and propelled me towards the ward.

"Stuff it! We haven't got time."

I wondered if she knew more than she was letting on. We ran over the snow despite my fear of falling. I couldn't have an accident now and I was also desperate to get to my father. I used to work at this same hospital as a junior manager. I used to know it like the back of my hand but it had changed fundamentally. There were new buildings everywhere with signposts to match. We struggled to find the ward but eventually we arrived at the nurses' station.

"I've come to see Frank Howard," I blurted out.

The nurse, a large black guy with sad eyes looked at me in gentle surprise.

"He's dead."

I spun round to face my brother.

There was no "I'm sorry mate but," or "Come into the waiting room I need to talk with you."

My brother is not the subtlest of souls.

"You missed him."

Perhaps he struggled to find the words but the ones he chose pinned me to the wall with blame for failing to arrive in time. I raised my hands in horror conscious that the nurse was watching us as my mouth gaped open. My mother appeared from behind my brother's wide frame and I put my arms around her and held her in silence.

"There's a quiet room just round the corner," the nurse said gesturing to his right. "It'll be more private."

I walked towards it in disbelief. Dad's death had been happening slowly in front of me for weeks but it nevertheless still came as a complete shock. We sat there silent and motionless.

"He had a massive stroke."

My mother's lips trembled and she looked at me imploringly as if she were asking me to stop what was happening.

"You can go and see him if you want. He's lying on the bed."

I turned and saw the drawn curtains across the corridor. Without speaking I got up, walked towards his bed and stopped. I stood at the foot of the bed looking at the body of a frail old man lying with his mouth open. I had been so afraid of him and now all that remained was the silence, the stillness. I sat down and found myself talking to him.

All that anguish, all that fear, all that guilt lay there motionless. It had all come to nothing. I resolved there and then never to regret anything again. I resolved not to repeat his mistakes. I had made some in bringing up my children but there was so much more I could do as a granddad.

I looked at him and shook my head.

"You never stood a chance did you?

It was all stacked against you. I caused you so much worry and there was no one to advise you. There was no support system whatsoever. You couldn't cope.

I understand."

I paused. I could see life continuing outside the window completely unaware of the drama unfolding inside. Car lights danced on the snow as they turned round the corner. Orange street lights pierced through the steam as it rose from one of the hospital's boiler rooms and drifted across the glistening rooftops before dissipating into the air. I caught a sight of my own reflection in the dark window pane and I could see the mirror image of my father's other side. He looked like somebody else.

The way his head lay flat on the mattress without a pillow for support, his mouth open reminded me of the only other time I had seen a corpse. As a trainee administrator in the Health Service I had to spend a week working in every department to get a taste of all aspects of hospital life. As part of this training programme I worked for a week in the mortuary. Somehow I had managed to avoid seeing a body for three days but on Thursday at 2.00pm I ran out of luck. The porter had just gone on a message, leaving me alone with the dead and the smell of the mortuary. An undertaker's van pulled up outside the front door. They had come to collect someone.

"Hello. We've come for Mr. Albert Jones."

I looked at him gormlessly trying to hide my fear and horror. He hesitated.

"Mr. Jones?"

I quickly gathered myself. I was frightened but I didn't want to look stupid. I looked along the row of names and found the person required on a middle shelf. I opened the door and pulled out the tray before letting it down to the floor. It sat there at an angle of about 30 degrees.

I was mindful of a news item that had appeared on the news the week previously. It had told of a woman who had been found on Morecambe beach. She had been pronounced dead and was transferred to the mortuary for a post mortem to determine the cause of death. As the doctor leant over he noticed a tear drop in her eye. This was a sign of life. She was rushed into Accident and Emergency and amazingly made a full recovery. The dead had apparently come back to life.

I had these thoughts swirling in my boyish mind as I ripped open the shroud. Before the body could be released from the hospital I had to check the name and case sheet number that was written on Mr. Jones's arm in indelible ink. They had to match the details written in the undertaker's file. I was struck by the way his mouth lay open and his stillness. I stood and stared.

"OK that's our man." I turned to check his documents when the most horrible thing happened. For a few seconds the force of friction must have been stronger than the force of gravity until the latter took over. Then the body began moving down the slope of the tray. I saw it move out of the corner of my eye. The dead had come alive again! I uttered the manly sound of "Yoops!" as I jumped into the undertaker's arms knocking his glasses askew on his nose.

"Steady on lad."

"Oh I'm sorry I thought he was moving. I thought he was alive."

The two men grinned as they loaded their client into their van and departed. I did not go into that mortuary again.

As I looked at my dad he reminded me of that man. Somehow even in death he didn't look relaxed. It seemed like he was hanging onto life, despite its obvious absence, like the woman on the beach. There was to be no resurrection however. I began speaking to him again.

"I remember the look on your face when you saw me on a push bike. I must have been about 11. Your mouth dropped open and you completely forgot that you were driving a large vehicle. I was so delighted that I could ride. I waved at you as you passed by but your face told me that I would be in trouble when you got home. For that moment I didn't care. I was riding a bike! You'd spent a whole week's wages on a train set in the hope that I'd play with it quietly in the house in safety. £12 was a lot of money and you were always afraid of being short of money.

I appreciated the sentiment even then. I know I didn't play with it and I'm really sorry but it wasn't for me. I did my best dad. I really did try to play with it. I know you weren't angry, not really. You were just frightened weren't you?"

I paused.

"I just wanted to say I'm really sorry."

177

Tears began rolling down my cheek.

"I wished I could have known you differently. It would have been nice to have had normal problems in our relationship. You never stood a chance did you? I mean they couldn't even tell you what was wrong with me. You never had any help at all did you?

It must have been really difficult. I'm so, so sorry."

I looked out of the window as yet more steam drifted upwards past the street lights. After a few seconds I turned to him once more and whispered,

"I understand dad. I really do and do you know what?"

I hesitated.

"I forgive you."

I wanted to take hold of his hand but was afraid to. I didn't know what it would feel like and I supposed he wouldn't have wanted that gesture anyway so I didn't. I wanted to feel close to him in death in a way that I had never managed whilst he was alive but I simply sat there instead.

"You're free now aren't you? It's all gone. No more worrying."

I wanted to tell him that I loved him but I didn't go that far. I respected and admired him but I had always been too frightened of him to say that I now loved him. He was too uncompromising in general for that. I admired his intelligence. I respected his honesty and integrity but I can't say I loved him.

"I'm sorry."

My father was damaged and in turn damaging. He was

simply unable to cope with what life had thrown at him.

There was nothing more to say. Eventually I stood up and turned to leave. At the corner of the curtains I stopped, looking at him for one more time,

"Thanks" and left.

My medical problems had damaged my relationship with my father. During his life I had always felt him to be hard and uncompromising. I blamed him for his anger and feared him throughout my entire childhood.

Writing a book can give you the strangest of experiences. I edited the above yesterday. I have worried all night that I have been unfair to my father.

It is now Sunday morning. I have just had a shower and am naked except for a golf cap that I have found in the clean linen. I am wearing it so that I don't forget to take it downstairs to my trolley. I catch a glimpse of myself in the bathroom mirror and stop dead in my tracks. I am looking at the image my dad.

"Look it's your daddy! I can hear my young mother's voice as if it were yesterday. I am four years old and can see him high up on a building site as we walk past with our mum. He is separated from us by a safety fence, which encloses bags of cement and mounds of sand that are being raised upwards in a lift. He takes his peaked cap off and waves it at us. It is the same colour as the one I am wearing now. I recognise his smile and we wave at him.

Then for some reason I see the same smile again but now his face is much closer. He is sat by mum as they both face me. They are smiling sweetly and talking softly. I am 10

179

years old and have just burst in through the front door.

"Mum!!Dad!! They want me to play goalkeeper for the school team next week. I'm good mum. I really am. Can I please? Nigel and Julian said they'll lend me some shin pads so I'll have two thicknesses. I'll be OK won't I? I won't get cut. Can I play mum please? I'm asking mum because I already know what my dad's answer will be. Maybe she can get round him.

They sit me down and reason with me. Mum doesn't come to my aid in the way that I had hoped she would. They don't tell me I can't play. They are too sensitive to do that. Instead they ask me if I think it's really sensible knowing how easily I get cut. They let me make the decision. My smile fades. I know they are right but I am bitterly disappointed.

Next morning I trudge to school. As I enter the school gates Nigel the captain is waiting for me. Immediately he waves the shin guards and runs towards me and I deliver the bad news.

It is the worst day of my young life. I never played for a school team.

My dad destroyed my dreams with that smile. His kindness and consideration smashed my hopes. He wasn't a monster but to a ten year old he seemed like one. He deserved my love but he didn't get it and its now much too late as I sit at my desk, still naked, save for the peaked hat that looks like the one my father wore, throwing these words at the page.

Chapter 21 Victor

Victor is my non-identical twin brother. He too has been affected by Ehlers Danlos syndrome but in different ways to me. When he was very young he suffered from a hearing impairment caused by a laxity in body tissue in his ear. Fortunately it improved as he moved towards his seventh birthday. His speech development was hindered due to his hearing problem and as a result I became his ears and voice box. I seemed to understand what he was trying to say even when our parents couldn't work it out. Unfortunately this gave me a certain degree of dominance in our relationship that lasted well beyond his immediate physical problems.

This was not helpful to Victor. I was a very angry little boy who had also suffered a fair degree of trauma. I was angry at the controls placed upon me, angry at the pain I was enduring and damaged by the anguish within my family. I was also frightened. As a result I was not the best-equipped person to deal with Victor's problems. I had too many of my own

Just as my father took his anguish out on my apparent stupidity I vented my anger on Victor's gentleness and acquiescence to my authority. In short I was a bully. I hit him regularly for the slightest misdemeanour's that incurred my wrath. I hit Victor regularly and he had no defence.

To make matters worse he was often forced to go and play football or rugby with me on the basis that he understood about the danger I was in. Victor was not expected to hurt me like other boys might but he hated any kind of sport and resented having to look after a brother who was better at those things than he was. For my part I couldn't bear the fact that he was apparently normal and didn't want to play. I would have given anything to have had skin like him and be able to play the games he hated. I resented his apparent wastefulness and was impatient with the difficulties he had whilst playing so unenthusiastically with me.

I considered him lazy and a fool and was so angry with him. Now Victor was and is most definitely lazy but he's no fool. He is a wasted talent and I feel that my behaviour in our childhood played a considerable part in the damage he suffered. It is a sorrow and a guilt that still lingers and will probably do so for all my life.

Victor has not suffered the cuts and bruises nor the number of dislocations that I have but he has had quite serious trouble requiring surgery on his knees. He was a bus conductor but could not cope with the constant climbing of the stairs. The company tried to re-train him as a driver but his knee collapsed under the pressure of operating a heavy clutch. As a result he was retired on medical grounds and has not worked since he was 24.

He suffers from depression, weighs about twenty stone and has lost all his teeth. I'm not responsible for all his problems by any means but I have been a major contributor. In more recent times I have tried to recover the situation but he is unyielding and does not even manage the basic niceties when I phone my mother and he answers with nothing but a grunt.

Ehlers Danlos Syndrome doesn't just affect you physically. It affects who you are and your relationships with others. I was a damaged little boy and so was Victor. I have tried and will continue to try and build some sort of relationship with him but I am afraid that all my attempts will continue to fail.

I'm sorry. What else is there to say?

Chapter 22 Mum

My mum was always the person who I felt understood what I was going through. We now know that she has Ehlers Danlos Syndrome. She always knew that she had something wrong with her skin also but it was not diagnosed in her until I had been diagnosed correctly. In her youth girls didn't undertake physical activities in the way they are encouraged to do now. This meant that whilst she had some cuts and bruises, the punishment she took was not on the same scale as I endured. It was nevertheless significant.

Mum seemed to understand what was happening to me.

Whereas my dad couldn't understand my love of sport, she did. Her father had been an active sportsman and had even had trials with St. Helens Rugby League club before an offer of work on ships took him away. Later a damaged ankle, a result of a motorbike accident had finished altogether any lingering hopes of a rugby career.

She understood. That didn't mean she wanted to allow me to play rugby but she was always trying to find ways to accommodate my desires. She was always sympathetic and approachable and she acted as a buffer between me and my dad. I will always be grateful to her for that. Unfortunately my medical problems helped to cause a rift in my parents' relationship. Mum was faced with the impossible task of dealing with a medical condition that had been misdiagnosed, a husband who was terrified of its consequences and a son who just wanted to be a normal little boy.

In her old age she has had many medical problems. She has recovered from breast cancer. She suffers from diabetes and is considerably overweight which has placed significant stress on her hyper elastic joints. As a result she is in constant pain. Mum has also had considerable problems with her digestion. She suffers regular bouts of vomiting and diarrhoea and is regularly confined to her bed.

These problems are a warning to me. The laxity of tissue in the intestine does cause problems for some people who have Ehlers Danlos syndrome. It results in the fact that food is not absorbed efficiently through the intestinal wall. This is manageable if you are otherwise well but mum is not. She put on a considerable amount of weight through a combination of poor diet and a total lack of any significant movement. She has tablets for diabetes, vomiting, diarrhoea and pain. I don't think that 10, sometimes more, pills a day does her fragile intestines any good at all. She has many significant health problems but she has compounded them by a lack of care to herself.

My relationship with my mum has been affected by our shared condition. I could not understand why anyone with EDS would allow themselves to put on excess weight. The joints hurt enough without an extra burden being put on them. As a result of their problems both my mother and brother have sought refuge in the arms of doctors to such an extent that they have become "medicalised" but doctors can't cure everything.

About five years ago I arrived at their house at about 1.00pm after spending some three hours on the M62. I had journeyed from Hull to their home in St. Helens. I spent all afternoon and evening with them. At about 10.00pm I started to feel pains in my feet. I took off my slippers and socks and was horrified at what I saw. Both feet had swollen alarmingly. I pointed out to my mother and brother that that had happened because I had been sat down for the best part of 12 hours without movement. I suggested that they had regular problems with swollen feet because of their lack of movement. They looked at me blankly. My response to this problem was to go for a walk despite the discomfort and very quickly my feet returned to normal.

My mother and brother remained seated, watching TV. Their response was to take water tablets to relieve their problem. They don't need tablets. They need to move. At 5'1" my mother weighs about sixteen stone whilst my brother weighs about six stone more than I do.

Last year mum stayed at our house for a week. One day we visited a garden centre and had lunch in its cafe. I had a salad and my mother had a Panini cut into two halves.

"Oh I really enjoyed that but I can only manage one of these," she said.

Mum proceeded to wrap the uneaten half in a serviette so that she could take it home for supper. I had spent the last 90 minutes pushing her in the wheelchair with one hand whilst pulling a trolley full of plants with the other and still felt hungry after my salad.

"I think I'll have a scone."

"Oh so will I."

"But I thought you said you were full?" I asked.

"Oh I could manage a scone," she smiled.

I said nothing.

The scones duly arrived. On the plate beside the scones were a portion of butter, and two little dishes containing in one, jam and in the other, clotted cream. I selected jam and clotted cream. My mum used all the butter and then topped it with all the jam. Finally she smeared on the cream. I couldn't believe that someone who complains about her aching joints so much and takes an inhaler for her "bad" chest could eat so much especially after she had just said she was full.

Again I said nothing. I did not want to row with my mum. I managed to resolve my concerns for her welfare by reasoning that at eighty-one she was entitled to do as she pleased. If she wanted to enjoy food and gain so much weight that she suffered pain in her already damaged joints then so be it. Other people smoke. Would we tell them off for being stupid once they had been diagnosed with cancer? We might have thought it but we wouldn't have said it. So why should I tell my mum off?

I had just worked this out and felt really good. I could now move forward to enjoy a more pleasant relationship with my mother. She could be what she wanted to be, do what she wanted to do.

The following day we travelled back along the M62 to St. Helens. It was blisteringly hot and my car's air-conditioning had stopped working. We stopped at some services to let my mum have a break as she was struggling to breathe and needed some air. As we passed a shop she said,

"Do you fancy a Magnum ice cream?"

It was the first test of my new attitude.

"Yes OK, why not?"

We sat in the car with the doors open and the fan blowing

at maximum and enjoyed the ice cream together. It was very pleasant. Before long we resumed our journey. An hour later she began to struggle again so I pulled into the services for a second break. I unloaded her wheelchair once more and pushed her round the complex to get some air. As we passed a shop she said,

"Do you fancy another Magnum?"

"No," I replied sharply.

"If you're hot get some water."

She sat like a scolded child and I felt guilty. I didn't know what to do. Did I have the right to tell her what she could and could not eat? Of course not but equally did she have the right to talk to me about how ill she was, how she suffered with pain and breathlessness and fear of dying? I didn't want to watch her damaging herself and I certainly didn't want to suffer the stress she was causing me. In addition pushing someone in a wheelchair, who is two stone heavier than oneself is not a reasonable expectation especially when it is totally avoidable.

I felt like a bully and a victim at the same time. I was in turmoil again. Then something profound struck me from out of the blue. I realized that I was not only frightened for my mum's health; I was frightened for my own. I have been advised to make certain I don't put weight on so that my loose joints don't suffer unnecessarily. I have been very disciplined in this regard. I exercise regularly, perhaps too much sometimes and I watch what I eat. I count the units of beer I consume. I never eat a sweet when I go for a meal in a restaurant. At home if I have a sweet I reduce the portion of my main meal. I NEVER buy biscuits. I know that if I did I could eat a whole packet so I won't have them in the house. I am determined not to suffer unduly in old age.

 My mum's attitude to her own health represents the sum of all my fears writ large in front of me, mocking me. She has become everything I am determined not to be. This is not fair on her. She is entitled to do what she wants and must be allowed to bear the consequences of her actions. Equally I have not been unreasonable either. Our medical condition has put strains on our relationship. I am confused generally. I want to be sympathetic but on the other hand I feel that both my obese brother and mother are acting irresponsibly. They know they eat too much and seem determined to actively ignore the consequences and blame others for their predicament.

My brother once saw a consultant about pains in his chest. The doctor told him to lose weight and stop smoking. On the journey home he turned to my mum and said, "Well he was a fat lot of use wasn't he?" He had expected to be given a pill to sort out his problems rather than taking responsibility for himself.

They have become trapped. They both have a medical problem like me, which causes pain in their joints so that it hurts when they are active. Their response to such pain was to reduce their activity. As a result they gained weight and this added to the discomfort in their joints causing them to become even less active. Consequently they gained more weight, suffered more pain and the cycle continued.

When my mum comes to stay with us she loses half a stone in a week and stops coughing. She is physically capable of much more than she allows herself to do. Both my mother and brother are depressed and their individual depressions rub off on each other, multiplying their problems. They both need to find some activities, which separate their lives somewhat but it is very difficult to get this to happen. Recently my brother decided to take up fishing, something he has always had an interest in. He baulked however at the fact that he would still have to pay the full annual registration fee despite the fact that half the year had elapsed when he enquired. He therefore decided not to apply for a permit until the following year. I pointed out that £24 for the remaining 6 months was still only £4 a month for a day out and was still a cheap activity but he would have none of it. He therefore refused to pay and did not go fishing, remaining sat in his seat.

My brother is not mean. He was pretending to do something whilst doing nothing because he was afraid to get out of his rut. I don't think he wants to be unhappy but I'm equally sure that he is afraid of the changes that will take him out of the rut.

Telling someone that they need to change is all very well but it's like telling someone who is ill to get better. Sometimes we need an outside intervention. That can often be something as simple as a friend or partner who keeps you on the straight and narrow but what if you haven't got one? The physically disabled, the mentally ill and the elderly are often socially isolated. They can't or don't get out as much as others might. They have no one to go out with. If they don't go out or have nothing to do they can get depressed. When they get depressed, they can lose even more social contacts and so the rut deepens into depression.

Add into this mix the fact that my mother and brother, like me, suffer considerable pains in their joints that are themselves tiring and depressing. In this situation creating change can be very difficult. Recently mum collapsed at home and was taken to a community hospital. On admission a bright young doctor said "You will not go home until we've sorted out your problems."

Seventeen days later this optimism was reduced to, "You have a multitude of problems. Ehlers Danlos being the main one and it affects everything else. I think you should go home and take life easy."

She was discharged with a new set of stronger antibiotics and a prescription for even more tablets. The doctors didn't know what to do so it's not surprising that my mother didn't either. One thing is certain a person's attitude to their disability is as big an issue as the disability itself.

My friend John and I have discovered golf in our retirement. I never thought I would be playing golf. I had played it once when I was twenty nine and got so frustrated with my inability to hit the ball more than fifty yards that I never looked at it again until now, some thirty years later.

A cold February wind was biting at us as we walked up the eighteenth fairway towards the last hole and a warm drink. As I limped forward on painful feet John stopped half way towards his next shot. With one hand on his golf trolley and the other on his knee, he leant forward trying to take in a breath that the wind was stealing from him.

He has suffered from severe asthma since early childhood and cannot remember life without an inhaler. He did not let it stop him from being active however and he has always attempted to live life to the full.

"You and I both have reasons not to be on a golf course today," said a biscuit pointed in my direction. We were sat in the warmth of the clubhouse asking each other why we put ourselves into difficulties.

"We both could have said, 'I can't do that' and not bothered and we would have been right."

"But" added the biscuit pointedly,

"We would have been damned. We have a choice. We can die in our beds or live on a golf course." He paused, "Even if we are crap at it."

Just at that moment part of his soggy biscuit that had been dunked in his tea fell into his cup. We laughed but the humour of the moment did not diminish the seriousness of his words.

John's experience of a medical problem has been totally different to mine. He was confronted with a shock that changed his life fundamentally and forever. It must be very difficult to have something and then have it taken from you. I had my medical problems from birth and knew nothing else. What unites us both, however is a desire not to be beaten by these problems.

This may sound very positive but in truth it is a very difficult line to draw. "Living your life to the full" is a lovely cliché but it ignores many difficulties. The very drive that keeps us going is the very thing that could kill us. John has been so ill on occasion and I have been badly injured. What on earth was I doing up a ladder with knees that dislocate? I should have said "I can't do that," but I was too afraid to admit it to myself. John was right. We are "damned".

A friend once said that the aim should be to push your self and not punish yourself. This is a very fine balancing act and good balance is not something possessed by people who have Ehlers Danlos syndrome. It is simple to give in and easy to overdo it.

My mother and brother gave into it. When they got hurt they lay down. When I was injured I got up but my positive approach has not been without cost. Victor has not been in hospital as many times as I have. He has not had to endure the pain I have. I cannot say who is right and do not judge those who are defeated by injury, pain or illness. It is their right to feel that they cannot deal with it. There is no simple answer.

My mum has been foolish. She has let herself become inactive and overweight and as a result has endured many health problems but that's not a crime. There are millions like her. It is just that EDS punishes every weakness or "misdemeanour".

The attempt to be "Normal" to deny my vulnerabilities has not only caused me much pain and injury but it has also damaged my mental health. My mum and brother are depressed but so am I. In my attempt to be "normal" I have placed myself in situations that produced inevitable failure and self-doubt coupled with self-loathing as a result of my failures.

I now realize that mum needs support not criticism. That is not easy. It is very stressful listening to someone complaining about their problems as they tuck into another sweet that they shouldn't be eating. Trapped by pain she has sought consolation in the pleasure of food. I need to understand and rebuild some bridges burnt by my well-intended but nevertheless unhelpful criticisms.

Chapter 23 Doctors

Mine is an inherited medical condition that will stay with me all my life. As a result I have been in regular contact with members of the medical profession. I owe my life to their knowledge and dedication. That is not to say, however that I am totally uncritical. Some doctors have been excellent. A couple have been less so.

One doctor in particular had a profound effect on my life. He was a junior doctor assigned to give me a medical as part of my application for a job in the Health Service. The examination was nearing its end with nothing untoward found.

"Any particular problems?" asked the young man.

"Nothing much." I replied. "I have haemophilia."

"Really?"

"Yes. I've had lots and lots of cuts."

I told him about my list of injuries. He listened intently and frowned.

"You cut easily but you don't bleed a lot?"

"No, my dad has always said I hadn't got haemophilia but the doctors told him he was wrong."

Doctor Barker examined the myriad of scars on my virtually skinless knees.

"It's paper thin," he said.

I sensed a growing interest, even excitement in him.

"I don't think you've got haemophilia. I'm not sure. It could be one of two things."

He played with the scar tissue again.

"I need to check it with my professor. Can I get back to you?

"Of course."

Was someone actually going to tell me what was wrong with me? What would be the implications? I was surprised, elated and confused and a little worried.

Three weeks later I walked into a wood panelled lecture theatre at Liverpool University's

School of Medicine accompanied by my mother, father and brother. We had been invited to meet Professor Clarke who was then the President of The Royal College of Physicians.

"Nothing much," was what I had said to the young doctor when he had asked me if I had any medical problems. I was used to getting cut and bruised. It was nothing special. Injuries were a fact of life. I had come to accept them as part of normal living. To me it was all very ordinary and yet now the President of the Royal College of Physicians had come from London to see me.

"Interesting. Very interesting." They all said.

"Well done." They beamed, at their young colleague who glowed with pride.

They turned to my parents and he explained their findings. As I remember, the fact that I hadn't got a blue tint in the whites of my eyes eliminated one of the alternatives.

"We are pretty sure you are suffering from Ehlers Danlos Syndrome. As far as we know there are 87 recorded cases."

They explained the details of the condition. It was very

tense and exciting. After 19 years someone was describing symptoms that I recognised. My father had been right all along and the doctors had not listened to him when he told them I hadn't got haemophilia. He was vindicated. I felt liberated. People would now know how to help me. I would no longer be so alone.

It was a wonderful moment and marked a fundamental change in my life. Doctors now knew what the name of my condition was even if most of them hadn't got a clue what that name signified.

Evidently misdiagnosis is still a common problem for sufferers of EDS but back then there was no support group to provide information and challenge ignorance amongst the medical staff. We had been on our own.

From that day on my relationship with doctors changed. My condition had a correct name. I wasn't accident prone as my GP had suggested to my father and I certainly wasn't clumsy or a fool. It would take many years, however, before I could come to terms with the effects of those labels.

This was not to be the only contact I had with Liverpool University. In December 1972 I was working at Whiston Hospital on Merseyside. It was a huge hospital with over 1000 beds. I arrived at Linda's parents after finishing work. It was cold and raining as I jumped out of the car and ran towards the front door. The tarmac of the road met with light grey concrete of the gutters and kerb but the pavement consisted of yet another strip of tarmac and then light grey concrete paving stones. In the darkness I couldn't make out where the road and pavement met. I stubbed my toe against the kerb and fell forward onto the pavement. As I fell my shin rolled over the top of the kerb. I knew immediately, without looking, that I would be paying another visit to hospital. I hobbled up the steps to Linda's front door and banged as hard and as fast as I could.

"Linda I'm cut. I'm cut!"

I could hear a voice coming down the hall,

"Be quiet you'll wake my dad!"

"I'm cut. I'm cut!"

"Stop shouting. My dad's asleep!"

"Open the bloody door!"

Linda opened it.

"What's the matter?"

"I'm cut. I'm bloody cut. Stuff your father!"

I hobbled and hopped into the front room where Linda's dad was waking up to the commotion.

"What have you done?"

I threw my right shin onto the couch and the rest of me followed it at speed. I pulled up my trousers to reveal the blood and my shin-bone beneath the broken skin. Linda and her sister Glynnis were both nurses and greeted the sight that lay before them simultaneously.

"Aaaargh!" was not the confidence inspiring sound I had hoped for.

"How did you do that?"

"I tripped over the kerb."

"How?"

"Does it matter? Get me to hospital!"

I attended the casualty department at the same hospital I worked at. I was stitched by a doctor who happened to lecture at Liverpool University. As a result of our meeting I became an exam question on several occasions at the university medical school. There is a picture of my scarred knees somewhere in a medical revision text book although I have never seen the finished publication.

On one occasion I attended a medical training session in my lunch hour. Most of the young doctors were excellent, very polite and caring. On this occasion, however, one fool said about my hyper supple joints, "have you ever considered joining a circus?"

Now it is true that some of those contortionist act probably have EDS to some degree or other and joining a circus or going on stage is their choice. If they can create something positive out of a problem then good luck to them but I am not a circus act and never wished to be. I know it was an innocent remark but anyone in a professional position, be it a doctor, teacher or social worker cannot make such comments.

Patients present themselves to doctors in a position of trust. Such comments are unacceptable and hurtful. One careless comment overwhelms dozens of positive comments or acts. I was very young and in front of an audience I did not feel confident to tell him where to shove his circus tent. I had been through very troubled times. I was not a circus freak. Yet again I was having a negative label thrust upon me that affected my self-esteem.

Such comments reign totally dominant in the psyche of the

vulnerable. I am still angry about it today. The simple lesson is that people in positions of power should guard their mouths at all times.

The medical profession was more than anxious to learn about my condition. I have been asked on several occasions to be a question in a medical exam. I would sit on a bed and medical students would be asked to identify what medical condition I was suffering from. I did not mind helping out in the slightest. In fact, if I'm honest, I quite enjoyed being the centre of attention but soon the novelty value wore off.

I kept hearing the word "interesting" crop up in conversations with doctors. It may be interesting to the doctor but living with it is definitely not interesting at all. I refused to be involved any more after I attended a medical symposium at Liverpool University. I was sat in a bay in a large hall. In other bays sat an albino, a dwarf, and a giant plus others. The "exhibits" for that is what it felt like, sat as doctors walked past looking at them as you would animals in a zoo. One American doctor apologized as she looked at me in horror.

"Don't you feel embarrassed?" was her only comment.

Education for doctors is essential of course but the needs, self-esteem and dignity of the patient are paramount. My experience in that display booth was definitely not interesting at all. Doctors should never treat a patient as "interesting" because it reduces the patient to the role of an also ran, someone on whom the doctor acts with his or her knowledge. Every doctor must remember at all times that patients must have a say in the whole medical process and that the patient is more important than they are. When a person is in a position of power over others it is that person's duty to be humble.

Several years later I was lying in a hospital bed recovering from ruptured knee ligaments. The consultant came round with a bunch of students to show them this "interesting" case that had come in. Not for the first time I was put on display. He described my current injury as if it were the only one I had ever had. He then described the details of EDS in general as if I weren't there. He didn't refer to any other problems that I had had nor did he ask any questions of me. He didn't refer to the then 150 stitches I'd had inserted in my body, the dislocated knees, the broken bones or the inverted base of my spine. He knew nothing of these injuries. It didn't stop him from going on to say to his class as he smiled at me,

"It is a disability but if I had to choose a disability I would choose to have this one."

I thought to myself,

"Well you can have it then."

Now I know I am not confined to a wheelchair. I know my medical condition is, in itself, not life threatening but this statement showed crass ignorance. I have always said that one of my problems was that I was not confined to a wheelchair. I am not volunteering to be either but my problem was different. As a child I could run, I could play sports. I could also, however, fall over and require 10 stitches in a cut or suffer severe bruising to my shin resulting in the fact that I was hospitalised for over a week.

I estimate that over the course of my life I have spent over a year confined to a bed or settee and have spent even longer being reliant on crutches. His words also ignored the fact that a lot of these injuries occurred to a child. Being split or ripped open is terrifying when you are any age least of all a young child. My childhood was littered by a series of traumatic events. This unthinking doctor also ignored the fact that for 19 years my family was given the wrong advice and sometimes the wrong treatment.

Finally his statement ignored the fact that different people react differently to the same problem or illness. My brother hated sport of all kinds. I don't think he would have had the troubles I had simply because he wouldn't have placed himself in the situations that I got myself into. Gender is another issue as well. My daughter is affected in very much the same way as I am but she did not attend a boys' grammar school which placed such emphasis on physical contact sports. She had fortunately other avenues to express her femininity. I struggled to express my masculinity. In fact I failed completely.

It also depends on whether the patient is an artist or a footballer as to what impact a disability has on an individual. A damaged hand may not be as important to a footballer as it is to an artist. Lifestyle is an important factor to throw into the disability equation.

Doctors are on very dangerous ground if they treat their patient merely as a set of symptoms and that consultant failed miserably with his throwaway comment.

The danger lurking for doctors is that they interact with people only when they are sick. They must avoid seeing people as a set of symptoms. This must be very difficult to do. It's rather like a policeman who sees mostly the dark side of humanity and forgets that most people are law abiding and nice. Patients are not symptoms. They are people.

When that consultant said, "If I had to have a disability, this is one I would choose," he was being crass. He had no idea what it felt like to fall and as you fell think "oh no will I be cut yet again?" He had no understanding of what it was like to be frightened every time your daughter moved too quickly. He had no right and no ability to make that statement. In my view it was totally unprofessional

I had a similar experience with another consultant many years later. My daughter had been referred to a plastic surgeon by our GP. Sarah was 14 and becoming self-aware. She had become concerned about the scars on her legs as they were inhibiting her from wearing skirts. We had originally seen our doctor to enquire about the use of creams to disguise scarring. It was his decision to refer us to a plastic surgeon.

We turned up at the clinic full of hope. The fool of a consultant gave us 2 minutes of his time before destroying her dreams. He walked in, took a brief look at Sarah's shins, moved the scar tissue between thumb and forefinger and muttered, "Nah. There's nothing we can do. Somebody has been wasting my time." He didn't even look at Sarah as he got up and walked out. I was gob-smacked and torn between comforting my crying daughter and punching him in the mouth. We were dismissed before I had chance to formulate some objections. To this day I regret not being stronger. I suffered the curse of being grateful to doctors and felt unable to demand my rights.

I print words I should have said here, to remind doctors that they have a responsibility to their patients which goes beyond the ability to diagnose an illness. That responsibility is to listen, be aware of the feelings of their patients and take note of their concerns. They have a power over the patient, which they must exercise with sensitivity. The patient is not just a set of symptoms. That "doctor" left my daughter in tears watching his back exit the room.

"Excuse me! Do you mind? Have you seen the state you've left my daughter in not to say myself? You are highly intelligent, highly educated and highly paid but you have the manners of a dog. You've let your professional status override your humanity now get back in here and treat your patient, a young girl with some respect!"

There, it may be twenty years too late and he's probably dead now but at least I've said it.

Doctors should not lose sight of the fact that they are the patient's servant. I give thanks to my current GP and the other doctors who have genuinely helped me but after that GP calling me accident prone, the consultant dismissing my condition as the one to have and that arsehole smashing my daughter's hopes I shall never bow to doctors again and I will never forgive that bastard of a plastic surgeon who hurt my daughter.

It would be nice to think that things have improved and I think they have but the medical profession still has a long way to go. I still hear accounts from people with Ehlers Danlos Syndrome referring to mistaken diagnoses or an unsympathetic attitude by their family doctor who has mistaken the symptoms as lethargy, laziness or clumsiness. Of course it is a rare condition but it is a case of the doctor not listening to the patient and presuming he or she knows best at all times.

My current general practitioner has been a breath of fresh

air however. At our first meeting I informed him that I suffered from EDS and he said,

"Right I've heard of it but you'll have to explain your details as I've never dealt with anyone who's had it."

This was so important, a doctor admitting that I probably knew more about the specific issues than he did. I remember thinking,

"This is a man I can trust. He won't give me bullshit."

There have been several occasions when I have had a problem. He has informed me of the general issues and I have talked about my specifics. We have then discussed ways forward together. This has been so important to me. I was 50 years of age before I felt that I was getting the service I needed.

He won't know it but on one visit to his surgery he said something that completely changed the way I looked at myself and unwittingly contributed to the development of this book. I had dislocated my right thumb whilst doing some work in the garden.

We talked about the need to continue doing my own thing for as long as I could. He suggested seeing a consultant with a view to obtaining some supports that I could use when gardening and doing household repairs. He dictated a letter into his Dictaphone whilst I was still there so that I knew exactly what was being said about me. In the letter he said one sentence that was so important to me.

"Mr. Howard who has coped magnificently with the effects of Ehlers Danlos Syndrome is now having some difficulty in using his thumbs during heavy work."

I cope magnificently! I'm not accident-prone! I'm not

clumsy! I'm not a failure! I'm a success! With such words we lift or condemn people. There is a line in Shakespeare's Julius Caesar where the conspirators are discussing who should live and who should die. They have a list in front of them and one of them says, "I damn him with a spot."

So it is with one word or sentence that we can destroy or create. This applies to professionals but it also applies to all of us. When my children were small I made a point of finding something to praise them about every day. One small incident serves as a good example of how we can help or damage others. One evening Andrew, who was then about eight years old was taking a bath. He stood up to get out. I held up a towel for him when he paused, got back in and proceeded to wash himself between his legs. I realized that at 8 years of age that little boy was thinking about his personal hygiene. He was being very good and conscientious and yet a careless adult could have easily smashed his self-confidence by shouting at him and telling him to hurry up. I made a point of praising my children whenever I found an opportunity. It doesn't take much to destroy a child and it doesn't take much to lift them.

I am not trying to make myself out to be a saint. I have made many mistakes but one positive thing about having EDS is that it has made me think about how I act. I have to continuously make certain I am physically safe and as a result I am very conscious of my own persona. This also affects how I relate to others around me. It is something that all of us should think about however.

My G.P. is the only person to have described the way I have dealt with my difficulties in such a positive light and I am eternally grateful although I have noticed an improvement amongst younger doctors in recent years.

Chapter 24 My Children

It never entered my head that I would father children. My parents had always instilled in me the belief that I should not have children when I grew up. When I told my parents that I was getting married their first words to me were, "Does she know that you mustn't have children?" I reassured them that everything was fine and that Linda understood the situation. I shared my parents' fears, as I was terrified of what might happen to them. I did not want anyone to endure a childhood like mine but Linda changed all that.

Sarah was born in1975 and from the moment she started walking it was obvious that she had inherited EDS. She has had several cuts and her shins are permanently bruised. Her feet are very flat due to the hyper flexible ligaments in her feet and her major joints "tremble" on a regular basis although, to my knowledge, she has not had a full dislocation.

If she had been brought up in the same circumstances as me I think she would have had the same trouble as I did. Luckily she was not into sports as I was and was not under pressure to be a "man". She was never interested in climbing ladders, digging gardens and weight training.

On talking to her however, I find my memory is flawed. She listed a whole series of cuts to her knees and shins that I had completely forgotten about including one horrific cut to her shin. She had fallen against a wall whilst messing around with some friends and cut herself. A young man, one of her friends had carried her home to get help. It was virtually a carbon copy of my accident when I was thirteen and yet I did not recollect it at all.

I can remember being by her side in casualty but I can't remember taking her there. The young nurse was very pleasant and matter of fact as she took off the bandage that someone else had put on. I know I hadn't bandaged her leg because I can recall clearly the feeling of shock as I saw her injury for the first time. I was horrified when I saw the mixture of bruised and torn skin. I didn't want to alarm Sarah but could not stop a gasp slipping past my lips. I turned to the nurse silently imploring her to help and I can recall the look of surprise on her face as I appeared to her as a desperate father begging her to help with a simple turn of his head. I was able to look at my reaction for a split second from outside of myself. I thought, as I looked at that nurse's expression, "I've just made you realize that you don't just treat an injury you treat a person. You deal with many injuries and although you've seen them many times you have only just understood the anguish that people go through. I have made you a better nurse."

There's always something positive to be gained, I suppose.

I cannot explain why I had forgotten such awful moments. Have I attempted to bury them? I found watching my lovely children suffering injury and pain on an all too regular basis far more difficult than facing such trauma myself. Sarah suggests it may have been forgotten because we deliberately tried to reduce the drama in order to protect her. There is also another factor however. Maybe such injuries and pain are so normal to us it is difficult to remember all of them.

"The other day I was at the till in Asda," Sarah said. "I dropped a can of beans and it hit my shin puncturing the skin. It wasn't a bad cut but it bled quite a bit. The member of staff was really upset and wanted to get a first aider to help. I just put Aisha, (her youngest) in the trolley, got some steri-strip that I always carry and fixed it there and then. When I was done I wiped the blood and continued paying for my stuff. I just dealt with it as a normal event. I was more concerned that I'd got a spot of blood on my new Ugg boots! I realized last week that we tend to normalise it when Indira said, "Mummy why do you say 'ow' so much?" My joints click and it hurts for a second but then I carry on. Maybe it's not normal but we just deal with it as if it is."

I'm not so certain about this. I agree that we do normalise something that others would get upset about but I can still remember my major injuries. Have I forgotten her's because I wanted to make Sarah's injuries go away? The pain your children suffer is always worse than yours.

I have always tried to hide the horror I felt from my children. I didn't want to make them worry about getting injured as my parents had done with me. I felt that this would create a self-fulfilling prophecy that would contribute to further accidents. I decided that as the adult it was my responsibility to reduce the burden on my children as much as I could. I was desperate to ensure that they would suffer only physical and not emotional trauma as I had done.

Does this suppression of my feelings contribute to my constant feeling of tension throughout my body? I am constantly anxious.

Sarah and I have a much better relationship than my father and I did. We have had our problems as a result of my generalised state of anxiety but the general, loving and supportive atmosphere in which she was brought up has more than compensated for any harm that might have been done. She also had more advice than I ever had. My parents were not equipped to deal with a child with a mad keen interest in sport and a serious medical problem that no one had identified correctly. I grew up being told off and was often given a good smacking. It was a recipe for resistance and anguish.

I do not have a perfect record as a father. I did have some problems at first. When Sarah was naughty I smacked her. I dealt with Sarah this way because that was the way my father controlled me. When I got smacked I thought I had done something wrong. I associated a smack with my wrong-doing. As a result a smack was intended to put me back on the straight and narrow. In my mind I was not doing anything wrong. In fact I thought I was being a good father. In contrast Linda's parents never smacked either her or her siblings. She was horrified at my behaviour and we had several fights over this.

Somewhere inside me I knew she was right. I associated being smacked not only with correction but my feelings of being a victim, of having been wronged but changing your behaviour is not that easy. I was listening but I was confused.

One day when Sarah was four I told her off. She ran upstairs away from me. I chased her and she sat on the bed screaming in frustration, her little hands clenched into fists too weak to deliver blows. I thought to myself "What am I doing? I am not a bully. I don't want to be a bully. This is a repeat of my treatment of Victor. I've suffered enough violence either from my father's anger or my injuries. I want this to stop." I picked Sarah up and cuddled her. I apologized to her and told her I was wrong to chase her and that I would never do such a thing again. I told her I loved her and I never smacked any of my children again.

I don't believe in it.

Adults should talk to children who have done something wrong. They could withdraw a freedom but above all the parent must explain. I was the adult and I didn't understand my behaviour so why do we expect children to always understand theirs? We have to work it out. We hit children because we can. If they were 6' 3" we'd talk.

I suffered due to the stress my father was under and the violence of my accidents.

I didn't want any more pain in my life and I didn't want to inflict it on anyone else.

Most victims of abuse first thought is to ask "What did I do to deserve that?" They often blame themselves as I did, especially when they are children. They think they must have been naughty. They rarely think of themselves as an innocent victim. That's why they repeat it themselves when they become an adult, as I did. They associate smacking a child with correcting naughtiness and repeat the treatment they received on their children. It's very difficult to unpick it all. My experiences were distinctive. I have always had to be self-aware, watching for any potential danger that I may get into. I am constantly appraising my situation and behaviour in order to avoid harm. This specific mental process has trained me to think more widely about my general behaviour in a way that most people don't do. As a result I was able to analyse and challenge my behaviour as a parent. Unfortunately not everyone can work it out.

Despite my early problems one of the things that has bound Sarah and me together is the fact that we share a hereditary medical condition that hardly anyone knows about. She is very close to her mum but no one can break our link. It is unique. Unlike my father who could not advise me at all, we have had many chats about what was going on. I was able to advise her on her choices and the possible consequences of her actions without getting into a conflict situation of dos and don'ts.

My experience taught me that such an approach was totally counter-productive. When Sarah told us that she was pregnant with her first child I said nothing to dampen her enthusiasm whereas my mother's reaction was "Oh God no. Is she going to have it?" It was not my place to tell Sarah anything. She knew the score. She understood the demands that could have been placed on her and the unborn child. There was no point in agonising over it. Our role was to help the best we could despite my fears. Zac is a beautiful young man and I am very proud of him. Luckily he displays no symptoms.

Sarah has gone on to have another 5 children and is a wonderful mother. The children are fantastic and are well known in the village.

What is striking about Sarah is her toughness and determination. She lives life to the full. Her large brood keep her busy and she often works in their shop. She intends to train as a teacher when her youngest, Aisha, goes to school. She has got a very good head on her shoulders and I'm sure she will be more than successful as she has a very determined and professional approach to everything she does. I am very proud of her.

She has passed on her courage to her children and has taken her parents' attitude of positive encouragement one step further. Only Indira has been affected by the syndrome. She has never been dissuaded from doing anything or steered in certain directions in order to protect her.

My parents tried to control my behaviour. I tried to allow Sarah choices but guide her in the direction I wanted my child to go in. Sarah's attitude is that neither form of control, no matter how well intended is possible anyway and only leads to conflict as it did with my father. In being positive she has never passed on a sense of fear to Indira as my parents did to me. As a result she has only had two bad cuts; one to her arm and one to her knee and she has had 15 stitches in total. That's distressing but it's less than her mother and me.

Doing it Sarah's way has not been easy but Indira has learned to manage what she can and cannot do. Sarah has talked to her. They have gone through the possible implications of her actions whenever she has decided to undertake things. Indira knows she has "delicate skin" but it has not stopped her riding a bike or going horse riding. She is careful without fear. If she has an injury she is never told off. She has never been told she is stupid for wanting to do something that might cause her harm. She understands her situation and has managed herself very well.

Luckily she has never wanted to play rugby, football or cricket. I think Sarah's approach is a very good one. Whether it would work with a little boy such as I was I don't know. I don't think I played rugby as an act of defiance at being told not to. I don't think I had children because my parents said I shouldn't.

It has always worried me that I was not as good a father to Sarah as I was to the boys; that my anxieties over her welfare got the better of me. Despite all this angst Sarah says she has happy childhood memories; that her memories of me are of a loving and supportive dad who often rescued her when she was badly hurt.

I am pleased that Sarah enjoyed her childhood. I take it as a sign of considerable success on my part and it is something I take great pride in. Despite my fears and shortcomings I was able to help her establish a happy and successful life. I managed to help her create a positive outlook with a high level of self-esteem; something that was denied to me.

Robert is our middle child. He is about 5'8" tall and weighs 14 stone. In his spare time he does weight training and as well as being a driving instructor he is a qualified self defence coach. He and his friend are planning to open a school in the near future. It isn't a sport. He teaches street fighting techniques as originated by Bruce Lee. It's totally uncompromising involving head knee fist and boot. His lessons include defence against sticks and knives where they put motorbike helmets on and attack each other. He absolutely loves it.

Rob is really fit and amazingly strong. I think that had I not had this disability I would have been doing similar physical stuff. He is the man I would have liked to have been.

He is a very loving and caring person when he's not hitting people with sticks. We are really good friends and go out for a pint together every Sunday night. I love him to bits. Obviously he has not been affected by the condition.

Andrew is the baby of the three. He's younger than Robert by some seven years. He also displays symptoms of Ehlers

Danlos Syndrome but in different ways to me. A syndrome is not an illness. It is a combination of factors, which on there own can mean nothing, but when combined, form a condition and they can combine in a variety of ways. Andrew is having serious difficulties with his major joints. The hyper elasticity means that he has had several dislocations.

One of his wedding photographs shows him standing with his new wife Kim in the entrance of the church. They are looking over their shoulders back towards the camera inside the church. It is a lovely picture. If you look closely however you can see that Andrew's knees bend backwards to an incredible degree. It looks like his knees are facing the wrong way. As a result he doesn't stand straight. This will give him difficulties later in life if he is not careful.

Until recently he worked at Morrisons supermarket in Holderness road, Hull.

He was originally working as a general store worker, delivering goods to the shelves from the warehouse but found this work too demanding as his flat, unstable feet hurt considerably As a result he was switched to the tills. Unfortunately he began to have difficulties with this work as well. The repetitive twisting of his forearm as he took items out of a basket and put them on the collection point resulted in the fact that the two bones in his forearm; the radius and ulna banged into each other causing severe pain. He has had a lot of time off work and has had several warning letters about his absences despite the fact that they are caused by a disability.

The problem is that, like me, he doesn't look disabled. He doesn't need a wheelchair or a stick so he doesn't fit in with peoples' stereotypical view of what disability is. The letters only stopped after a solicitor's letter referred his employers to their obligations under the Disability Discrimination Act. Despite his requests for a transfer to office work they failed to even give him an interview when vacancies occurred and he has since left. In my view he should have sued for constructive dismissal. He was harassed out of the job.

The other day we had a conversation in which he said he didn't think he was disabled because he can move quite well. This is because he doesn't look or feel disabled. I never did until the injuries had built up. I thought hurting yourself was normal. In saying what he said Andrew is, like me, reducing the pain he is in to normality. He is also forgetting the difficulties he had coping with work and the harassment and stress he suffered as a result.

Andrew has had few cuts however and for that I am thankful although he did suffer one very nasty injury when he was a baby. I suspect he hardly remembers it but that didn't stop it being one of the most traumatic days of both Linda's life and mine.

He was about 18 months old. We were watching the Roland Rat show on children's television and Andrew was dancing to a song. As he swayed from side to side he kept turning to us, smiling and clapping. He, we were having a lovely time. Then he over balanced and tipped forward, banging his head on the drawer of a unit. I was sat behind him and went to pick him up intent on soothing away his tears. Linda was to his right and as I picked him up she saw it immediately. "He's cut. He's cut!" I can still feel the panic in her voice as I sit writing this some twenty-six years later.

She snatched him off me and I saw the half moon hole in his forehead as the blood began to trickle down his face. The skin had exploded as it does in someone who has EDS. Linda gasped and began to shake all over.

"We need to get him to hospital." Linda did not respond. She just stood there holding him tightly, shaking. Andrew lay silently in her arms in obvious shock. He didn't cry.

It was a repeat of my first injury. I could almost feel the pain myself but I remained disciplined. I knew I had to look after mother and child despite my own anxieties. I took hold of her. "Linda go and get dressed now. You have to do this. If you want to help him you must go now."

Linda responded to my instructions and was back down dressed before I'd had chance to find my car keys. On reflection we should have called an ambulance but it never occurred to us. Both of us were too upset to drive. Nevertheless I got the kids into the car in seconds. All I remember about that journey is trying to keep everybody calm whilst driving at sixty miles an hour through thirty limits. As I sped towards the huge hospital that now came into view along the dual carriageway I realized I was biting my thumb. I told myself to stay calm and slow down. Most of the time I have difficulty with everyday life. I can never find my keys and am always forgetting my phone or wallet but I'm very good in a crisis. I stopped outside the entrance to casualty and dropped Linda off. "Don't run!" I shouted as she speed-walked into reception. I waited for a moment to check she was OK. Andrew had been clinging to Linda's dress but the force of her movement forced his arm away and it was heart wrenching to see his little arm flailing about her side. I turned the car and headed for the car park.

217

What happened next was awful and something my parents never experienced. It was something I would not wish on anybody.

I had to sit there whilst they examined him with a penlight. He was lying silently on the bed with a hole in his forehead as the nurse lifted his arms to inspect his ribs. I knew they were caring for him as they checked for signs of child abuse but this was nonsense. They could have examined him after they had dealt with his injury. Any bruises would not have disappeared. I just wanted them to see to our little baby.

Then the real implications dawned on me. This was his first injury and Andrew was completely unknown to the hospital. He hadn't been formally assessed as having Ehlers Danlos syndrome. If they suspected abuse I would be the first suspect.

"I've got Ehlers Danlos syndrome," I blurted.

"What's that?"

"Christ," I thought I could be in serious trouble here.

"I cut and bruise easily. It looks like my son has it. I showed him my scarred forehead." The male nurse stared at my head. He said nothing.

Then a doctor came to examine him and we began to talk about Ehlers Danlos syndrome. He looked at my forehead but said nothing. An age seemed to pass before the doctor returned with a colleague. Fortunately she knew about it and was sympathetic. She told Linda and I that Andrew would be taken to theatre to have his head stitched and he would be put under general anaesthetic. They wanted to do very fine stitching and didn't want a baby wriggling and screaming in fear and protest. We waited for an hour in that side ward.

"They are taking a long time."

"Yes." I had no words of comfort. I wanted to support Linda but I was worried that I might receive a call from the police. I didn't know why it was taking so long and I was just as frightened as she was. I could see yet more years of stress and worry ahead and I was powerless to stop it.

Then a trolley appeared at the window and began to roll past.

"Is it him?" Her voice was desperate.

I looked at the empty trolley and was about to say no it's empty when I saw his foot at the far end. He was curled up inside a blanket fast asleep oblivious to his parents' fears. He looked so small and vulnerable. The nurse lifted him off the trolley and handed him to Linda who had shot past me whilst I was staring fondly at him.

She held him for an age until he woke up. I can't remember how long we had to stay but eventually we got him home. He recovered far more quickly than either of us did as children do and he was helped by the fact that he had four protectors. The kids were wonderful and played with him for hours without complaint. The police never called.

I looked at my three children as they played together. I was frightened. Was this another beginning of a catalogue of injuries? Would I ever be able to relax? We had managed the situation with Sarah very well and with two children I thought we had got away with it. Then, seven years after Robert's birth, Linda had decided she wanted another child. In having Andrew had we subjected another child to unnecessary pain and suffering, as my parents had feared?

I looked at Linda comforting her child. I wondered what she was thinking. Was she worrying for the future like me? Did she feel any pangs of guilt like I did? Despite my anguish I could not feel angry with her.

Miraculously, Andrew has only had one cut. He is happily married to a lovely young woman and they have had three beautiful children. Andrew has had his problems but they have not been to the same level as mine and for that I am grateful. It seems like all the worst elements of the syndrome were combined in me and have weakened in my children. I'm pleased that I have been the one who had to deal with the worst of it. I would not wish my life on any of my children and I couldn't imagine how difficult it must have been for my parents watching me dealing with the things I went through.

I am so pleased that Linda and I had our children. They are lovely, kind caring people. I am very proud of them all. Without being conceited I can say that my relationship with my children is excellent. I have been and continue to be a wonderful father.

I did not allow the fears engendered by our medical condition to damage my relationship with my children. I have been very courageous and disciplined in the face of constant anxiety. Not only am I proud of my children. I am proud of myself.

Chapter 25 Women

Some of my friends and colleagues will laugh when I say this but I am actually very shy. I appear loud and confident but I'm not. The brashness is camouflage.

Several years ago the college I worked at organised an industry day. Over a period of time we made arrangements so that people from industry and commerce came into college and prepared and taught a lesson in their subject area. The person assigned to me was the husband of one of our senior members of staff.

As part of the preparation for his lesson he came in to observe me teach. He told his wife that he couldn't believe the change in me when I walked in front of the class. We had first met in the conference room along with all the other people involved. He told his wife that he thought I was very diffident and quiet. He had said to himself "God how can this guy be a teacher? He's not said a word." When we entered the classroom things changed completely. "The place exploded," he told her. There was an immediate surge of energy that you could feel and the kids responded to it immediately."

This sums me up completely. I'm a good performer. I'm loud out front but a wreck "backstage."

I was like that with girls. Now most boys are shy around girls. That's normal. It's an enormous strain to be the one who is supposed to make the initial moves and to appear as if you know what to do. They can say what they like in this age of equality but young women do not like hesitant and shy young men who look like they have no confidence in themselves. They might say they dislike the cocky guy who thinks he's God's gift to women but being shy gets you absolutely nowhere. I was 21 before I had a serious girlfriend. Actually I was 21 before I had a girlfriend.

I never met girls. I went to an all boys' school. I had one sibling, my twin brother, so there was no sister to bring her friends round. This was quite normal in the 1960s but I had additional problems. I was often sat at home bandaged and on crutches. I had a far more restricted social life than most of my contemporaries.

The main problem was however that my legs were badly scarred and my skin was soft and to me very unmasculine. I don't like to touch my own skin especially when it is close to the bone as on forearms and shins. I can feel the vulnerability. I can't stand people touching my arm. I feel that the softness must be a shock to them and that I am repulsive. I have always found it difficult to believe that girls would find me attractive in any way.

I had such a poor view of myself that when girls dropped hints or even plucked up the courage themselves to ask me out I simply couldn't believe it. I would treat it as if they were joking and dismiss it. I never gave myself the opportunity to feel good about myself because I was frightened of what they would think when they touched me. I felt very inadequate and out of my depth around girls

When I was 39 and working in a college, a female student pinched my bottom. Notwithstanding the fact that she shouldn't have touched me at all, she made a comment that destroyed any self-confidence that I had managed to develop.

"Oh it's a bit flabby. What a disappointment!" Now I am not flabby in any way. She had grabbed the skin and pulled it further than normal skin would move. I should have been angry at being touched against my will but I was too devastated by her words to do anything.

Until recently I have rarely worn shorts. In hot weather I tend to wear cool linen trousers that hide my scars. If I did wear shorts I used to watch women's eyes as I approached them. I saw them move down to my legs and stare. I always thought they were appalled by the disfigurement. I felt like a freak show, ugly and unmasculine.

I laughed when a student said at an end of year leaving do that I had better legs than she did. I thought she was joking. I then realized that she was serious. Then I put it down to the fact that she was looking at the back of my legs and had not seen the scarring on my knees and shins. I couldn't believe that any woman would find my damaged body attractive.

Maybe the women were looking at my legs because they weren't that bad to look at after all? None of the things I worried about seemed to bother Linda. Andrew has produced three kids although he does not have the scarring that I do. Sarah has given birth to five. It does not seem to have hindered her but I just couldn't get rid of negative thoughts towards myself

If Linda and I ever parted I've no idea how I would approach relationships with women. I couldn't imagine going through all those explanations again. One good thing about the onset of old age is that I hopefully I won't have to.

Chapter 26 Linda

Meeting Linda Joyce Parry was the best thing I ever did. She has seen me through some very difficult times. Sometimes our life together has been wonderful. Sometimes it's been down right bloody awful but I think that my life would have been a lot worse without her.

When I first saw her, Linda was 5'2", curvaceous and very feminine with beautiful wavy dark red hair and blue eyes that twinkled amidst an array of freckles. She was lovely and she still is.

I first saw her as I passed through the pharmacy when I was a trainee hospital administrator. At seventeen she was a cadet nurse, too young to work on wards but employed around the hospital to get used to its environment. I noticed her immediately but was far too shy to say a word. I was six months out of a boys' school and had one brother. I had had no contact with girls. What I didn't know was that she fancied me and that some of her colleagues were trying to drop hints in order to get me to ask her out but I missed all the signals.

I spent a week in pharmacy. As I left on the Friday night I saw her at the bus stop but avoided her in fear. As I turned away and began my walk home I thought to myself, "She's lovely; the type of girl who'd make someone a nice wife."

A month later she turned up at the local drama group where I was already a member. She came with a young man who had recently joined. I was really unhappy to see her with someone else even though I'd not seen her in the intervening weeks. At least I thought I hadn't seen her. She now says that she said "hello" to me on the main drive and that I walked past her without saying a word. I don't recall it at all.

A month later she and the other guy stopped seeing each other. A fortnight later we were engaged.

I hadn't planned to ask her to marry me on the day that I did. We had been going out for a fortnight when we went to the Lake District for the day. I had started walking in the Lakes about two years earlier when a friend from work had asked me if I fancied a walk in the Lakes. I had never been and had no idea what I was going to. The walk was very taxing. It is very rocky and steep and water rushed down the gill with deafening force. I could see a ridge up ahead and thought it was the top. When we arrived I couldn't believe what lay in front of me. The ridge hid a tarn that contained beautifully clear water. Behind this lay an array of peaks waiting to be climbed. We had reached only half way. It wasn't really the place for someone with my physical problems. One slip and I would have been in serious danger but I fell in love with it immediately and still visit as often as I can. It was just the place to take a new girlfriend when you had no idea whether she'd enjoy it or not. We hadn't even been for a walk in the park together. Luckily she did enjoy it and we had a lovely day. At one point however, I offered her my hand to help her up. She took it and then cautioned me (I'm being polite here) about my sexist condescension to a woman. I tried to explain that I was only taking note of the fact that she hadn't done anything like this before and that yes I would have offered a hand to a male friend. On reflection maybe I wouldn't have. Maybe I just wanted an excuse to hold her hand.

I couldn't understand why she'd taken my hand and then complained about it being offered to her. Why hadn't she simply said, "No thank you, I can manage"? It did not occur to me that this kind of thing would continue for the rest of my life. Before I knew it however she was expressing the same wonderment at the scene as I had when I first saw it. She stood there, taking it all in. We sat down at the side of the tarn in a little dip sheltered by rocks and ate a sandwich and drank a welcome hot cup of tea. It was simply lovely and I was at peace with the world. Before I knew it I said the words "Will you marry me?" and she replied "yes". We sat there for an age, comfortable and cosy. It had seemed the most natural thing to do. It was the sweetest hour of my life.

Then I said some very important words that were less romantic.

"We can't have children you know."

"I know".

I couldn't believe it. I had found a woman who was beautiful and caring who loved me, shared very similar interests and understood about my fears over my medical condition. It was all too perfect and it did not last.

After two years of happy married life Linda suddenly told me that she wanted a baby.

"It wouldn't have to be like you and your mum and dad would it? We know about it and as a nurse I could deal with any problems. We'd manage it much better than your mum and dad could have done. What do you think?" She was pleading with me. This was a complete surprise to me. After all I had been perfectly open about the situation when I proposed to her and I thought we were in complete agreement. It had never, at any point, occurred to me that I would be a father. It just hadn't entered my mindset.

I was so surprised that somehow I found myself agreeing to it.

Linda's mum supported her in the idea that it would be OK. I'm sure they both felt that it would be. They had no means of knowing what I had been through as a child. On the Ehlers Danlos website it says that one of the problems that sufferers have is various degrees of depression caused by the difficulty in convincing people that something is wrong. I could walk, run and swim. I was a very active young man and despite my difficulties, very fit. Linda had never seen me have an accident. Indeed for a while in my early twenties I seemed to be a picture of health. I was bigger, stronger and more careful than I had been as a child. There was every reason to believe that "things would be OK". In the end I thought they would be as well so I can hardly blame Linda. She was twenty-one, in love and it was perfectly normal for her to want a baby.

My mum and dad were horrified and telling them that Linda was pregnant was a very difficult conversation but there was nothing they could do. They were faced with something they had dreaded all along. They had hoped to avoid it but there was no turning back. Linda was determined and I followed in hope and love. I was genuinely pleased for her and hopeful for me. I was hopeful that our optimism would be fulfilled but it proved far more difficult than either of us imagined.

Sarah was born on the 19th of August 1975. Linda was ecstatic. I tried to be but there was a cloud of doubt hanging over me. I was trapped between my wife's joy and my parent's fears. I closed my eyes and hoped for the best. The legacy of my childhood injuries lay heavily on me and the prospect of being a parent of a child who cut easily frightened the living daylights out of me. Every time Sarah fell over my heart was in my mouth. Every time she tottered Linda smiled but I grimaced.

I suffered constant anxiety and tension and I was perhaps too strict with Sarah. I didn't want to pass on my fears to her as my father had done to me but at the same time I was desperate to protect my cherished daughter from harm.

I was in a constant state of fear and worry not only for my child but for me as well. I was constantly reminded of the childhood pains that I thought I'd left behind. I could not escape. Through all this my reaction was to joke. I suppose I use humour as a defence mechanism. Not only did it defend me against the pain I had endured it served to disguise it. I suppose Linda never got a true indication of the constant anxiety I suffered. It was therefore difficult for her to manage the situation in a way that would have helped me and our relationship. I think she thought I bullied our daughter and sought to defend her against me.

Linda proved to be an excellent mother. She is a very maternal person. She is, like many women, very defensive of her offspring sometimes to the detriment of her relationship with their father. If ever I told the kids off she leapt to their defence with the utmost passion courage and vigour. I sometimes faced a torrent of abuse when she felt I was being unreasonable.

Once she had a row with Sarah who was then 14 years old. Linda stormed out of the room.

"Stupid fat bitch," muttered Sarah behind her back.

"Don't you dare speak to your mother like that. Don't you dare!" I shouted.

Before I knew it Linda had re-entered the room with as much force as she had left it. She was screaming at me to leave Sarah alone. It was absolutely awful. I had defended Linda completely and was being laid waste as a reward.

This was not the only occasion that this kind of thing happened. There are too many times to describe them. I am not trying to apportion blame. The rows were a reflection of the tension in our relationship. They show how disability can affect peoples' relationships. Everyone has their own personality that they bring to a partnership. Over the years, if the relationship lasts, each person has an affect on the development of the other's character. That process is hopefully a healthy one and is to be welcomed.

The issue of disability inevitably shapes the interplay between two people. This can and often does strengthen a relationship but for that to happen the non-disabled person has to understand the situation and outlook of the disabled partner. That is not easy at the best of times. I understood Linda's desires. They were perfectly normal. She found it difficult to understand my fears. They were not normal. I don't look disabled and for the majority of our marriage I have never referred to myself as such.

I was faced with being a father of children that I had had no intention of producing. That placed me under strain. I needed Linda to understand that and help me deal with the consequences of her motherly needs. Unfortunately she was not able to do that.

Linda's urge to have children was too strong for her to resist despite the fact that she had agreed not to in that romantic moment on the mountain-side. She was a young woman in love and genuinely believed that she could make it work.

Recently she told me that if we hadn't had children we would have probably split up. I smiled at the use of the word "We". I would not have left Linda because we hadn't had children. What she really meant was that she would have left me for someone else who would have given her children.

Unfortunately love can't conquer everything.

There was one moment when I felt Linda began to understand. We were on a caravanning holiday in Devon. I used to enjoy being in the caravan but it always took me a day to get used to the confined space. I was always bothered about knocking myself. Linda thought I was just bad tempered after driving. Early into our stay I woke up in the middle of the night needing to go to the toilet. As I stepped out into the darkness of the awning I felt a sharp pain on my left ankle. Still half asleep I was a little confused. What could it be? I put my hand down to the pain and felt the warmth of my blood.

It sounds ridiculous to describe but I had cut my ankle on the zip of a suitcase that Linda had left by the door! As we drove to the hospital to have seven stitches inserted I tried to explain to Linda.

"You know I'm not in a bad mood. I'm under stress as a result of being in a confined space. If people don't put things away I'm in trouble aren't I?

"Yes love. I know you are."

It was the first occasion she had actually seen me get a cut. Seven stitches from a collision with a zip was unbelievable. It was obvious I was in trouble and she could not be angry with me. Linda was lovely to me for the rest of the holiday. Unfortunately it didn't transfer to the rest of our lives until years later.

All of these tensions placed an inevitable strain on our relationship but life has never been as difficult as it has been during my most recent injury. The worst moment occurred when Linda came home one day from work and I was enthusing about some money saving techniques I had seen on television. She exploded with rage.

"Shut up! Shut up! Shut up! I take care of the bills! Don't you bloody well interfere! Shut up! I've just come home and you're on about bloody money!"

I could not believe the force with which she delivered these words or how angry she was with me. I only wanted to talk to her about something I thought was a quite simple issue. Her reaction seemed completely over the top. In reality it probably was but the tension between us was caused by the fact that we were both living in completely different worlds.

I was asleep for large parts of the day. I was lying in bed recovering from a horrendous and dangerous injury. I was alone all day for over four months. I didn't see anyone apart from when I was visited by a physiotherapist and the occasional ambulance driver. I was becoming very isolated and I was beginning to worry about money. Teachers' sick pay arrangements are very good. You have half a year on full pay and a further six months on half pay but we were nearing the end of my full pay period with no foreseeable return to work. I was worried, weak and very vulnerable. I must have jumped at Linda like a puppy does to its mistress when she returns home.

I was in no position to realize the difficulties she faced when I was in hospital. Linda was spending her working day dealing with children with serious behavioural problems before coming to visit me. Often she sat there waiting for me to wake up. Sometimes I didn't. She would then drive the twenty miles home. She had no time to rest and often fell into bed at nine o'clock only to wake up and do it all again the next day.

Things became even more difficult for her when I came home. I was delighted to be back in my house but Linda had to do everything for me. She had to get all my meals prepared, sort out my urine bottle and give me a bed bath. In addition she had to be cheerful for me during my moments of consciousness.

Linda had had a motherhood of worry nursing our children's injuries. She had also had to care for me through a lifetime of injuries

She had dealt with it all without a single word of complaint but suddenly listening to me prattling on about money proved too much. This brief, harmless conversation proved to be the straw that broke the camel's back. Her anger was a product of the difficulties she had faced throughout all our life together not just the immediate issues she was facing. I sympathised but at the same time I was in no state to deal with her shouting at me.

We were both under tremendous strain. I knew that it had been hard for Linda but I had never asked for any of this to happen. I felt very threatened with no one to talk to. It was the loneliest day of my life.

At two o'clock I hesitated and then picked up the phone.

"Hello Samaritans."

The voice was warm and calming. Immediately I felt safe. I whispered into the phone.

"I'm not suicidal but I've had enough and I need someone to listen to me."

I paused, half expecting to be told not to bother with him. He had more pressing engagements from people with real problems.

"What's your name?"

"Philip, Phil." I corrected myself.

"Hello Phil how can I help?"

"I'm not suicidal but I've had enough and I need someone to listen to me."

I blurted out the words, embarrassed at my repetition but I felt I had to say it again in order to justify my claim on his time.

There was another pause.

"Go on," he said encouragingly.

Words came out of me that I didn't know I was going to say.

"I fell off a ladder on New Years Day and I've broken my femur. I've got a metal nail down the centre of my thigh-bone. On top of that I've got Ehlers Danlos syndrome. It means my skin and joints are hyper extensive. I cut easily and I dislocate my joints. I've had 200 stitches. I've dislocated both my kneecaps, ruptured the ligaments in my left knee, dislocated my shoulder, broken bones in both feet. I sprained my right ankle broke my scaphoid and I bruise a lot and now this."

The words spat out in rapid fire as I said them without drawing breath.

I continued:

"My wife shouts at me. I know she works hard and is stressed out but I really need her to stop screaming at me. If she needs a rest she should go off sick but she won't. I can't cope with her shouting at me. I have had enough. I've just had enough."

Suddenly the hail of words stopped. I could hear him measuring his response.

"You've been through a lot."

"Yes".

"What do you want to do?"

I talked. He listened. He allowed me to formulate a plan.

I would talk to Linda about having a rest. I needed to tell her my concerns over money. The way to stop a rift developing between Linda and me was to be open about our feelings and fears. He suggested that the reason Linda had not gone off sick from work was that teaching probably took her away from the strains at home and acted as a safety valve for her despite its demands.

I decided to focus on happy things and ignore the fears about money. We had enough money. I had to recognize that I probably had too much time on my hands and had begun to worry about trivia. It was time to re-evaluate my situation and become more positive.

I thanked him and put the phone down.

Something else had happened in that phone call.

I realized that the Samaritan was right.

I had been through a lot.

That single comment began to change my life. I had been so busy lying down that I hadn't understood the severity of my situation or that my life had been laced with difficulties. To me it had all been normal.

It wasn't.

I had never understood the effect my medical problems had had on me as an individual and on my relationships with other people, particularly my wife. I was not to blame and she most certainly wasn't.

"You have been through a lot," was as simple a statement as it was profound.

I had been through a lot. I'd never said it to myself before. Suddenly I had permission to say that I needed help, that I couldn't cope on my own. It was time to begin the process of changing my life. Before that could happen successfully I had to analyse and understand my life in a way that most people never have to do with theirs.

It turned out to be much easier to say than do.

Amazingly our marriage has survived and is in fact still very strong. I can see the strength and support that Linda has given me. As I said at the beginning of this chapter, I am so glad I met her. She is my best friend. The plain fact is that without her, I wouldn't have survived.

Chapter 27 Philip Howard

I am a liar.

I have lied about myself all through my adult life. It's not a big lie. It hasn't hurt anyone, except me, but the lie has been fundamental to how my life has been lived.

Most of my friends and contacts now live in and around Hull. They know nothing of my childhood in St. Helens. Recently my close friends have come to understand the details of my medical condition but for many years although they knew I had a problem I was seen mainly as being accident prone and a little clumsy. Only recently did a former colleague describe me as a "Walking disaster".

Whilst in Hull I set up rugby league teams in a school and later at the sixth form college. I also coached an under 13s side in a local village on the outskirts of the city.

When asked by the kids who I had played for I made up names of teams in St. Helens. How could I explain to them that although I was teaching them the basics of the game I had never actually played in a team? I told people I was a half-back and when they learned about my injuries they assumed I got them through playing rugby. I let them assume it.

I have never worn rugby boots and club colours and I never played for a school team. I did play a lot of rugby but it was always out of sight of teachers and parents and often as a prelude to a visit to hospital.

Just after my fifteenth birthday I suffered a bang to my right knee, which resulted in one of those blue/black bruises that so often have decorated my limbs. Before it healed I knocked it again so that it bruised even more. It was really painful but it did not stop me from playing football and rugby. Unfortunately a week later I banged it once again and a hole appeared in my skin on top of the bruise. I was cut from underneath. I was bandaged and limping for several weeks. One day my mother happened to pass by the field I was playing football on and saw me running about.

"Oh Philip! Why are you playing like that with your bad leg?"

"I'm not playing. I'm the ref."

She walked on satisfied with my answer.

I lied then as I did when I got the chance to play cricket for the college staff cricket team. I had never played whilst wearing whites and pads. I had never faced a proper cork cricket ball. When I played as a child we used tennis balls.

I had two awful injuries whilst playing for the staff team. One was a severe bruise to my left hand caused by my jarring the bat into the ground. I bandaged it in order to disguise the size of the swelling from my wife and friends and when asked, simply said that I'd knocked it. No one ever saw that the back of my hand was swollen to twice its normal size.

The other injury was the result of a direct hit on the inside of my right ankle. Everyone laughed as I hobbled off but when I got home and took off my shoe the ankle, like my hand had been, was almost double its normal size. Luckily the bruising disappeared very quickly and after a couple of days off work with a "cold" I returned to my colleagues. I didn't tell anyone. I knew it was stupid but I didn't want them to say, "Hey don't you think this is a bit off? Look at those bruises. You shouldn't be playing with injuries like that."

I presented myself as a fit and active sportsman and couldn't bear to face what I perceived as my weaknesses. I paid for this attitude in pain and injury. On reflection I realize that my whole behaviour, playing sport, doing DIY, and lying about my achievements was a sign of a deep-seated unhappiness. I didn't like what I was and couldn't accept the limitations my medical condition placed on me. It stopped me from being the man I wanted to be and I couldn't find an alternative path for two main reasons. Firstly as a child no one knew what was wrong with me. The diagnosis was completely wrong. As a result I never received any advice on how to manage my medical condition. There was no professional counselling available and my parents were equally in the dark and unable to help. I was in constant conflict with my desire to be active and the restraints put on me by my parents, schoolteachers and doctors. I was completely isolated.

Secondly my medical condition did not stop me from putting myself in danger. Had I been confined to a wheelchair life would have been much simpler (I'm not suggesting for one minute that it would have been better).

My problem was not that I couldn't walk, I could but when I did I fell. It wasn't that I couldn't play sports, I could but when I did I ended up bloodied and bruised. I was living life in a permanent state of frustration, which only served to ensure that I was unhappy with myself. In fact I now think for large parts of my life I have been depressed. I didn't look like I had a problem and it was difficult to convince people that I did. It never occurred to me that I might even be seen as having a disability.

I believed all the things people said about me because there didn't seem to be any other way of looking at it. I thought I was stupid, clumsy, an accident waiting to happen.

So I joked and then I lied. It made life a lot simpler.

My life had been a constant battle and as I lay at the bottom of the ladder it was a battle I knew I was losing. Now I can see that I never had a chance of winning. I began to examine my behaviour and it wasn't a pretty sight. I didn't like who or what I was. It was time to find a way to like myself and to understand what I had achieved.

Instead of hiding from my problems I began to try to identify and understand them. I wanted to work out what was causing all my accidents. I had a medical problem of course but it wasn't that simple. I was vulnerable to injury but I had to get into a situation where I would be injured in the first place. Placing myself constantly in danger said something about my personality and my reaction to my life situation.

If I couldn't understand what was driving me into danger I would never be able to avoid it. I knew that if I failed in this task I would soon be dead. Not only did I want to stay alive, I wanted to be happy.

Part 5

Understanding

"I don't know why. It just seems that you are one of those people who accidents just happen to." was sat on a low-slung visitor's seat. Last time he had visited me he had been laughing and joking at yet another piece of apparent stupidity on my part. Now his face was etched with concern.

"At first I thought it was just a case of your being a silly bugger again but two colleagues have said that a broken femur is a very serious business."

He paused.

"You can't go on like this you know."

"I know."

I knew he was right but I hadn't then got the strength to tell him that I was already well into a process of trying to work out what the hell was happening to me. The incidents/accidents that I have described are by no means a complete list. They merely give a flavour of what my life has been like. I was in turmoil and living in a constant state of stress.

The more I have thought about it, the more I have come to realize that a number of factors that have caused me problems. The medical ones are the root cause but they are not the only ones. I couldn't change my medical situation but I could change my responses to it. I had to understand how my emotional and physical states related to one another before I could begin to unravel them all and take the steps I needed to ensure I had a successful and safe future. I identified several factors that needed addressing.

Chapter 28 Misdiagnosis

To be fair to the medical profession Ehlers Danlos syndrome is very difficult to identify. Even now people with this condition report that they had difficulties with obtaining a correct diagnosis. The problem is that it can present itself in so many different ways.

It was only when I was in my late thirties when I cut myself on holiday that I learned that I might have a problem with my joints. I had slipped on a wet rock and fell to the floor cutting my elbow on adjacent stones. As the doctor inserted the seven stitches into me he explained the nature of Ehlers Danlos syndrome to the nurse who was assisting him.

"Patients have a problem with their joints," he said.

"Hang on a minute." I said. "I don't have problems with my joints."

"Well you're lucky then. Many people suffer several nasty dislocations." I thought, "You haven't even mentioned my skin cutting. Look at all the scars." I was annoyed. Then it dawned on me as I lay on the casualty bed. "My knees used to dislocate when I was a kid. They haven't dislocated since I ruptured the ligaments and had an operation. Maybe I do have a problem with my joints" My son Andrew has had few cuts but his major joints are loose and he is abnormally supple and has suffered dislocations of his major joints. When I dislocated my knees no one ever connected the dislocations to my wider medical state because I was supposed to have haemophilia. In fact I don't think I ever reported them. My knees dislocated and then went back into place and I carried on without seeking medical advice at all.

As I enter my sixties I am experiencing significant difficulties with my major joints and they cause me far more problems than my skin does.

A couple of years later I noticed another problem had surfaced. I had bought a pair of summer shoes with styled cuts in the sides. They were very light and comfortable. Unfortunately I began tripping over thin air to, once more, the amusement of others. I couldn't understand it. I felt such a fool.

"It's because your ligaments are loose," said my GP. "Your brain thinks your foot is in one position but it hasn't actually cleared the ground properly and therefore you trip over yourself."

I was 51 and only now had discovered why I had had so many falls as a child. I had a medical condition that caused me to stumble and fall. This was repeated over and over again in my childhood resulting in cut after cut. Nobody spotted it. Now I have shoes designed to remove the problem. I could have been spared much pain and anguish.

The doctors got it wrong. I don't blame them. That was the state of medical knowledge at the time.

Chapter 29 Bad Luck

Sometimes I have just been unlucky. Last summer I went for a walk on the beach at Spurn Point with Andrew, his wife Kim and their three children. It is a lovely place, unspoilt except for the remnants of wartime defences, which dot the landscape.

The Yorkshire Wildlife Trust maintains it as it is a haven for wild life of all kinds. We got out of our cars and walked down on to the beach from the road. All of us had a lovely time building sandcastles and collecting some of the brightly coloured stones that decorate the beach.

Then Maia let out a yelp. She had been stabbed in the foot by a two foot length of thick wire bent at both ends. It bruised the bruise she had already acquired during her attempts to ride a bicycle earlier in the week. Her shins were now black and blue along their whole length. Maia has inherited the condition and seems to be prone to having accidents and resultant injuries in the same way as I do. At six years of age she has already had eight cuts and had more than twenty stitches inserted in her legs

She too has a medical problem but why did it have to be Maia who hit the wire? It had obviously been there some considerable time waiting to attack her. No one else had seen it. It was an insignificant proportion of that huge expanse of beach and yet the one person vulnerable to the dangers it presented stood on it.

It was almost a repeat of my accident on the bench in the park. I had soft skin but why was it me who fell through it? Why hadn't someone else fallen through it? Why had no one repaired it before it too attacked me?

It could be argued that I am over cautious. I may be now but I wasn't then and Maia has never been made to feel inhibited by her medical situation.

Sometimes I think I have simply been unlucky but I can't help feeling there's another explanation. It's not feasible to believe that someone can be constantly unlucky throughout his or her entire life and why would the "bad luck" be repeated across generations?

Everybody has accidents. It's just that when I do I suffer more injuries than would otherwise be the case. Perhaps people with Ehlers Danlos Syndrome don't have bad luck, they have bad consequences.

Chapter 30 Gender

A third factor, which shaped how I dealt with my problems was my gender.

I was brought up in a society in which the roles of the sexes were quite distinct. Mothers stayed at home and dads went out to work. This put very clear limits on what the sexes could aspire to.

I grew up in a working class family in an industrial town in the north of England. My dad was, at different times in his life; a bricklayer, a plumber and a manual labourer in a factory. I could not do any of these things.

At school the height of honour was to play first Team rugby in winter and cricket in summer. I could not do any of these things.

Later I married into another working class family. Two of my wife's brothers were miners and the third was a mechanic working on heavy industrial vehicles. Yet again, I could not do any of these things.

In the midst of all this I was a boy with soft skin. In fairness to my teachers I was always met with kindness and sympathy but the societal pressure to be a man in the conventional sense was enormous. I was so keen on sport they allowed to be a touch judge or an umpire but it couldn't assuage my disappointment. I felt that I didn't match up to my understanding of what it was to be a man. As a result I have carried a sense of failure with me all my life.

No alternative form of success compensated for this sense of failure. When I qualified as a teacher I was met with comments from certain members of my wife's family which compounded my sense of inadequacy. In their eyes teaching was not seen as a proper job. I could not seem to gain any form of success. I constantly felt the need to try and establish myself as a man.

I should never have been up a ladder with knees that are prone to dislocation. It was a recipe for disaster. I should never have attempted to play football and rugby. I paid for my sense of weakness with injury after injury, which merely served to confirm my weakness. I was on a treadmill of anguish that I couldn't get off and the more I tried, the faster it seemed to go

I did try to find alternatives. As a 35 year old newcomer to Hull I knew no one. When a neighbour invited me for a game of badminton I accepted readily despite never having played the game. Half way through the game I thought to myself "This is a bloody good game." I had never had the chance to play it.

They introduced swimming into the curriculum on a regular basis when I was 17. I am a very good swimmer and once came second in the 200 yards breast-stroke in a Lancashire Schools competition. It received a mention in assembly. That is my one sporting success. Unfortunately it was at the end of my school career and was far too late to prevent me having already suffered innumerable injuries. I could have been steered in all kinds of directions that I never ventured in. Schools now teach so many alternative activities that were not available to me in a 1960s Grammar School.

Recently I have discovered golf. I take my grandchildren for lessons and we played our first game together last month. I never had such opportunities at their age. If I had been brought up in today's society which is far more tolerant of alternative ways of life there's a chance that I wouldn't have been so focused on rugby and I wouldn't have suffered so many injuries.

Some people have said I was downright stupid for trying to play sport. I knew I'd get hurt and if I did it was my fault. Why didn't I learn? Why couldn't I try to alter my behaviour? Why didn't the pain stop me and make me behave differently? The strange thing is that in some ways the injuries benefited me.

The damage I received gave me considerable kudos amongst my peers. People shook their heads in disbelief and sympathy each time I returned to school on crutches. The Head of my primary school described me to my parents as "the toughest little boy he had ever come across". Nurses described me as a brave boy. Denied any opportunity to express my masculinity in a conventional way the injuries provided proof of it. I wasn't a weakling. The scars were my medals. Of course I didn't get hurt on purpose in order to prove the point and I certainly wasn't conscious of this process but there was no incentive to stop me carrying on as I did. Injury was an acceptable risk and perversely it brought rewards. It made me a man in my own eyes.

When I was about 15 I saw a Humphrey Bogart film, which impressed me greatly. It struck a huge chord with the way I saw myself. In "The Harder They Fall" Bogart plays a boxing journalist who becomes caught up with the Mafia. They employ him to promote a huge but limited boxer from Argentina. All his fights are fixed so that he wins and is lined up for a world title fight in a contest he has no chance of winning. The Mafia lay heavy bets against their own man and stand to make a fortune when he loses.

From the very start of the fight the hero is subjected to a brutal assault. He is knocked down several times but refuses to give in. Bogart pleads with him to stay down but the simple, honest challenger can only say "But what would my people think of me?" Time after time he gets to his feet only to be knocked down once more. Bruised, cut and battered he never gives in but suffers great punishment.

When I was a boy I found myself sympathizing with this character. I didn't need to be in a boxing ring to understand what it felt like to suffer cut after cut, blow after blow. What is significant about the hero is that he is not a winner. In fact he is very much a loser. He fails completely in his mission to become a champion.

This represented what I felt about myself. Despite all my best efforts I was doomed to fail in everything I tried to achieve. I couldn't play rugby, cricket or football. I couldn't do typically masculine jobs and I couldn't find alternative means of success. One possible avenue would have been academic success but I was absent from school so often that this was always bound to elude me.

The countless injuries I suffered were my compensation. I was the champion of accidents and no one faced them with greater bravery than I.

Chapter 31 Silly Philly

It was difficult enough dealing with the limitations imposed on me by my own body. Labels imposed on me by others who were my friends but did not understand only served to make things worse.

When I was a child I was seen by my father as naughty and rebellious even a little stupid for wanting to play rugby, football and cricket. Teachers, although kind, saw me as a problem and my GP saw me as clumsy and accident-prone.

My brother in law, Richard, once said that when he watched Basil Fawlty's disastrous escapades in the television programme, Fawlty Towers, he always thought of me. Again I was seen as a comedic figure. The pain I had gone through wasn't noticed.

When I severed my knee ligaments as a result of falling down stairs a friend bought me a "Mister Men" cup as a present to cheer me up. I still have it today. Mr. Bump sits on the window ledge in my study covered in bandages whilst holding a walking stick. Even the cup is now damaged. Its rim is chipped as a result of being dropped.

Mr. Bump seems to look at me as if to say, "I understand. This all looks funny, doesn't it Philip? Everyone thinks it's a bit of a laugh but you and I know differently don't we? I don't want to be portrayed like this, a clown on a children's cup. You don' want to be seen as the fool, someone to be pitied or laughed at. These accidents hurt don't they? Not just physically but emotionally. You're not a clown are you? You're a victim."

On moving to Hull I began a different life with people who knew nothing of my medical problems or my life history.

As the number of accidents mounted they were greeted with comments like "Oh not again!" "What are we going to do with you?" I became seen once more as a bit of a joke; as being a problem rather than having a problem.

In November 2011 I stood on a small stone that was lying on a concrete path in the garden. I sprained my ankle and broke a metatarsal bone in my foot.

I announced my accident to my friends on Facebook. Listed below are the responses I got. They sum up everything about my life and how people perceive me. I have removed peoples' names for privacy:

Phil Howard

Bugger! Just paid £407 to join a golf club and have fallen over in the garden. I've broken a metatarsal

bone and am in a pot and on crutches!. No golf for at least 6 weeks!

•

Only you phillip only you

Oh Phil, Phil, Phil - what are we going to do with you?

hahahaha i remember at school when we started the rugby team and you being the teacher wanting g to show us pupils how it was done joined in 10 mins later on ya way to hospital with a broken ankle lol Phil stick to Chess lol

ouch!

Blimey Phil - not good at all.

Oh Phil it could only happen to you! Hope you're OK x

Phil you plonker

nooo! phil that's so bad! instead of playing golf you will have to add this new chapter to your book. we will come and visit you next week. I bet if you call the golf club they will put your membership on hold for compassionate reasons. x big love xx

I'm sorry to hear your in the sick bay again, silly philly.

I recognise fully my contribution in this process. I had just broken my foot for the third time and sprained my ankle in the process. It was very unpleasant, yet I informed people in a flippant manner, seemingly more concerned about the golf than my discomfort. I invited such comments by my presentation of myself but that presentation in turn was a product of people's previous reactions to my injuries throughout my life. Joking about my situation has been a defence mechanism. Trying to explain to people what was happening and why was very difficult when I didn't fully understand it myself. People were not nasty. In fact they were very sympathetic but I was growing tired of a joke that wasn't very funny and was becoming less so as the injuries mounted.

I am NOT clumsy. I have never been so. I was a very good agile goalkeeper when I was a teenager. I have very good hand to eye co-ordination. When I mess around with my son who is 32 he says that I am very fast and accurate. He should know. He teaches martial arts. When I retired all the staff had an end of term lunch together. As I sat down my knife slipped off the tray. My colleague said, "It's true isn't it? You are clumsy." What he didn't notice was that as the knife fell through the air I caught it before it hit the ground. I didn't bother trying to explain and challenge his comment. I just nodded and smiled. It is the way people see me and I've grown tired of trying to explain myself.

Cracking jokes deflected criticism. It was better if people thought I was funny rather than stupid.

Unfortunately I then had no way of telling people what my problems were. They thought I was dealing with my problems quite happily but I wasn't dealing them at all. Jokes both shielded me and harmed me at the same time.

It was clear that something was wrong. The bandages and crutches were obvious but no one could help and no one, including myself, had understood the effect that injury after injury was having on my mental health. As I entered my fifties I was in a bad place and could see no way out.

Chapter 32 Depression

Recently I visited a sports therapist because I had injured my back whilst pushing my mother in her wheelchair. After three weeks of sleeping on the floor and with no sign of a Physiotherapy appointment I was desperate for some relief. I was trying to avoid painkillers because I wanted to know what my body was doing so that I could reduce the risk of causing further damage. As time passed however I had found out what my body was doing and I didn't like it.

My son recommended the therapist but I still went with some trepidation. He applied elasticated adhesive tape to the areas of pain that now included my back, shoulder and knee. The therapist explained that the tape pulled the pain receptors off the injury and allowed the damaged parts of my body to function normally, which enhanced healing. Pain restricted movement and limited recovery. To my surprise the pain disappeared very quickly.

What was significant about the removal of pain however was the change produced in my general demeanour. Physically I felt much lighter and stronger; mentally I was brighter and happier. I suffered no pain and painkillers had not dulled my senses. Although the relief was only temporary my new-found freedom made me realize what a negative impact constant nagging pain had had on my whole outlook on life. I had not been aware of how depressed I had been feeling until I began to feel so well. I realized that I had been depressed for a considerable period of time

When I read the psychology booklet on accidents that my colleagues had given me when I was in hospital I began to see that my accidents weren't simply accidents at all. They were much more complicated events than those created purely by chance. I began to look at my personality in a way I had never done before. It was a disturbing view but as I looked, a number of apparently unconnected features of my life began to pull together. I have dislocated my right shoulder twice in the last ten years. The physiotherapists who tended me both made the same comment when they tended my aching limbs."You are very tight. You need to relax. I was not aware I was so tense. My body was in a permanently clenched state ready to defend itself from injury.

I am constantly in fear of getting hurt. In 1985 I was issued with some fairly strong surgical tights to support my ankles, which used to swell a lot by the end of the day. Swelling in joints is nature's way of providing a splint. It stops unnatural movements in the joint. The side effect of wearing these tights was that, for me, it acted as a second skin. Suddenly I wasn't vulnerable any more. I have had four major injuries to my shins involving cuts requiring 17, 13 stitches twice and 11 stitches. I have also had severe bruising that required an operation to remove the blood. When wearing these tights all the fears of hidden dangers lurking unseen, waiting to injure me disappeared in a moment.

I had just started work as a teacher. As I walked along the school corridor one morning I sensed a new confidence in me. Wearing these supports lifted a heavy burden from my shoulders. There was a sense of euphoria, of newly found freedom. I had a new skin that wouldn't tear. I was ready to take on the world.

Unfortunately I could not continue wearing the tights as they cut into my soft skin and made me sore. It seemed that there was no escape and I returned to my feelings of insecurity. As well as my own fear of injury another powerful factor contributing to my damaged mental state was my parents' fear. In an attempt to protect me they tried to stop me doing things I wanted to do which only served to make me want to do it even more. Unfortunately their fears did not stop the accidents. Indeed they only served to make matters worse.

I knew I was "a problem" to my parents, teachers and doctors. When I was 17 my school organised a trip to Russia. As the son of a member of the British Communist Party I desperately wanted to go but I was turned down flat. The organizer of the trip was Mr. Rimmer the man who had been working in the tuck shop some four years earlier when I thrust my bloodied shin in his face.

"Howard you are a lovely young man. There is no one I would rather take than you. I'm sure you'll be jolly good company but there's no way I can take the risk. I'm sorry but I can't take you." This was a devastating blow to my morale. As a child I recovered from disappointments fairly easily before flitting on to the next one. As I grew older I was becoming increasingly frustrated by the limitations being placed on me. I was learning that if I let it, my medical problems would seriously limit my life experiences.

I knew that I frightened my parents and teachers alike. I felt sorry for them and guilty that I was the cause of so much anguish. Although I had plenty of friends no one knew that I felt desperately alone and my self-esteem collapsed.

I developed a psychology of over-caution, which served to

cause further accidents. I became so careful and nervous of hurting myself that I got into the habit of checking my behaviour constantly. Some years ago I was walking along a cliff top path with a friend. He commented that I was not looking at the lovely coastal views but seemed to be watching my feet, trying to prevent a fall. I seemed to be guarding myself. He was right. I was constantly tense and aware of potential danger even if none was apparent.

As a result I created a situation where I had accidents just in the manner that the psychology booklet had referred to. I began to "predict" situations that might be or become dangerous and then found myself in those situations. I couldn't seem to get accidents out of my head. I'm not saying that I deliberately hurt myself; far from it but it seemed that when I predicted accidents that then actually happened I gained some control over a life that frightened me. In some strange way I was able to cope with an "accident" better than I could the fear of one. In much the same way that people who say "I never win anything" seem to be happy when they lose. Their accuracy gives them control over uncertain events even when that accuracy does not benefit them.

My stressed mental condition produced negativity in me that I have only recently begun to overcome. This poor outlook has created some strange experiences. I've never admitted this to anyone but as I began to raise my foot up to climb that wall at school I looked down at the wet concrete and for a microsecond I thought "I bet I cut myself here." This kind of thinking in a thirteen year old child have shows that I was already beginning to show signs of a deep-seated state of stress in my personality.

As I have written this, my left hand has shot to the sky, my back has arched against the chair and I have let out a muffled cry of pain. Flashbacks like this occur on a regular basis. I can be driving down a road and suddenly the moment of pain flashes into my head for no apparent reason always with the same reaction. This is when I feel most vulnerable and at my loneliest.

Other strange dark thoughts have entered my head with some very unpleasant consequences. Some years ago I was watching my favourite television programme when a popular presenter was speaking. I thought I heard something in his breathing and it alarmed me. I thought to myself "Oh you don't sound very well. You sound a bit chesty." Imagine my dismay some two weeks later when I heard on the radio whilst on holiday in Wales that he had died of a heart attack.

I had a similar disturbing thought about a colleague of mine. We had a sports event in college and I saw Tony in shorts for the first time. His legs looked white and thin. I thought, "You don't look very strong." I had a very strange feeling about him. Shortly afterwards he died suddenly from a heart attack.

These thoughts continued. About a year after Tony's death I went to school to pick up my children. A young woman was waiting by the door. I didn't know her at all but I immediately had a very uncomfortable feeling when I looked at her.

"I thought to myself "Your life isn't up to much is it?" I looked away, annoyed with myself for having such thoughts, angry that I would make such a judgemental statement about anyone. I discovered a month later that, to my horror, she had been hit by a car and had subsequently

258

died.

At the time I had no idea why these thoughts occurred but they naturally disturbed me greatly. I'm not superstitious in any way. I have never attended a psychic reading or shown any remote interest in anything like that.

None of these events had anything to do with me but my mental state must have been one of great turmoil. I must have been very unhappy with the world and my life and in particular traumatized by my accidents. I was in a continuously stressed frame of mind and negative, dangerous thoughts oused from my every pore. I had to find a better way of living, a more positive mind set.

I began visiting a counsellor in my late forties. During one of our sessions I began talking about my physical difficulties. I found myself talking about the very serious cut that began this book. I told my counsellor about how I had joked about the nurse's breasts pushing into my face as she held me down. For years I'd presented that experience as a bit of a laugh, a chance to feel a woman's breasts.

"It hurt. It really hurt."

"It sounds like it did."

That simple statement was the first time I had ever told anyone about how desperate I had felt at that moment I pulled down my sock and saw the extent of the damage to my shin. Everyone talked about what a tough little boy I was. They assumed I was able to deal with everything that happened to me but I had never come to terms with any of it. Not only did I have to face the injuries but I also had to face having stitches inserted into soft, weak skin without any anaesthetic.

That admission to the counsellor was the first time I had expressed anything about how I really felt and her kind reply brought to a head forty years of silent anguish. I knew then that the joking had to stop. The problem was that the accidents didn't. I had to find a way to deal with them and quickly, to stop them. I had to begin by rejecting the labels that others placed on me and to stop the jokes. Before people could take me seriously I had to take myself seriously. I had to stop pretending that I was OK. I clearly wasn't.

My physical problems were having a serious impact on my mental health. I was in a terrible state. I was full of anxiety and possessed by dark thoughts but I kept these emotions hidden. I knew I had to break free even then but changing your core self, your basic personality is a very difficult thing to do. Nevertheless I had to set about reconstructing myself if I was ever to achieve personal happiness. Effecting this change is not a single event. It is a process that can take a considerable period of time and for me it involved a number of realizations that occurred haphazardly. The skill is to recognize them when they occur and seize on them, making sure that you gain maximum benefit from them.

I was beginning to develop a more positive outlook but right until the time I fell of the ladder new, strange thoughts had begun creeping into my head. They were no longer dark thoughts of death as they had been previously but they were still disturbing. I had started thinking "I haven't had any accidents for a while now." This eventually translated into, "I wonder when my next accident will happen?" I then began to have awful feelings of foreboding. "Something bad is going to happen. It's time. I'm due one." I knew that I still had a long way to go if I were to achieve a long lasting peace of mind. Falling off the ladder proved that.

A significant step along the way to developing a more positive outlook was initiated by the then Principal of the college where I used to work. It was one of the most useful conversations I have ever had. I had originally gone in to complain about the fact that I had been overlooked for a promotion yet again. She was very kind and was able to put my troubled mind at ease. She turned the conversation away from just work into one about my life in general.

"Do you have any lights in your life?" she asked.

"No."

"None at all?"

"I can't think of any."

"I think you're depressed."

I knew she was right. I had thought that I suffered from bouts of depression but suddenly in the midst of this conversation I realized that I didn't have bouts of depression, I was depressed. The website for Ehlers Danlos syndrome refers to depression being a common feature in people who have the condition. One of the main causes is that they seem to be perfectly all right and can't get people to understand the difficulties they have. Andrew, my youngest child had this difficulty at work. They often thought he was malingering when he took sick leave and had several disciplinary hearings as a result. I could see how it upset him but I didn't detect it in myself.

I don't look as if I have a disability and I have never referred to my problems with that title. I was labelled as clumsy or stupid because people only noticed when I had my accidents. They didn't see the day-to-day issues I had to deal with. They didn't lie just in a physical injury but in the nagging fear of being injured combined with a constant feeling of weariness that I experienced. Throughout my life people have asked me if I was feeling ill, as I looked tired and drawn. I always told them I was fine. Now I realize that I wasn't. I had begun to find full-time work very tiring. I was exhausted and as a result of all these factors I became depressed. Life as I was living it was becoming too demanding. I knew I wanted my life to change but I had no idea what to do. I was making some progress but it was a stumbling uncertain journey and it was proving to be much too slow.

The Principal's final words were, "My dad used to say that life is a gift. It is our duty to enjoy it." As I walked down the dimly lit corridor that led from her office a shaft of light dazzled me. I knew she was right and was determined not to wallow in self-pity. I thought to myself, "If I have no lights in my life, I'm dead." I had a choice. I could submit to it all and die or I had to find a light in my life. I resolved there and then to find one. It was quite simple really. I asked myself what do I enjoy in life? One thing came into my thoughts; my grandchildren.

My doctor signed me off work for nearly six months. During that time I began to cycle up to their school to greet them as they came out at the end of the day. Their smiles lifted my spirits and my mental health began to improve. It was like looking at the night sky on a cloudy night. You might not see a star at first but once you do another one appears and then another. That simple and fairly short conversation with the Principal helped to change my life. It was only one of many such moments but it was the key, which unlocked all the rest. I had made a decision to liberate myself from depression.

Carrying it out, however would be another challenge altogether.

Part 6

Changing

Chapter 33 Making Plans

Although I hadn't realized it at the time my outlook on life and my ability to deal with my problems had already begun a very slow, unconscious and unfocused process of change when I was about 24 years of age.

I was watching a game of rugby on television between France and Scotland. The BBC's Bill McLaren was commentating when a French player received a gash to his thigh. As they carried him off on a stretcher McLaren said in his broad Scottish accent, "Oh that's a horrendous injury!"

It looked to me like he'd need about 7 stitches. I thought to myself "Horrendous? I have had two or three of those a year for as long as I can remember." McLaren's words sent a slow fused thunderbolt through my perception of who I was. Whilst it had been 'normal' for me to attend casualty on such a regular basis that they knew me by name and spend several weeks recuperating from broken bones, dislocated knees or cut shins it wasn't normal for anyone else. Although it may sound ridiculous to say, I hadn't realized.

In the middle of writing this book I have remembered something that I had completely forgotten existed. Thirty years ago I wrote a play and then left it in my desk drawer. It's now lying somewhere in the attic. I have no idea why I did not try to get it published. I finished it just as I moved to Hull to take up a teaching post and the upheaval in my life must have stopped it being a priority.

I suddenly remembered it last night. It came as a complete surprise. The play is called "I'm not Frank Spencer". The main character is a man who bumbles from one accident to another as the character Frank Spencer does in "Some Mothers Do 'Ave 'Em". He is based on my life experience and whilst the television show presents Frank's antics as humorous events the play suggests that, on closer examination his situation is far from being funny. The man is obviously suffering from severe stress and anxiety in all features of his life. He is never relaxed and is tormented by all kinds of demons in his life.

Unfortunately the play merely describes these events but it doesn't attempt to explain them. What it does show is that even then, I was concerned about both my physical and mental health but I wasn't capable of explaining them. Thirty six years later I have finally made some progress in this matter and I now have a much clearer understanding of my situation but it has not been a simple realization, more the gradual demisting of a fog that has enveloped me and stopped me from seeing the true reality of my life – that most people don't get hurt as much as I do and doing so is definitely not normal.

There have been several other occasions in recent years when it has dawned on me that the events I have experienced have been, what others might consider, difficult to say the least. Lying on the floor of my garage forced me to realize that these accidents were more than mere inconveniences. My situation was very serious. I couldn't afford to suffer another injury. This was confirmed by the slow healing of my leg. Age was now a factor. My body was telling me that I had had enough.

The most significant realization did not occur as a result of a serious injury however. This happened when I was on a bus returning home for an appointment with my podiatrist.

My feet are very flat due to the fact that my ligaments are so loose. As a result my feet don't fill a normal shoe properly. What this means is that I can't tie the shoe tight enough and the foot slips around inside. Consequently my feet rub on the sides and sole. Walking any distance hurts. I like walking in the Lake District but the only way I can do so is to strap up my feet and take double painkillers. I have to rest the next day as my feet are bruised and I could never contemplate a walking holiday where I walked every day.

The podiatrist I saw this day looked at my feet. She said, "Your foot widens abnormally when you stand on it. I think you need purpose made shoes." This was as big a revelation to me as when young Doctor Barker correctly identified that I had Ehlers Danlos syndrome. It is very difficult to be ecstatic when you are limping to the bus stop but I could not wipe the grin of my face as I thought about the prospect of having comfortable shoes when a shock wave passed through me.

"I have never, ever been comfortable." Was all I could say. It was a really strange experience. I could actually see the stinging pain that was growing in the balls of my feet. Being in pain had been a normal state for me. I hadn't considered it before but now that I did my feet began hurting even more.

As I sat on the bus I thought to myself, "Other people wouldn't put up with this."

Although I was hurting I also felt liberated. Somebody was going to do something to help me. The pain would go away rather than lie there, nagging at me, tiring me. When the man at Samaritans said "you've been through a lot" I had heard it but not understood it fully. Now on the bus I saw it

267

clearly. All those cuts and dislocations, the constant pain in my feet, the painful lower back, lying on the garage floor in rat shit thinking 'this has got to stop'

Then another thought struck me. "This has got to stop" were the words of a victim. I was now thinking "This will stop."

This change of words was really significant. It meant I was taking control of my life. I was going to stop doing things that hurt me. I was going to stop feeling the need to impress people. I was going to be strong enough to say "I can't do that and it doesn't make me any less of a man if I can't".

I really enjoyed that journey home. It was the best bus ride a boy ever had for I was still a little boy, trapped in his memories, his fears and his pain but now I was going to become a man. I had begun to formulate a plan of how to change my life. I couldn't do anything about my medical condition but I could begin to understand its implications for the first time. No one had ever been able to help me. Even I have never met anyone else with EDS but now I sensed that a change was occurring and I was determined to create a new way of living. It would take time and as it turned out, would be a lot more complicated than I first thought. Nevertheless as the bus neared the end of its journey I was beginning a new one.

A cloud of diesel fumes swirled around me and began to disperse as I stood in the village square. I bought a chocolate-coated Magnum ice cream from the local newsagents and sat on a bench enjoying it in the sunshine. I was free from anxiety, stress, self-doubt and some of the pain. I actually felt the cloud of depression, hidden and sinister begin to lift from me. It swirled around as the diesel fumes had done minutes earlier before rising upwards to be burned away by the warmth of the sun. I had never felt so happy. I was 59 years old and for the first time in my life I had thought, "The pain is going to stop," and I knew that my life was going to get better.

No ice cream ever tasted so sweet.

I could now see that it might be possible to stop or reduce the number of injuries I was suffering. My life was going to improve because I had resolved to turn it around but I was still at a loss about how I was going to do it. The podiatrist's actions were going to remove the pain in my feet and I had changed a few things in a piecemeal fashion but the accidents hadn't stopped by any means. The problem I faced was that the more I thought about how to avoid accidents the more I seemed to be thinking about accidents and I had already identified this thought process as one of the problems causing accidents in the first place. I was stuck. Then I read a book that helped me considerably.

"A Beautiful Mind" is an account of the life of John Nash, a very important mathematician who had serious mental health problems. He was diagnosed as a paranoid schizophrenic and was hospitalised on several occasions. As part of his treatment he was prescribed drugs in an attempt to stabilise his condition but they produced little improvement in his long-term situation. When his wife was later admitted to hospital with mental health problems she began to understand the inadequacies of purely medical approaches to mental illness.

When she recovered, she vowed never to have her husband

taken into hospital again. A breakthrough in his life came when he learned to recognise the demons that lurked in his mind. Instead of using drugs to destroy or anaesthetise his demons he learned to recognise them for what they were; his enemy. Instead of blanking out his demons he learned to understand and manage them. I decided that I needed to address my demons in a systematic way and defeat them.

Gradually over a period of weeks I drew up all the different strands of thoughts about my life and produced a plan.

First of all I decided that I had to recognise that whilst I have never been so ill as Nash, I have had a stifled depression for a large part of my life. My injuries have fundamentally affected my mental health. My wife has often complained that I am always cracking jokes and that it's very tiresome. Jokes have been my only defence. They covered up all my feelings of traumatisation and anguish and got me through the pain and anguish but they could not solve the problems I had and I now wanted a solution not a mask.

Once I recognised what the jokes were about I was able to begin to control them. I haven't got rid of my sense of humour but I know that I don't have to make a joke about everything in order to negotiate my way in life. I used to throw jokes at everyone for any reason even when there wasn't really a joke there and a former Principal once explained to me that I hadn't got a certain job I had applied for because, "I was too much the clown." I was not a clown. The jokes were a sign of stress.

Now I have identified what my problems have been and faced up to my weaknesses and accepted them I am far more relaxed now and more discerning. I no longer feel the need to be humorous. I am also more sensitive to how my jokes may affect others to Linda's considerable relief.

I still have flashbacks to my injuries. They can happen at any time without warning. I can be sat watching television and an ambulance siren will sound. Before I know it I have let out a gasp. My head has arched backwards and I am grabbing my leg in an attempt to hold a cut, which no longer bleeds.

I now know however that having flashbacks is a perfectly normal response to a series of traumatic events. I am no longer afraid of them or angry with myself for "allowing" them to appear. I have simply made a decision to accept them for what they are; images in my head. They are a picture of reality and not reality itself. You can change a picture.

I now see myself differently in the pictures I have of myself. I can now see that I am a person who overcomes difficulties rather than being damned by them. When the flashbacks occur I think about how brave I've been. I have fought and won and suddenly the memories hold less pain for me.

Everyone has difficulties in life of one kind or another. Life is about how you deal with them. Translating this into "Everyone has accidents at some time. Thinking about them isn't bad. It's perfectly natural in your situation. You are not weird. You just have to take sensible precautions. When you do you'll avoid most of the accidents that you worry about. They simply won't happen. Make them go away like Nash did." When I begin to think like this I begin to win. It's a wonderful feeling.

If I am frightened of a forthcoming situation or if I find

myself worrying that something bad is going to happen I no longer lie in expectant fear. I change the outcome. Instead of seeing my grandchildren crying I see them smiling. I tell the demons, the bad thoughts to go away. If I find myself worrying about falling down the stairs or cutting myself I stop and imagine how it could happen and I change the outcome. Soon such behaviour became a habit. The jokes had become a way of thinking, a habit. I changed my habits.

It isn't easy and I didn't believe in all the "psycho babble" of envisaging positive outcomes but it works. It takes time and must become a habit, a way of living and thinking but it has considerably enhanced my life.

I have just had a phone call from my daughter asking me if I can look after Aisha, the youngest of her children, for the afternoon. I had planned to do some more of my book so my first reaction was "Damn this is terribly inconvenient." This is how people always react to unplanned events. The positive view was to stop thinking the negative thoughts and change the picture. "How can I get something good out of this?" Then I found myself thinking "I haven't seen her for a while. I can always do the book tomorrow. It would be nice to talk with her. My car needs washing. I'll do that instead and she can help me. Then we can have a ride into the village to pick up a paper, which I was going to do anyway. I probably need a break anyway. I am also pleased with myself because I started early on my book which means I have already done two hours on the book I have done well."

By the way, Aisha and I had a lovely time.

Chapter 34 Becoming a Man

My life had been under a process of change for some time but I hadn't connected all the different strands together. Now I understood things more clearly I could see that it wasn't just a case of being more careful or taking painkillers to alleviate pain and its consequent depression. Neither was it simply about telling myself to stop being afraid. All those things were necessary but I had to address much more fundamental issues in my life before I could deal with those just mentioned.

More than anything else my view of myself and my masculinity was probably the major demon in my life that I had to confront.

My body is softer than normal. My skin breaks or bruises easily. As a result I couldn't play the contact sports I wanted to and I certainly couldn't do any of the traditional male jobs such as a bricklayer or mechanic. I am lucky in that I am fairly well muscled and this has helped to keep my joints under control when the ligaments didn't but in some ways my natural athleticism only served to exacerbate the problem. I nearly could have done the things that I wanted to do. I have described myself as a sports car with flat tyres. The engine's fine but the car struggles to go anywhere.

My grand daughter has often told people that she has "delicate skin". She is quite comfortable in saying that she is unable to do something. She does not see it as a failure on her part but that was a very hard thing to say when I was a boy growing up in a world full of rugby, cricket, John Wayne and Rambo. I have never felt very manly. In fact I have always carried with me a sense of inadequacy, which has contributed to my depression. I wasn't the man I wanted to be and I didn't like the man I was.

As I have aged I have gained certain benefits. It is now easier for me to admit to my apparent failings. I'm no longer expected to climb ladders as I used to. It's acceptable to say that I can't do certain things any more. No one expects me to play for the staff football team. I no longer have to make excuses because I can't admit that I'm frightened of getting hurt. The last accident has provided me with an excuse to give up the battle. I can say without fear that I'm too frightened to climb a ladder and people don't laugh. They think such a fear is quite reasonable. Suddenly my perceived failures have disappeared in a cloud of dust and rat droppings, silenced by the clatter of falling aluminium.

As a result I can now reflect, not on what I couldn't do but on what I have achieved. If only I had had the wisdom that age brings when I was younger. If only the society I was brought up in had been as tolerant and understanding as today's I might not have felt so badly towards myself.

I thought of myself as weak and yet not one of my teachers was anything less than kind and protective towards me. None of them ever said anything to make me feel inadequate. In fact my feelings have come entirely from my perceptions of myself.

I once told a very dear friend about my feelings of being a failure. Alan said,

"You've nothing to prove to anyone after what you've done with your life. I don't understand why you feel that way about yourself. No one else thinks like that about you."

But I didn't or couldn't value comments like this at the time. I was so damaged that I didn't believe or want to believe the compliments. They didn't fit with my view of myself. I was suffocating in a maelstrom of emotions. I had a view of myself and of manliness from a variety of sources but some were more powerful than others. It's clear that the views of me as clumsy, stupid and inadequate were stronger than any positive views that might have existed. I had spent my life in fear; fear of injury and fear from others reactions to me. I was stressed and depressed and couldn't see a way out of my problems.

In these circumstances most people are faced with a choice. They accept the way things are or they decide to change. I knew that if I didn't change the way I saw myself I would continue to have more accidents and would soon be dead. I didn't want to be hurt any more and I didn't want to be seen as a figure of fun. Just as I found my stars after speaking to the Principal, I decided to find some good things to say about myself. In doing so I redefined myself as a man. I sat down and wrote a list of things to be proud of. At first it was a very short one but just like the Principal's stars, the number of items on my list grew the more I looked.

Despite my problems I have achieved many fine things.

All my working life I have helped people. As a teacher in A Sixth Form College I helped mould young people into adults. Hundreds of students have passed through my hands. Not only did I teach them my subject but I had a very strong input into setting an example of how to be a good person and a good man. I never condemned people for their weaknesses and immaturity. Instead I always tried to take people to a higher level. I have been told on several occasions by young people that I inspired them to achieve far more than they thought possible.

As the Head of Special Needs I felt that I gave strength to vulnerable people. I supported them as they faced serious difficulties and helped some of them prepare for death. I helped their families to deal with their pain. I supported teachers' aides who had to face the emotional stresses caused by such work. They looked after such children on a daily basis for two or three years at a time. They acted as scribes in class, fed them and toileted them. They waited patiently when a taxi failed to turn up, unwilling to leave them alone. People who help the very vulnerable need looking after as well. I think I was really good at that. Strength doesn't always lie in muscles or thick skin.

I have saved my son Robert from serious injury twice. One summer evening, when Robert was four, we were sitting on the front step enjoying the sunshine. The house opposite had just switched on their new fountain and my son wanted to go and have a look at it. I watched him across the road and was enjoying his delight. Suddenly the neighbour's seven stone Alsatian dog appeared menacingly in the front doorway. I could tell by the look on its face that it meant business but it moved too fast. It ran across the short length of the garden before leaping over the low wall and head butted my little boy. As Robert rolled over on the floor it sank his teeth into his right buttock. I ran across the street in my bare feet. I screamed and roared and instinctively raised my hands as high and wide as I could. Luckily it backed off and cowered in the corner enabling my son to get up and run behind me. It's frightening to think what would have happened had it bitten me. My skin would have come away easily but I had no time to think about that. The only course of action I had was to save Robert from further harm. He tells me now that even as a small infant he knew I was the one to get behind.

The second event took place in the local swimming pool some two years later. Linda sat on the side, nursing our newborn son Andrew whilst I was in the water with the other two. I told Robert to stay where he was and to keep hold of the side rail whilst I escorted Sarah on her first completion of a full breadth of the pool. I was busy praising her for her achievement when she said,

"Dad mum's shouting."

I turned to see Linda pointing frantically at Robert whose bulging eyes were starting to disappear below the surface on the opposite side of the pool. Such was her belief in and reliance on me that she had not thought to tell the attendant who was sat next to her. I dashed across the water sweeping Robert onto my shoulder and lifted him out of the pool onto the side.

"Oh fanks dad," he said rubbing his eyes.

Linda was so relieved. No one in that packed pool had seen him struggling. Robert remembers it well and describes how safe he felt as he saw my arms ploughing through the water towards him. My children and I are good friends. I know I have been a very good father but I am a wonderful granddad. I know because Floyd told me so. In my retirement I have discovered golf. I never thought that I would be playing this game but I absolutely love it. I play once a week and would do more but for the pains in my feet. I am so enamoured with the game that I have taken my grandchildren for lessons. On one wet and murky Saturday afternoon I decided to hit a few balls whilst they had their lesson. I was lining up my shot when Floyd who was then seven years old turned to his friend and said "Oh granddad's taking a shot. Watch this. He's awesome!"

I wanted to tell him that I was only a beginner but I saw the look of admiration in his eyes and I knew that I was doomed. Nervously I set myself and unleashed a mighty blow. Unfortunately the club head hit the ground before hitting the ball. As a result the ball shot upwards and travelled further vertically than it did horizontally. Fortunately, in hitting the ground the club made an almighty noise and the ball disappeared from view above the roof line of the driving range. My grandson turned to his friend and said "See. I told you!"

I am awesome!

Since I was about fifteen I have been politically active. I was the trades union representative at work for a number of years and helped several people with serious problems facing the wrath of the Principal on several occasions without flinching. For a number of years I was an active member of the Anti Nazi League and was involved in organizing physical resistance when the National Front attempted to march and gain credibility as a political force. One occasion took place in Stockport. It was anticipated that three thousand members of the racist group were going to march. Fortunately more anti-racists turned up and the police allowed only the National Front's leader to march bearing a placard protesting against his denial of "freedom".

Both these events were potentially very dangerous for

everyone involved. I could have been facing the possibility of serious injury. I could not bear however to see what I considered to be a serious threat to innocent members of our community go unchallenged. My concern for others was stronger than my concern for myself. I think I have been very brave.

As I began to write this chapter the number of stars in my sky began to grow even if other people didn't always appreciate my efforts.

Linda had decided to come to the Lake District with me before she went on holiday, without me, to Turkey. She didn't want me to be alone on holiday as I had been the previous year when she went to Turkey for the first time. Although I welcomed her on the holiday I doubted whether she would enjoy walking up Sca Fell Pike. It is the highest mountain in England and probably the toughest in Britain.

Unfortunately she had forgotten to bring any thermal underwear. I suggested buying some locally but she insisted that she'd be OK and so we ventured forth against my better judgement. Linda is a very strong person but she would have done better to listen to my advice.

As we left the car she said, "Shall I take my purse?"

"No. Where are we going to spend any money?" I convinced her to leave her money in the car. This turned out to be a bad decision on my part.

Four hours later we arrived at the top. I wanted to stop and take some photographs of the fantastic views stretching to Morecambe bay in the west and Scotland to the north. I also wanted to stop and have a cup of tea and something to eat. It was important to rest. Linda was having none of it. She didn't like the top. There were some flies hovering around some discarded food left by unthinking walkers and she didn't want to stay. I pleaded with her to stop somewhere and have a rest and a drink. Without her thermal underwear she was becoming very cold, as I had predicted.

"If I stop I'll never start again," was her understandable reply but it was misplaced. The fact is that had she stopped and had food and drink she would have been re-energised and more capable of carrying on. Her mind was made up however and off she went without knowing where she was going. I did not realize she had gone as I was busy taking photographs of what were a series of wonderful views. This was my fifth visit to the top of Sca Fell. I had seen nothing but thick fog on the previous occasions and this was the one time I could see what I had come up to see. It was beautiful. I sat there in awe.

"Wow isn't that wonderful Linda? ... Linda?"

She was nowhere to be seen. I stood up and saw her tasselled hat bobbing from side to side. I gathered my things together as quickly as possible and ran off to catch up with her. As you come off from the top and head towards a place called Esk Hause, the land is drowned in a sea of rocks and boulders and the path rises steeply and uninvitingly before it begins to descend. I thought Linda would have a fit if she saw that rise. I was confident in my ability to stumble in the right direction but chose to follow Linda in an attempt to pacify her. I didn't want her to be angry with me and panicked. We turned left onto a descending path that quickly petered out into a walk over rocks. The terrain quickly became very rough and dangerously steep. We were completely lost and Linda was exhausted. After a huge effort we left the rocks behind and began to move over wet grass. It was still precarious underfoot. Suddenly the last remains of strength drained away from Linda and she began crying and sobbing. I have seen her cry and shout in the middle of a row but this was different. She was at the end of her tether.

"Get me off here! Get me away! Get me off here! I want to go home!"

"OK love OK. I'll get you off but stay calm and do as I say."

"Get me off here! I don't want to be here! Get me away!"

I held her shoulders but she wasn't listening. I tried to stay calm but inside I was more scared than I have ever been in my whole life. I could not however, let Linda see this. I looked at the grass, wet and shiny and had a brilliant idea.

"Sit down."

"What?"

"Sit down!"

"I want to go home!" She was screaming and in a state of total panic.

"I'll get you home! Trust me. Sit down."

Linda sat down, her face contorted with anxiety.

"Push yourself!"

"What?"

"Push!"

With that I began to toboggan on my backside down the slope. I stopped after twenty yards and turned to encourage Linda to follow. She was shaking her head and crying. I climbed back up and held out my hand. "We'll be alright. We'll be alright. Just follow me."

Linda took my hand and I pulled her towards me. She began to slide forward and could see that it was a way to get off the mountain. We slid 300 feet down the side of the mountain and came to rest near a path of sorts. Linda and I had soaking wet bottoms. To make it worse we were covered in sheep shit and looked like we'd had serious personal accidents. We were however feeling safe and could see a way to a clear path. But Linda was still gnashing her teeth in total distress.

"If we follow this we'll be fine."

Unfortunately it turned out to be the wrong path. I had been looking for a tarn that I wanted to use as a reference point but missed it. The path took us round in completely the opposite direction to the one we wanted. I couldn't make sense of the map. Stupidly I hadn't brought a compass as I thought I knew the area like the back of my hand. Clearly my confidence was misplaced. I must have turned my head to check on Linda as the tarn came momentarily into view before disappearing again. Whatever the reason I missed it. I was struggling to find our location and did not realize my mistake until a lake came into view in the distance.

"There's no lake here," I said to the map. It was undeniably there however. There was no beach or water line of any kind. The mountain just descended into the water. "That looks like Wastwater but we're not near Wastwater," I said to myself as a large "W" on the front of Wasdale Head Inn emerged out of the gloom.

"Shit. Shit, shit, shit!"

I looked at the map and realized my mistake, my huge mistake confirmed by the sign, 'Burnside Cottage' that sat on the wall on my left. We were walking by Burnside Beck. I searched the map frantically and found it. It was in the wrong place!

"Shit. Shit, shit, shit! How the hell do I tell Linda who was completely exhausted? We stumbled onto a beer garden bench that had been placed conveniently for our weary limbs.

"Get me a pint!" demanded Linda completely oblivious to our difficulties.

"I don't remember this pub."

"Ah well er we've got a problem."

"Get me a pint," she said staring menacingly towards me.

"Er have you got any money?"

"No. Haven't you?"

"No."

"I asked you should we take some money with us? You said no we wouldn't need it."

What was I supposed to say? I decided to tell her immediately.

"We're in the wrong place."

Linda suddenly became alive again.

"What?"

"We must have turned the wrong way."

She was speechless.

"I'll sort it out." I said, not knowing what the hell I was going to do. I patted her on the arm.

"Get me a drink."

I went into the hotel and came back later with two glasses of water. Linda looked at me in disbelief.

"Let's go inside."

Linda followed me into the packed bar and we sat on a wooden bench in the corner as I explained that we were on the other side of the mountain from our car. I explained what our options were. We could walk back some two hours round the foot of the mountain. Linda's look immediately showed that that was not an option. The second was to stay at the hotel overnight at a cost of £80 and try to convince them that we'd bring the money in the morning. The third was to get a taxi.

"This happens more than you think." The barman smiled.

It did not reassure Linda who dissolved in to tears, real tears. I was so sorry for her. People began looking over at us as I tried to smile my way through it. Linda could not stop crying however. She was exhausted, hungry and in desperate need of a beer. Water just didn't impress her at all.

"Right this is a bad moment but we'll get out of this. I'll phone a taxi."

I managed to get hold of a taxi after ten minutes searching. It was Sunday night in the middle of nowhere.

"This happens more than you think." The big guy grinned as he loaded our bags into the boot. Linda was not able to smile. It took us an hour and a half to get round the Lake

284

District and cost us £85. We dropped Linda off at our hotel in Keswick before driving back to the car. Then I drove in my car, followed by the taxi, back to Keswick to get some money out of a hole in the wall in order to pay the driver. My misery was not yet over however. On the way back I turned first left at a mini roundabout instead of taking the second exit and found myself in a car park. All I could see in the rear view mirror was the driver's teeth as he grinned at me.

"I bet he thinks I'm a right knob head." I whispered to myself.

Finally we got to a hole in the wall outside Barclays bank.

It was out of order.

Luckily I got the money from another bank. As I handed him the cash I said,

"I'm not being funny but I hope I never see your face again."

He laughed again as he said his goodbye. I returned to our hotel bar where Linda was sat drinking her second pint of lager. A pint of bitter sat on the table waiting for me. Linda smiled a "You're a wanker," smile. She has not been to the Lake District since.

When we got home I was the one who got blamed by all Linda's friends and relatives. They all saw it as my being accident-prone again. To this day Linda does not acknowledge any responsibility for what happened. In everybody's view I got us lost. The fact that she ignored all my advice is completely lost. Things go wrong in all kinds of situations in life and no one seems to have noticed that despite being in a situation which terrified Linda I did not panic. Far from being 'typical Philip' when something went wrong on the mountain I got us home safe and sound.

My family and personal life has not taken the course that I envisaged when I began married life. I was fully convinced that I would and should never have children. I agreed to my wife's request however. I met her needs as mine were forgotten. The constant anxiety I felt was always about by my fears for the safety of others, never for myself. When Linda mistook my stressed behaviour as anger or awkwardness, I absorbed the stress. I know that she has had a very difficult time in many respects. She too was worried about her children and I suspect had feelings of guilt. I dealt with the shouting and the tears. I have been very strong in caring for my loved ones and have put my own anxieties after the needs of others. In fact I have never spoken about them until I began writing this book. In doing so I have come to redefine myself as a man.

Despite my physical difficulties I've held down a responsible job, looking after the most vulnerable of people. On many occasions the demands of a full-time job left me exhausted but I have never let my family down. We could have lived off unemployment and disability pension but my children would not have had the start in life that I was able to give them.

When I finished writing this list I realized that I had much to be proud of but I hadn't recognised this at all. I saw a man who I thought to be ugly and scarred, unable to hold down a "Real" man's job, incapable of following "manly" pursuits. My difficulties had produced a demoralising negativity in my psyche. I didn't like myself. Now I feel completely differently. When I look at myself I am really content. I have done well.

Finally and most importantly to me, I can call myself a man because I have had a pile of shit thrown at me, literally and metaphorically and I'm still standing. I have faced my demons and defeated them (almost). I don't feel inadequate or guilty or angry anymore.

I couldn't be the man that I wanted to be. I'm not a rugby player or a footballer but I am a good dad; a fantastic granddad; an awesome golfer. I was an excellent and inspiring teacher. I am a good husband and a loyal friend; a reliable member of the Hull Male Voice choir. In fact I have many fine qualities but in my depressed state of mind I saw none of them. My failures, as I perceived them to be, outweighed everything else.

The problem with depression is that it makes you depressed. With my new-found positive attitude towards myself I could begin to take control of my life and enjoy being me. I was looking forward to it.

Chapter 35 A Different Future

Re-defining myself as a man has enabled me to listen to my body more clearly. I need to give myself permission to stop living the way I have been. I need to give myself permission to "fail" and I need to admit that I can't do "it" and enjoy something else. Some sort of plan was, at last, emerging but it was not fully formed, more a series of ad hoc ideas.

Whilst I was recovering from my broken femur some seriously stormy weather ravaged Sunk Island where I live. It is located on the eastern edge of Britain and there are few trees or buildings to protect us. The wind had taken down a large section of cast iron guttering. It fell to the ground and shattered. It could have killed someone. Concerned about any further falls and the amount of water gushing down my wall I asked my son in law and his dad for help. My son in law's brother in law came to help assess the job. He looked at the size of the task and said without hesitation, "I can't do that. It'll kill my back." I looked at him in surprise. I didn't know Richard had a bad back. I had never heard a man in my circulation say that he couldn't manage to do something. My dad always seemed to tackle everything. Richard has no idea how his few words helped change my life. What a relief. It was OK not to be able to cope. It was OK not to want to climb a ladder. Like many men I have spent my whole life doing DIY jobs around the house for which I had no training. I had been under constant pressure trying to work out how to do things only learning how to do the job by the end of the task, never to do it again. Unlike other men, however I had been in constant physical discomfort, kneeling on floors that bruised my knees, cutting myself on metal, dislocating my thumbs whilst grabbing pliers.

Richard's words removed a huge weight off my shoulders. The next thing I did involved a very significant decision. I claimed and succeeded in obtaining Disability Living Allowance. In doing so I was admitting that I needed help. I would use the benefit to pay somebody to my household repairs. I was now saying not "I'll do things more carefully" but "I can't do those jobs. They hurt me and I'm afraid." It was not a lie. If I'm honest I've always always afraid.

Anthony and his dad did the gutters for which I was so grateful and I am never ever, ever going up ladders again!

I have a large garden pond that I dug out by spade several years ago. Recently it had developed a leak in the lining and was losing water. I called in a local company who relined it for me. It took two men, many years my junior, six hours to complete and cost £350 paid for by my disability living allowance. I also recently paid a painter and decorator to paint the outside of my house. I had asked for help. It was liberating experience.

Applying for Disability Living Allowance did something else. It made me start referring to myself as having a disability. I prefer the term medical condition or something like that but it allowed me further scope to deal with my issues. I wasn't the problem, the medical condition was. The next stage in the creation of the new me was to take early retirement. I was a very successful 'A' level teacher and for a number of years derived a considerable amount of satisfaction and enjoyment from my work. The last few years however had been an increasingly difficult struggle, which eventually became a nightmare. I was constantly tired and could no longer deal with the demands of full time work. I had to admit that I was washed up.

I finished in July 2009. A month later I was lying on the grass in agony. I have always loved gardening. I remember being 13 years old and helping my dad with the allotment at the back of his garden.

I entered retirement with the intention of writing my book and enjoying my garden but in the first week I dislocated both my thumbs. I had been lopping branches off some overgrown bushes and sat down on a bench for a rest. I had my arms folded and was enjoying a moment of solitude when I began to notice a dull ache in both my hands. I looked down and my right thumb was lying awkwardly across the palm of my hand. It was out of its socket. I stared at it in disbelief as the pain began to intensify. It looked really strange. It was just lying there. I then saw that my left thumb had done the same thing. I picked up the thumb of my left hand with the fingers of my right and gently manoeuvred it back into place. Then I used all of my left hand to pick up my right thumb and put that back into joint as well.

About three days later my left thumb did it again. This has had more serious consequences. My thumb no longer moves properly due to arthritis. It seems to have come on all of a sudden as a result of this injury.

There has been one comic side to this. I am a member of the Hull Male Voice Choir. We sing using our music books. But I don't have proper feeling in my left thumb and cannot do something delicate like turn a single page of paper. I was singing in rehearsals one day when I clumsily over hit the booklet with my damaged thumb. It propelled the book out of my hand and it struck the back of the chap in front of me. As I tried to rescue it I mishit it again and it took off landing on someone else's head. They were most perplexed. It's not everyday that you get hit by flying choral music! It looked hilarious to everyone who saw it and wasn't hit by it but it was another case of my looking clumsy and a bit comical. It was anything but funny. I was in pain and losing control of my left hand.

In the first weeks of retirement I had a second problem. I was lopping some branches off overgrown trees and bushes. I have loppers that are designed to give extra power. I was cutting one branch that proved a little awkward. I squeezed on the handles a little harder. A pain shot across my back and up and down my torso. I dropped the loppers and let out a gasp. It was agony and I thought I was having a heart attack as I fell to my knees. It was a desperate feeling. I was completely on my own and thought I was going to die in the garden that I loved. Linda was not due home until gone 7.00 pm. In the brief moments I imagined lying there for hours until she arrived. I had to move and get help. The pain was indescribable but when I turned towards the house to take my potentially last steps it eased. Feeling slightly ridiculous at my state of panic I stood up wondering what the hell had happened. Heaven knows what I looked like.

I began to walk to the bench where I had sat after dislocating my thumbs. The pain returned. Although it was not as severe it stopped me in my tracks once more. Eventually I made it to the bench. Sitting down was a very painful movement. I got my backside onto the seat. I realized that I wasn't dying and I sat there panting as I tried to work out what was happening to me. I eventually worked out that I had torn a muscle in my back and popped my shoulder at the same time. I have suffered both injuries before on separate occasions but never simultaneously.

I was in disarray. I limped because of my feet. My hands hurt because of the dislocated thumbs so that I couldn't pick things up properly and now my back hurt at every movement and limited my ability to turn my head. I was in acute discomfort and moved like Quasimodo. I had only been retired a week or so. All my plans of a carefree time, doing what I wanted, when I wanted, were in tatters.

It felt like I'd been beaten up and given a good kicking all over my top half and I was very sore for over a week. It was yet another sign that my whole lifestyle had to change and I was receiving reminders by the minute.   For sometime I had been assessing my life and had been trying to accommodate my disability rather than fighting it. Now I felt I wasn't even going to be able to do that. I now wear supports that have been provided by the Health Service. I wear them when I am gardening. I don't use them all the time. What they have done is to make me think about what I am doing. Because of the hyper extensibility of my ligaments my limbs move into awkward positions naturally. I now think about what I am doing. I try to control this more. It's not easy. I am constantly watching my own behaviour. It's not natural but so far I've had no similar incidents. When I use secateurs I deliberately move in a more controlled way.

As painful as it was the worst thing about it was the extreme sense of loneliness and fear. I couldn't move to get help and on Sunk Island during the day there is no help available anyway. It is a lovely but remote place and my vulnerability had been exposed totally. I spend a lot of time on my own. I quite enjoy not speaking to anyone all day. This has amazed my family as they thought I'd find retirement depressing after spending all my working life dealing with people but I am never bored. I do the housework, write, play golf and from spring to autumn I spend a lot of time in my three large gardens. At the rear of the house I have a wildlife friendly garden with a pond, four silver birch trees and plenty of shrubs such as hawthorn and blackthorn. All the plants are native to the area, which makes them insect and bird friendly. At the side of the house I have a more conventional family garden. It has plenty of shrubs and flowers and the grandchildren play football on the lawn. I am always repairing the grass.

The front boasts a vegetable plot. I spend a lot of time outside.

Robert is constantly on at me to make certain I have a phone on me. He often rings me just to check. I think he's worried that I might have an accident or something! I started making certain I kept a phone on me just to pacify him but in truth I could see it was a sensible precaution especially after I nearly set fire to myself in Andrew's garden. I was busy cutting his hedges with my new petrol powered, industrial standard chainsaw. The motor sits on a frame, which is carried on my back like a rucksack. This design leaves both hands free to operate the cutting tools. I had just refilled the petrol reservoir and was busy reducing some of Andrew's overgrown hedging in his back garden.

"Wow that petrol smells a bit strong. I must have spilled a bit on the frame when I filled it up."

After several minutes the smell had not gone away. In fact

if anything it had got stronger.

"Bloody hell, that smell of petrol is strong.

Bloody hell, my shirt's soaking wet.

Bloody hell! Bl..., bloody hell I'm covered in petrol!"

I had not realized that when I filled the petrol reservoir up I had somehow forgotten to replace the cap. My natural reaction was to whirl round to see if I could see where the petrol was coming from. This only had the effect of spilling even more petrol onto my back as it flew out of the reservoir. I have never moved so fast in all my life. There were no naked flames near me but that was hardly the point. Once again I had found myself in a potentially dangerous situation. I have sprained joints, broken bones, dislocated joints, suffered severe bruising and some serious cuts. I have even suffered an electric shock on two separate occasions but I drew the limit at setting fire to myself. I pressed the quick release button on the waistband and removed the machine from my back.

In the end I managed to avoid doing any serious harm to myself but the incident, although now seemingly funny, was no joke. Although I had made a decision to change my life the fact remained that I was still living a lifestyle of calamity. It was not enough to do what I had been doing in a more careful way. I had to fundamentally unpick my behaviour patterns. I had to find a new life, a new me, in order to deal with the problems that my medical condition kept throwing at me.

I had to accept that I was too damaged mentally as well as physically to find a different way to climb the mountain. I had to avoid mountains all together and stay in the relative safety of the valley. My life activities simply did not accommodate the physical condition I had been born with. The change required was going to be more fundamental than I had ever imagined.

So now I carry a phone.

I did joke with Robert that carrying a phone would not solve the problem. Sometimes I have used a chain saw to cut down overgrown trees and hedges. What if the chain saw cut off my left hand whilst the phone was in my left pocket? I wouldn't be able to reach it. I'd be twisting myself round so that my right hand could stretch across my front towards my left pocket whilst blood would be spurting across the branches I had just cut down. It was clear that I had a choice. I could carry two phones, one on each side or I had to stop cutting down trees!

I am too vulnerable to injury to be using high-powered tools. I didn't forget the petrol cap because I'm stupid or clumsy. I forgot it because I have so much more to think about in order to avoid accidents. I then run into other difficulties like forgetting to put on the petrol cap. I am vulnerable and I need to take sensible precautions. I now carry a phone like an asthmatic carries an inhaler and I've sold the power tool.

Christmas was approaching as was the anniversary of breaking my femur. I sent this email to my friends ;

"This Christmas I am going to do nothing except sit on the couch and lie there all holiday. Linda will be doing everything and will serve me beer. I hasten to add that this is not the oppression of the female sex. It is a health and safety issue- my health and safety! Anyway, serving me beer will be a damn site less taxing than the running round she had to do last year. Merry Christmas."

A female friend replied,

" Phil – have a merry Christmas but please make certain that when you are merry you don't fall off the couch and break the other one!"

Little did she know how close to the mark it would turn out to be! I had enjoyed a very relaxed Christmas and New Year. So much so that after New Year I decided to decorate the bathroom. I had paid professionals to do my pond and paint the outside of my house. I had got relatives and friends to fix my gutters and help me in the garden. Surely I could manage to do the bathroom without risk to my health? After three days I had almost finished and was very pleased with myself. There was one more small area left to paint, over the toilet. I was silently congratulating myself about the fact that there had not been the slightest hint of an accident. Nothing had gone wrong. There wasn't even a splash of paint on the floor because I'd covered everywhere and prepared well. There was no rush and no urgency to get the job done. I was at peace with myself and my approach to the job had been more than sensible.

Linda had gone to a friend's house for the evening. I enjoyed a quiet cup of tea before covering the toilet area with a sheet and climbed onto the chair I was using as a ladder. Brush in hand laden with sea green emulsion I reached for the corner, stepping out as I did so onto the toilet seat which lay hidden beneath the covers. Unfortunately I had forgotten to put the seat down and my foot fell into the toilet catapulting me forward. Luckily I realized in a flash what was happening and lifted my foot up before I jammed it into the basin thus avoiding a broken ankle. Unfortunately such was the speed and force of my movement I could not stop my head hitting the wall. I banged my forehead and jarred my neck. Paint went everywhere covering the walls, sink and me. I suffered no serious damage but was very lucky. If I had knocked myself out whilst alone I could have been in serious difficulties not least because Linda would have killed me when she got back.

I couldn't believe it. I had been so careful. It was just like the problems faced by my character in my "Frank Spencer" play. Despite all the thought and analysis put in to stopping his accidents the screws securing his ladder still came out of the wall. The more I thought about not having accidents, the more I seemed to think about them. The more I seemed to think about them the more I seemed to have. My plan was not working.

When someone is trying not to think about not smoking a cigarette, all the time they are thinking about a cigarette. Making the decision to change your learned patterns of behaviour is only the beginning and in practice is easier said than done. I was in a catch-22 situation. I realized that I was still so afraid of accidents and injury that I was likely to cause them. Changing a lifetime's habits isn't easy nor can it be reduced to a single event. It is a process of continuous re-learning supported by dogged determination. It doesn't matter what the habit is. It could be over eating or smoking for example but the essential issues are the same.

The process is not a smooth one. There will be setbacks. The overweight person may succumb to a cream cake. I put my foot in the toilet. The point is to analyse and re-assess where you are going and to constantly accentuate the positive gains being made whilst making plans to control and eliminate whatever dangers face you.

My previous attitude of "I'll be alright, I can manage" is and always has been wrong. I have to admit that I'm vulnerable.

There I've said it. I'm vulnerable.

That's so hard for me to deal with and I'm crying as I write it. It's taken me 64 years of pain and anguish to get to this.

I'm vulnerable.

I can't always manage. I need help. I had felt I was making some real progress. I had started to ask for help but my resolve to make changes to my behaviour would be tested over and over again. In the next few months my determination would be put to the test repeatedly.

Chapter 36 I Don't Believe It!

At the end of the play "Frank", the man in trouble believes he has sorted his life out, that all his troubles have been deposited in the past. The new 'Frank' is confident, relaxed and happy. Against his wife's wishes, however, he climbs a ladder to begin painting the outside of the house. He takes his time. He is thoughtful and cautious, his moves planned and sensible. He climbs the ladder and secures it to the wall with a rope, which is attached to a hook that he has previously drilled into the wall. He is safe. The accidents are a thing of the past but as he begins to paint, the rope slips off the hook and the ladder falls.

Like Frank I had identified my demons and made plans to overcome them. I felt secure for the first time in my life. I had made plans and readjusted them in the light of experience. I had admitted to my physical vulnerability and had come to accept that even decorating was potentially dangerous for me. I was confident that I would begin to enjoy a future that was significantly different to my past. I would write my books and learn chess. I thought I was OK. I'd decided I was OK. Everything was going to be OK. It didn't turn out to be that simple. In twelve months following the creation of my plan to change my future I was besieged by accidents causing me significant injuries.

Falling off the ladder had forced me, like the character in my play, to re-evaluate my life. I knew I had to do less, use my strengths and accept my failings. I was, as they say, "in a good place" but it was an illusion.

Christmas Day 2010 was delightful. We visited Sarah and her husband and kids in the morning before returning to share our Christmas meal with Andrew and Kim and their brood. After they left we had a light tea and then watched Doctor Who with Robert. At about 8 o'clock Linda's mum was sat in the kitchen reading a book. Linda was upstairs wrapping presents for Sam and Will who were to visit us on Boxing Day. Robert was upstairs resting.

It was a very pleasant lull in the day's proceedings before we were to regroup in the evening to watch one of Linda's films.

I was sat in the lounge relaxing when I suddenly remembered the two penknives I had received as gifts. Unfortunately I had told my brother that I wanted a penknife and had then put it on the list that I gave to my wife. She must have told Sarah who also bought me one.

I decided to keep them both, one for my key ring, the other for the greenhouse. Although they were by the same manufacturer and were the same size they were not identical.

I pulled them out of my coat to compare them. Slowly I pulled out each and everyone of the blades, screwdrivers and bottle openers and displayed them on the arm of my chair. They looked like one of those diagrams that explain what every blade is for.

In actual fact there was only one difference between the two. Victor's had a fine, thin blade for whittling wood probably in order to make a fire. Sarah's had a Phillips head screwdriver. I put one of the knives away and was busy putting the blades away on the second when disaster struck. The larger of the two flat-headed screwdrivers wouldn't move. I pushed harder and felt it give a little but it still refused to close. I pushed even harder and this time it collapsed into position immediately.

Unfortunately as the blade fell away from my hand my finger shot across the knife and struck the largest blade, which still stood erect and inviting to any finger that wished to throw itself upon it. Blood gushed out of my finger. The cut was an inch wide and was deep.

"Oh shit, shit shit! I don't believe it!" I shrieked a la Victor Meldrew.

I thought, "I have done Casualty on New Year. Now I'll have to go on Christmas Day!"

I dashed into the kitchen leaving a trail of blood on my trousers and the floor. I screamed Linda's name and alarmed her mother who was dozing over her book. Her hands jump up in semi-conscious shock and I nearly laughed as I ran to the sink to run cold water on the wound.

"Linda!!! Please now. Now!!"

"Oh what have you done?" cried her mother, which made Linda realize that something was seriously wrong. She and Robert both appeared from nowhere in rapid succession.

"Oh bloody hell. What have you done?"

"The bloody knife!"

"What knife?"

"The bloody pen knife."

"How did you do that?"

"Does it bloody matter? Help me!"

Linda sat me down on a chair that appeared from nowhere. I was alarmed but hadn't yet felt any pain. Linda pulled the cut apart to see how deep it was.

"Aahh!

301

Now I began to feel pain.

"Mmm. Oh dear it's very deep." She looked at me kindly. "If we can't stop the bleeding we'll have to take you to hospital."

She already seemed to be saying,

"I don't think I can help you."

She got some dressings from the first aid box.

"Press on it as hard as you can."

"Put some sugar on it," said Robert. It'll caramelise on it.

I had never heard of this. I thought salt did it but Linda agreed.

"We've no white sugar. We'll have to use this brown granulated stuff."

They poured it on and it immediately absorbed the blood. I was impressed until I began to feel the granules inside the cut.

"Bloody, bloody hell" I shrieked.

"Aahh Ffff Bbbb Cccc Jumpin Jehosifats" I don't know where I got that one from but I was doing my best not to swear in front of Linda's mother. I don't know why I was bothered; she knows every swear word that has ever existed but I nevertheless felt the need to avoid doing it.

"Aahh aahhh aahhh, good God Almighy Aaaggghh!"

Then suddenly the flow of blood slowed. I had completely bloodied three paper towels but it was now under control. Within a couple of minutes Linda was busy putting 8 steri-strips on the cut. We waited for five minutes and then for ten. The bleeding stopped and we all relaxed. Linda taped it up and we played a game of cards having forgotten that we had planned to watch a film.

The fuss ended as quickly as it started but if Linda hadn't been a qualified nurse I would have definitely ended up in hospital.

"Perhaps next year I should book a reservation."

I had responded to a potentially serious problem with a joke but then thought, "That's not funny. That is a perfect example of my using a joke to deal with a situation when in fact it does not deal with it at all. It merely masks my fears. In fact making light of it actually serves to ensure that I enter next winter's holiday period thinking "I hope I don't have an accident this year." It begins the process of creating an accident once more. Stop it now." I stamped on the first sign of negative thinking and removed it from my thought processes.

This was a real test. I could see friends laughing at my story. I watched myself laughing with them. One friend actually said, "Who bought you a penknife?" It was all very jolly but I was getting sick of it. People laughed at me because I had always given them permission to laugh at my imagined clumsiness. I had to change people's perceptions of my behaviour as well as the behaviour itself.

The first thing I asked myself was, "Do they even need to know about the accident?" The answer was of course obvious. They did not. "Why do I tell them then?" It was because laughing at myself had become the norm. It was the way I behaved. I didn't even think about it. I needed to start thinking more and planning my responses.

Obviously the results of some accidents are obvious. You can't hide 18 days in hospital for a broken femur but I didn't need to tell them about this cut finger. I began to plan my social interactions systematically. I imagined a social setting in which I didn't mention it at all. It was surprisingly easy. Then I put it into practice. I began to drive another of my demons away.

I returned to college for a few days exam supervision. At lunchtime I sat with my fellow invigilators. Normally I would have said "Hey do you know what I did over Christmas but I resisted and didn't mention it once. The result was wonderful. I didn't invite anyone to laugh at me and as a result nobody did. Therefore I was no longer that clumsy fool who just cut his finger on a penknife! He didn't exist!

As well as changing my behaviour and other people's perception of that behaviour I started to change my attitude towards myself. I decided to be a little easier on myself. Accident and Emergency Departments are full of people who have daft accidents. I was no different except that the consequences of those accidents were more severe in my case.

Chapter 37 The End (Almost)

I thought this would be the end of my story. I was now meant to be sending my manuscript to a publisher. I had imagined presenting it as a book about adversity, self-discovery followed by a resolution of my problems but as I said at the beginning of this section, changing your behaviour is not that simple. Sometimes life has a habit of biting you no matter what you do.

Despite some early setbacks in carrying out my plan I felt I had made some progress. After my initial problems I had settled into a most enjoyable life of retirement. Although I had nearly injured myself whilst decorating the bathroom I had in fact avoided an accident by my speed of thought and my cautious working. I had cut myself on the knife but it had been dealt with.

It was now February 2011 and I had not had a serious injury for some time. I had had a book published to some minor critical acclaim. I was very proud of my new me. The small success of the book had given me a real sense of personal worth. It couldn't have gone any better. I had been thinking only positive thoughts. I was retired and my time was filled playing golf, gardening and singing with The Hull Male Voice Choir. I was full of ideas for new writings and I didn't have a minute to spare. I was happier than I had been in a very long time and life felt good.

Then out of the blue and for no apparent reason my problems started again. I was getting ready to sing with the choir in Hedon, a small market town near Hull. I was looking forward to the performance as I had put a lot of preparation into getting my second tenor role right. I was confident, happy and relaxed. I finished showering and turned to get my towel, which was on the side of the bath. As I did so my ankles wobbled throwing me violently forward towards the bathroom floor. Luckily my right hand caught the grab rail and it saved me from falling.

I was unnerved for a moment and stood dripping on the non-slip mat that had not prevented me from falling. I took a deep breath and got out of the bath and walked into the bedroom to finish towelling myself down. I sat on the bed reflecting on the implications of what had just happened. I had been very lucky that I hadn't fall. My ankle had just given way without warning. I imagined Linda finding me unconscious on the floor having crashed through the shower curtain, taking the rail with me. I could see myself lying there with a broken neck and gashed shins, wrapped in a shroud of a white shower curtain.

I rebuked myself.

"It didn't bloody happen so stop worrying about it. You'll start making it happen if you don't watch out. You'll know next time to use the grab rail as a matter of routine. You put it there for your mother but you can use it as well. Accept your limitations. Take precautions. Think positive thoughts and you'll be OK."

I was fighting a constant battle with myself. All the time I was trying to be positive but thoughts kept creeping in which were symbolic of my understandable fears.

"I don't make things happen. Stop blaming yourself and get on with it."

I finished towelling and started to dress. As I put on my red bow tie I looked in the mirror and noticed the scars on my forehead.

"God I can't afford to add to those. If I had gone head first onto the floor."

And then another thought popped into my head. It's a thought that had been there for a while but I had managed to suppress it until now. It was an old friend, a thought that had often visited me but one I hoped had been defeated.

"I wonder when I will have my next accident?"

I was annoyed that I had allowed it into my head. I didn't want it nor did I seek it out. It had forced its way in. I tried to see these thoughts as John Nash envisaged his demons. I closed my eyes and told them to go away. The thoughts tailed off as I argued with myself once more. I opened my eyes and checked my tie before slipping on my dinner jacket. I looked very smart, as does the entire choir. We are a fine body of men and we make a really good sound. I was proud to be part of it. I couldn't wait for the show to start.

"Positive thoughts now; come on. It's going to be a good night. These thoughts are just natural fears of someone in your position. It doesn't mean that something bad is going to happen. You will be OK. You know what is happening and you're in charge. Remember this time it didn't happen. Positive thinking!"I smiled at myself in the mirror.

It was now six- thirty and time to go. I had to be in the back room of the village hall with the rest of the choir at 7.15pm. It would take about half an hour to get to Hedon from my house but sensibly I had allowed more time than I needed.

"Get there early. Don't rush. Take the pressure off. You always leave things to the last minute. You can't afford to do that. You, more than anyone need to be relaxed and unhurried. That way if things go wrong it means you won't

307

have an accident and then bear the awful consequences that others don't have to face in similar circumstances. Give yourself a break. Don't you like yourself?"

I smiled again in the mirror trying to convince myself that finally things were moving in the right direction. I was early and self-possessed. I was talking to myself all the time trying to get my life under control.

Although it might not sound like it I was pleased with myself. So much had changed for the better. I was comfortable with and proud of myself. I could not have said that two years earlier. I kissed Linda goodbye, wishing that she was going with me and got to my car. The journey to Hedon was uneventful but parking in this small town was, as ever, problematic. Eventually I found a spot at the top of a lane just a short distance from the hall. It was pitch black as there was no street lighting. I put on my interior light in order to change the shoes that I wore for driving and replaced them with my more substantial boots. I got out, locked the car and started to walk towards the church hall.

I noticed in the corner of my eye that the interior light was still on so I returned and pushed the switch before locking the door once more. I began to walk and again noticed that the light was still on. Annoyingly I had switched it to the wrong setting. I repeated the whole palaver once more and finally did it properly.

Nervously I checked my watch. It was 7.10pm. I was still in good time. I locked the car and as I put the keys in the lock I unaccountably slipped. It wasn't a stumble. Both my feet fell together into the gap between the kerb and the car. I banged my shin on the bottom of the door and knew immediately that I had cut myself. In the same instance I was thrown against the body of the car and banged my head on it before falling backwards on to the uneven concrete path. Despite being winded I sat up immediately and placed my hand on my sock to feel for the blood.

Luckily my instincts were wrong. I was not cut but I was very sore. My head, hands and shin were all stinging. I realized that time was passing and got up immediately. I collected my music book and keys off the floor and walked the 300 yards to the hall. I slipped into the toilets and tidied myself up as best I could. My suit was covered in dust. I beat it out with my stinging palms and reflected briefly on the fact that yet again I did not have my mobile phone with me. I know Linda and Robert were right but why did my fall have to happen precisely at the moment I forgot the phone? I made a brief mental note to check for it every time I moved. It's so important. I could have been stuck in the dark with any kind of injury and no means of obtaining help. I went into the back room as the choir was about to enter the hall still shaken and uncomfortable but determined to press on. I had been working hard for this. I felt confident that I would do well. We began to sing and for a while it went really well. The small hall was packed out and I hadn't made a single mistake but as the show proceeded I started to feel very hot. It was not helped by the fact that immediately behind me was a huge radiator blasting out heat. After an hour of singing I started to feel sick and dizzy as the effects of my fall started to show.

I was aware that my neighbour was looking at me with a concerned stare as the room started to sway. I was reminded of a similar feeling I had had when I was about ten years old. I was stood at the front of the school assembly when I realized I was leaning forward. I tried to work out why but before I could find a solution a stream of vomit splattered over the highly polished shoes of the headmaster. He was not pleased. I imagined vomiting over the heads of the front row and into the laps of the very nice ladies in the audience. I was so grateful for the interval.

I left the hall behind at the interval unable to continue. I gave my apologies and stumbled back up the hill to my car. It was really dark. I realized how lucky I had been not to injure myself there. I would have been in serious difficulty.

I sat in my car alone in the dark soaked in sweat, my head bowed against the steering wheel. All my best efforts were in ruins. I was so, so sick of it all. The night I had so looked forward to had turned into a disaster and my body was starting to hurt from head to toe. This accident really shook me. I couldn't understand what had happened. In my view I had done everything possible to take care of myself. I had been in a positive frame of mind and yet inexplicably it had all gone wrong.

I lay in the bath next morning, soaking away my aches and pains, trying to work everything out yet again. Despite having tried to formulate a plan to change my life I knew that change would not be simple. There would be gains and setbacks and I faced a constant battle that might never end. I would be engaged in a process that would not follow in a straight line. I knew that sometimes things would go wrong. My plan wasn't foolproof. I would have to re-double my efforts to improve things but how many times is it possible to re-double one's efforts? Living in fear of constant injury and my persistent inability to protect myself from harm was beginning to take a serious toll on my mental health yet again. I was at a very low ebb. I don't think I have ever felt as bad or as lonely as I did that morning. Suddenly after all the optimism I was close to defeat.

It was clear however, that defeat was not an option. I simply couldn't endure more injuries. After a good rest I resolved yet again, not to let the previous night's drama deter me from my goal of taking greater control of events around me. I worked out that I was still leaving my arrival too late. When I thought about it the accident merely confirmed that I had been putting too much pressure on myself all my life.

"I still didn't allow myself enough time," I thought to myself as I put more hot water into the bath. "If I had got there twenty minutes earlier the car park outside the hall would have had a space free. I could have parked without a fuss and simply got out from the car to the hall." I have to not only change my way of thinking about myself but also my actions in response to this new way of thinking. I have to allow myself to be vulnerable and not just think about it. This was difficult but I got out of the bath full of new resolve, determined not to be beaten. I ignored the nagging doubt appearing on my shoulder that had I got there earlier and parked in the car park I would have only tripped over the step and cut my shin. I couldn't afford such doubts any more. It couldn't just be a case of my dismissing these thoughts when they occurred; I had to develop a way of thinking that simply didn't allow them to appear at all. This was easier said than done but I had no choice. I gingerly finished towelling the bruises on my shins and arms and walked out to face the world once more.

The next week I felt very positive. I was enjoying retirement. I enjoyed a really good game of golf in the

311

February sunshine. I had taken possession of two pairs of new shoes purposely built by the orthotics department at Hull Infirmary. They were not perfect and required some alterations but were nevertheless a considerable improvement. I had never felt as comfortable.

The next day I was preparing for a trip to Wales for the weekend to watch some rugby. I was packed and ready at 11.00am. At 11.05 I was sat slumped in my car having collapsed in agony. Linda had used my car the day before and altered the seating and mirrors. For some reason the passenger side mirror had been knocked inwards to the body of the car. I leaned over and stretched out to knock it back. In doing so I popped my shoulder, the one with the shredded ligaments. It wasn't a full dislocation. The technical term is a sub-luxation of the joint, which moves too much and traps a nerve when it comes back into place. My physiotherapist had shown me how to move more easily in a way that would avoid any over extension of the joint but for one moment I forgot and moved naturally, to my cost. Despite the fact that my entire right side hurt, we had a really good weekend.

Over the course of the next week the pain reduced and I regained the full use of my arm but it was a clear reminder that I would have to be very controlled and disciplined in my everyday life if I were to avoid further injuries. Unfortunately it is not possible to maintain such a level of concentration regarding every single movement your body makes. The thought was creeping in that no matter how vigilant I was I would suffer further injuries.

By the end of the second week the pain in my arm had virtually disappeared and I was looking forward to the weekend. I had agreed to buy a second hand car from Bill, one of the caretakers at the college I used to work at. I bumped into him in the car park when I was doing some exam invigilation. He had looked at my tired old Fiat and said "You don't fancy buying a decent car do you? I'm selling mine soon."

"What is it?"

"It's a Mazda 6."

Now it so happened that I had been considering buying a newer car for some time and I've always liked Mazda 6s. It took me ten minutes to agree the purchase.

We arranged for me to pick the car up from his house on Sunday. I had planned to drop my old car off at my daughter's house in the morning and be at Bill's in Hull for twelve. To avoid any possible pressures such as those experienced in Hedon I intended to allow far more time than I originally thought I would need. I arranged to go to Sarah's early and spend some time with her and my grandchildren. She would then take me down to my village at 10.45am so that I would be at the bus stop at eleven; well in time for the 11.15 bus. There would be no rush. I would not put myself under pressure. I got showered put some nice clothes on, even some aftershave. This was all part of the new me. I was taking care of myself. I wanted to feel good and enjoy the day in all its aspects. As a result I decided to put my journey back one hour.

"It'll give me even more time. No need to rush. Take it easy." I said to myself. I had a really nice time with the kids and then Sarah took me down in good time to the bus stop. I stood there waiting, enjoying the pleasantness of a quiet English village on a Sunday morning. Time waiting was not time wasted. I was relaxed and confident. Soon the bus arrived. I boarded, paid my fare and sat reading a book. I was really well prepared and pleased with myself. The only problem was that my mobile phone, my life-saver was missing. After the fall in Hedon I now appreciated more than ever that a mobile phone was very important to my physical safety.

It was no problem however. I had left it in John's car and had arranged to pick it up when I had seen Bill. It would be an excuse to show off my new car to John. As arranged Bill was waiting at the bus stop when I arrived in Hull. We got in my lovely new car and he drove me to his house where we would exchange documents and money.

I began this chapter by saying that no matter how hard you tried to change things life had a habit of turning round and biting you. I was wrong. Life did not bite me.

Bill's dog bit me!

Bill had said to me as I got out of his car, "Take your hat off. Bob doesn't like people with hats. I think someone in the past must have treated him badly and worn a hat at the same time. He sees it as a threat."

I took my hat off, put it in my bag, walked in the front room and said "hello" and the bloody thing attacked me. It happened so quickly I had no chance to defend myself in any way. It bit my left knee but my jeans protected me. I could feel its teeth tugging on me. At the same time its left paw sank its claws into the right side of my left knee tearing away my skin without ripping the fabric of my jeans.

Bill and his wife pulled the dog off as I leant against the frame of the door clutching my leg. Bill's daughter asked me if I was OK. I replied that I was. I was hurting but my trousers weren't wet so I thought it couldn't have cut me. They moved me to the settee and as I did so I felt a jabbing pain. I pulled up my trousers and Bill's wife gasped.

It is strange how the body reacts. I experienced nothing but a dull ache until I pulled up my jeans. I thought I might have been bruised but when I saw the torn flesh with blood beginning slowly to emerge from the sides, the pain intensified ten fold.

I couldn't believe that after my morning's preparations this would have happened. I had analysed why I had accidents, taken every precaution to avoid them but to no avail. I wanted to cry or swear not just because of the pain I was now enduring but because of an overpowering sense of frustration and complete demoralisation. Anger burned inside me I wanted to kill the bloody dog but all I said was, "Oh that hurts." They bandaged my wound and Bill took me to hospital.

After a saline wash and an x-ray followed by a tetanus and antibiotic injections the young doctor said, "I think that the plastic surgeons will want to have a look at you. This isn't a full cut. It's more like a nasty scraping off of your skin." She spoke softly and gently, "They may and I only say may want to do a skin graft."

My reply did not match her sensitive approach.

During my treatment I found myself becoming very maudlin. The doctor's reassurances did nothing to assuage my depression.

"You're in pain Philip but we'll have you sorted out soon."

"It's not that doctor. I'm fed up. I really am. I've had so many injuries. I broke my femur two years ago."

315

"Oh gosh- not nice"

"I've had over two hundred stitches."

"Is that what these other scars are?"

"Yes I've got them all over. I broke my ankle, sprained my ankle, dislocated my ankle."

"Gosh."

"I've dislocated both knees and ruptured the ligaments in my left knee."+

"Gosh."

"That's a lot. What happened?"

"I've got Ehlers Danlos syndrome."

"Er that's extra supple skin and ligaments isn't it?"

I was pleased. At least she knew about it.

"I've never actually seen a case before.

"I think it's even more important that you see the plastic surgeons."

I must have looked even more depressed because she spoke quite gently as she dressed my wound.

"Hey Philip you're not going to let this get you down are you? You were so bright when you came in. Don't let it beat you. You said you'd retired. You don't look old enough to be retired. How old are you?"

"I've just turned 60."

"So you retired early?"

"Yes I'd had enough of teaching."

"So what do you do with your time?"

"I've written a book and had it published."

"Really? That's so impressive. What's it about?"

I began to tell her.

"Oh wow that's so impressive."

She was really pleased to have met an author. Immediately my spirits lifted and I began to feel more positive again. It showed two things to me. I needed to pursue my new definition of what it meant to be a man. I am an impressive person. It is just easy to forget sometimes. Secondly it showed how easily one can be defeated by events. I was in a very fragile state of mind. Having a disability of any kind can easily knock the confidence out of an individual. People who remain positive require considerable mental and sometimes physical strength but even they face a constant battle against depression and demoralisation. They are liars if they say they don't feel it permanently gnawing at their heels. Depression is easier to maintain than positive thinking although the rewards of the latter are considerable. The problem is it's not always easy to see them.

I sold another book but I'm sure there are easier marketing strategies.

Eventually the ambulance arrived to take me to the other hospital where the plastic surgery unit was located. The journey took twenty minutes. The driver asked me about my injury.

"Was it your dog?"

"No I'm not a lover of dogs." I said.

"Ah it probably sensed your fear."

I hadn't got the will to explain that I wasn't afraid of dogs I

317

just didn't like them particularly. I quite like horses but they make too much of a mess if they crap in your kitchen. I couldn't be bothered to ask if he was suggesting that somehow it was my fault; as if the dog couldn't help it.

When dog owners say "It's never done that before,"

Of course it hasn't. If it had it would be dead.

I concluded that he must have been a dog lover and didn't pursue the conversation.

The ambulance arrived at ward 4 of Castle Hill hospital and I was wheeled in to the reception area. It was now 5 hours since the injury.

"I'm afraid there'll be a wait of about an hour. The doctor's in theatre."

I smiled at the nurse. I have spent so much time in casualty waiting rooms over the years. One more hour wasn't going to matter but my anxiety began to rise as time passed. The television in the corner was showing a nature programme in which a bird of prey was tearing into the flesh of its victim. I turned it off as I didn't want to watch skin being stripped from the carcass. "At least it's dead." I thought to myself. I was surrounded by silence and my fears. I was in a very lonely place both physically and mentally. I was so looking forward to this day and now all my confidence in my new approach to life had disappeared once more down the empty corridor. The clock showed that an hour and a half had elapsed.

Somebody once told me that when they do plastic surgery the skin they plane from your body hurts more than the injury itself. I started to worry about whether my skin would be strong enough for the procedure. It tends to tear rather than cut. I imagined myself with a permanently open wound that could only be controlled by a constant stream of antibiotics and subsequent diarrhoea. All these thoughts passed through my brain at rapid speed. I really didn't need another stay in hospital. Then I remembered that my kids didn't know where I was. I'd only spoken once to Andrew on the casualty phone. I asked the nurse to let me use the hospital phone.

"Dad I'm not being funny but you need to look after your mobile phone. Look what happened in Hedon."

"I know. It fell out of my pocket in John's car. I realized its importance so much that I knew what had happened to it and was going to pick it up on my way home."

"Sods law then."

"Pretty severe Sod's law."

I sorted things out with Andrew. He agreed to phone his mum who was visiting her sister in Aylesbury and his brother and sister. I had still not spoken to my wife as I didn't have her sister's number. I was anxious to make sure that she did not worry unduly. There was no point in her dashing home early. She had been looking forward to her trip for ages and her coming home wasn't going to change anything. I turned the television back on again. Two lions were having sex.

"This is better." I forced a laugh.

After another hour a tall, young looking man popped his head round the door. He was dressed in green theatre garb and a light blue mask dangled round his chin. He was obviously a fourteen year old surgeon.

"Mr. Howard?"

"Sorry you've been waiting. I've been in theatre."

I followed him into the examination room.

"I'm getting old," I thought to myself as I took my trousers down and got on the couch.

The boy doctor looked at it studiously. I examined it with him. The wound was now much redder, angrier and bloodier.

"Mmm. You have EDS don't you?"

"Mmm." He squeezed opposite sides of the wound and blood trickled down the right side of my left leg.

"Mmmm"

"Tell me about it. Have you had lots of injuries?"

I repeated the list that I had detailed to the doctor at the other hospital.

"You've been through a lot. Do you have these injuries without much trauma?"

"How do you mean?"

"Well I take it that you didn't need much of a knock to have these injuries?"

I started to relate the story of the cut in our chip shop when I was 14 when my dad threw my skin on the fire. I had this inexplicably urgent need to tell people about my list of injuries. It was as if I was pleading with them to do something. It dawned on me that I might be in shock. I suddenly felt very alone. I was alone. It was getting late and I was tired. The memories of all my injuries flashed by. The strongest emotion these flashbacks produce has always been loneliness; lying in an ambulance with the bell

320

ringing; being wheeled into casualty and waiting until they brought my mum; being held down whilst they insert stitches without anaesthetic wondering when my mum will arrive; lying on a concrete floor in the dark; waiting in silence in outpatients and now this. Thoughts raced through my head during this brief examination. I could see that little boy alone in the room surrounded by medical staff discussing him as if he were not there. I saw him cry out, trying to be brave; refusing to give in but so desperately wanting to do so.

"Mmmm." Boy doctor stood at my side, his head on the back of his hand whilst his elbow sat on the couch.

"It doesn't look too bad."

"Do you want it then?" I joked. At least I think I was joking.

He laughed.

"Medically speaking, it doesn't look too bad. It's too wide to stitch. Ehlers Danlos skin won't hold the pressure of such a wide tear but there is skin left in the wound. It's not down to the bone which means the skin will grow back. It's not a cut. It's a very nasty tear and scrape but it will heal. I don't think surgery will do you any favours. We'll dress it and cover it with Anadine," (a gauze impregnated with a disinfectant based on iodine). Fortunately the dog (I can't call it by its name) had very considerately attacked the part of my knee that still had skin on it. Most of my knee is covered in scars, which would have presented more difficult healing problems.

I know that by the doctors' standards this was a minor injury but for me it was death by nine hundred and ninety nine cuts. Like the victim of that bird of prey on television

I had been gnawed at, ripped and chewed bit by bit. I had had enough. I felt my eyes welling up but as always I did not, could not give in. I was fighting an emotional battle as well as dealing with this specific injury.

"We'll see you on Tuesday and then in a week. I think you'll be OK but we need to keep an eye on you because of the EDS." They bandaged me up and gave me a cup of coffee whilst I waited for Bill to pick me up.

Whilst waiting in the main waiting room at Hull Royal I heard a number of people complaining about the length of time they had been there. The medical care was excellent but the public relations was diabolical. Earlier in the year I had spent 5 hours waiting with my daughter Sarah. She had fallen in the snow and cut her leg some days earlier. The wound was showing signs of infection so her G.P. referred her to Casualty. We were getting fed up waiting. No one said anything to us. When I asked about how long we had to wait I was told that they were doing blood tests for several blood disorders and it would take a couple of hours. By the end of our stay there we left feeling very impressed with the diligent care we had received. They had done everything possible to ensure Sarah was safe but nobody had told us that it would take so long. If they had done so we could have dealt with our situation more easily but it felt like nothing was happening.

I thought of a recent experience I had whilst staying with an old school friend and his mother in New York. Unfortunately she was taken poorly and was rushed to hospital. You could not fault the service. An ambulance, accompanied by a fire engine arrived within seconds. Evidently sending both vehicles is standard practice. They couldn't do enough for her. They offered her all manner of tests. It was very patient led. It was up to her to say what she wanted and they provided it. They discussed everything with the patient and informed us at all times of what was happening and how long we would have to wait. In fact there was very little time spent waiting, far less than in Britain. When my friend got the bill we found out why. For two and a half hours of care, including a brain scan, they charged thousands of dollars which was eventually paid for by insurance. It's not surprising that there wasn't a queue. Queuing for medical care occurs at Walmart where people wait to see the pharmacist.

I would rather wait for free than pay like that. I would never have survived in America. I doubt whether I could get medical insurance. I am so appreciative of the NHS and we should never neglect it. If only they could improve their public relations.

Bill duly arrived in my car. He was willing to drive me all the way home but I said that I was OK as I was able to bend my knee and had been told to use it as much as I could. I dropped Bill off at his house.

"I won't come in." I joked.

We said our farewells and I drove the fifteen miles to my home. After about five minutes driving I realized that I had made a mistake. I felt a burning sensation in my knee. I reasoned that it was either the Anadine or the pressure of the bandaging. Whatever it was I was in acute discomfort for the next twenty-five minutes but eventually made it back home at around 11.30pm. I limped and hopped into the kitchen and got a beer out of the fridge. About two minutes later I was enjoying another one. I was shattered but too tired to sleep.

It had been a hell of a day. I had set out in the morning full of confidence and optimism. I had made plans to give me more control of my life and as a result, provide a safer environment. Despite all my efforts I had still ended up on a hospital bed surrounded by medical staff interested in a medical condition they had only read about. I still had a lot to do to turn my life around. As I sat there alone in the silence of that empty house it began to dawn on me that I might never be free from injury; that pursuing an injury free life was filled with as many problems as living with injuries. Perhaps the problems I had could not be solved. Yet again I was in danger of defeat. I had one consolation that night. The car was very nice.

Unfortunately it would be another three weeks before I could drive it.

****

The wound took seven weeks to heal completely.

"Do you always heal slowly?" asked the consultant after three weeks.

I was about to say no. My parents had always told me that I healed well but faced with the still red gash sitting before me I was forced to re-think. On reflection I couldn't help thinking about the difficulties I had had with my femur and the fact that at one stage they were considering a second very unpleasant operation in order to rejuvenate the healing process. The cut on my right shin took eight weeks to heal because the skin couldn't hold the stitches under the weight of such a wide cut. My daughter has also said that we heal slowly but I have always disagreed. Maybe I had to re-think. The truth is I didn't know how quickly other people healed and had no means of comparison. I probably don't heal quickly at all. I think mum and dad told me a little white lie when I was a child in order to give me a boost when I was fed up.

"Yes I heal slowly," I said.

"Right. Keep on with the dressings and we will see you in a month. I don't want to say a fortnight and bring you back in only to tell you to come in again. A month should do it."

The doctor was correct. It took two months before I was discharged. Ironically this "minor" injury has done more damage than any other injury I have ever had. I thought I was in charge of my new life. I thought I was secure and would be safer than I have ever felt before. It was now clear that such hopes would not be realized. Despite all my efforts I was as vulnerable as ever. I was not angry or defeated but overcome with resignation, the realization that there was nothing I could do to alter my circumstances. More accidents would follow and I would never be free of the fear that was my constant companion.

Doctors can only treat the medical symptoms that are in front of them. They cannot deal with the way the injury affects a patient. This latest injury had unnerved me more than breaking my femur, which was a far more serious injury.

At the same time as I was wrestling with these emotional and physical difficulties I had to deal with people's reactions to yet another accident. As one colleague at my former college said, "He's the only man I know who could be downed by a Scotty terrier!"

I understand people's responses. I had changed my attitude to my accidents. I no longer initiated the jokes but I was trapped by the legacy of my previous behaviour. It seemed

I couldn't escape. The time for laughter had gone but everyone was still laughing.

That little Scotty terrier, that cute looking little bundle of fun damaged me both physically and mentally. I knew that I would never feel safe.

A physiotherapist recently advised me to use a walking stick to stop me from tripping up. It has another use. If a dog ever tries to attack me again I'm going to beat the living shit out of it.

Chapter 38 Plan B Or is it C?

I have plenty of time to think when I'm recovering from an injury but I didn't know what to think any more. Before this "minor" injury I had become really confident that I could face the future accident free. I believed that I had identified my problems and was making some serious progress towards solving them. I had to face the fact that I had been injured by a little dog and that the blow hadn't even broken the cloth of my jeans. There wasn't even a mark on them yet the pressure from the dog's paw had ripped a hole in my skin, an injury, which incapacitated me for seven weeks.

Only now did I realize how fragile my skin really was. It seemed that I was travelling on a journey to try and improve my life but had no idea where I was going or how to get there. Every twist and turn produced yet further dilemmas to be solved. I had no answers.

Maybe my dad was right all those years ago when he tried to stop me riding a friend's bike. Maybe Sarah was wrong to give her children free reign. I was not sure any more. I thought the battle was nearly over and now I found myself re-evaluating everything yet again.

No-one could have foreseen my being attacked by a dog. It made me realize that this and all the other events were not my fault. I was an innocent victim. From this moment on I changed tack completely. It happened quite suddenly. I woke up one morning and decided I couldn't fight myself any longer. This was my lot and I would have to accept the injuries and deal with them when they occurred. This acceptance gave me a peace of mind I had never known and it was this peace that gave me the chance to remove the accidents from my life once and for all.

So I re-gathered myself once again and formulated yet another new plan. I could not simply alter my ways of doing things. I had made plan after plan to try and gain control of my accident-strewn life but now it was clear that none of them were radical enough. I have begun to make adjustments in my life of a different kind. I had talked about accepting myself as being vulnerable but now I had to act on it. I had to go further than I had ever imagined.

Two weeks after being discharged from the hospital I was cycling in to the local village centre. On the way it was impossible not to notice the potholes that had been created as a result of the winter freeze. I counted seven of them all. Some of them were six inches deep lying there waiting to damage an unsuspecting cyclist. The previous night's local news had shown a story of a cyclist who was suing the council after falling from his bike and breaking his collarbone. I pictured myself falling from my bike. As I fell forward I arched my back into a swallow dive so that my knees didn't hit the ground and broke my arm instead. When I phoned the council to report them I found that no-one else had bothered to do so even though they lived much closer than me and must have had to avoid them far more than I did. Was I the only one to worry about or even recognise this danger? Was it a danger only to me? Was I over-reacting again only to create the accident I feared at some future date? My head was in a spin. I had tried for so long to act normally, to do things that other people did but the plain fact is that I can't. Cycling is too big a risk for me. I can't afford another knock of any kind. Cycling is not and never has been safe for me. It has become even more of a problem recently. I saw a specialist about the pain in my right knee. It is so badly damaged by the dislocations that I can have a knee replacement as soon as I say the pain is no longer manageable. Last week my knee locked on me. If I had been on a bicycle I would have fallen off and suffered broken bones and cuts.

"I must advise you against cycling. It is too dangerous." With a heavy heart I sold my bike. This was not a defeat. It was a realization. I didn't need the doctor to give me the excuse to say "I can't do it." Subsequently I have got rid of other dangers in my life.

We were planning to go to Italy for our holiday. I was now thinking "what if I have an accident?" How do I explain in English to an Italian doctor what Ehlers Danlos syndrome is when many doctors who speak my native tongue have never seen a case? How could I ask a foreign nurse to be careful taking plasters or tape off my skin because if you do it too fast my skin rips off with the tape? I obtained an explanation of my condition off the EDS website, translated it into Italian and carried it in my wallet.

In the end I went to Italy and thoroughly enjoyed it but I was on constant alert. I have decided that I won't go again. Is this a defeat? I will not look at it as such. I am not a person who likes to lie in the sun. I like to do things, visit art galleries, magnificent buildings and beautiful views. There are plenty of those in Britain.

I have also sold my petrol powered multi-purpose garden tool. Why am I trying to take down trees with a chain saw? It is ridiculous. I can see that now. I will employ the same gardeners who dug my pond to do any heavy gardening. I have also employed my grandchildren to help me with digging and mowing the lawn. I will be the designer and plant man.

So the battle continues. I have to manage my life even more carefully. As my doctor said I have and I do cope with the problems caused by Ehlers Danlos syndrome magnificently and I will continue to do so.

All through this book one theme has been ever present; that of my trying to come to terms with my unusual experiences, to understand how they affected my personality and to create a future life free of the stresses imposed on me by the past.

I have made considerable progress towards that aim but the process began long before the book was conceived, and before my broken femur. The book is merely the physical expression of a long struggle to come to terms with my experiences. The shape of my life has been affected by a disability but it is not the sole determinant. Everyone has their problems, self-imposed barriers that stop them from realising some part of their talent or personal happiness. It is too easy to put down one's problems to one sole problem. That is what many people do. The stronger attempt to place their difficulties (whatever they are) in the context of the rest of their life.

I have had a serious medical problem. There is no denying that. It has caused me considerable anguish and pain but like everyone I have had choices.

I could have chosen to do as my brother did and lie down when I got hurt. I was simply not able to do that. When I got hurt my response was to get up. I'm not saying that my brother was wrong. You have to deal with things the way you see it and in a way that is best for you. Indeed when I was lying on the garage floor I did think, "Maybe Victor is right. Maybe I ought to lie down more."

Getting up and fighting back produced a lot of further injuries that perhaps could have been avoided. Certainly I wouldn't be so badly scarred as I am and I wouldn't have the pains in my joints. On the other hand my outward looking character has seen me married with three lovely children. I've held a job of some responsibility and for a long while derived great satisfaction from it even though it did tire me considerably. I have many friends. I've been to America, Yugoslavia, Scandinavia Turkey Spain and Italy.

I've been an active trade unionist and helped many people. I have spoken at a national conference of the political party I was a member of. I have a lovely house in the country. I am retired and play golf when I want to. I have done very well. I need to keep stressing the positive features of my life and reduce the impact of the injuries. They need to be placed in a dark cupboard somewhere and locked away.

Life can be wonderful. It is worth fighting for.

Chapter 39 Maia

I have had my difficulties but thought I had overcome them. I re-formed my plans and then changed them completely to form new ones. Each time I made a change I felt that success was near only to realize that I had not yet achieved the peace I was looking for.

Now, as I write these words describing how, finally I had achieved a happiness I never thought possible I have discovered yet another issue, potentially more worrying than anything I had faced before.

Andrew's eldest daughter Maia cut her leg in January 2011. She tripped over and was taken to hospital. She had five stitches in her knee. This was not the first injury she has had and it was an indication that there could be more to follow, that my trauma could be repeated.

We visited her the next day. I entered the front room with trepidation but there was no need. What lay before me painted a beautiful picture. The atmosphere was very relaxed. Maia was sat on the couch, her leg raised and heavily bandaged. Violet, her younger sister was sat with her as mum read them both a story. Lucas the baby was asleep on the other couch, his head turned away from us oblivious to both our entry and our fears. Andrew and Kimberly deal with their crises in the same way that Sarah has done with hers. There is no gnashing of teeth, no anxiety shown. It is so unlike the trauma of my childhood.

Maia is a very talented girl who is on the school's "Gifted and talented" register. There are a lot of positives in her life and she will receive more support than my parents could have ever given me. Despite my fears none of my grandchildren have had anything like the number or severity of injuries that I faced. The condition seems to have reached its zenith in me and I am glad that it has been so. I would not want any of my grandchildren to endure what I have done.

They and I have a lot to be thankful for and as I looked at this scene I was overcome by a very strong emotion. I thought of my lovely daughter Sarah and her wonderful children. They were all in this room in my head.

I felt so happy.

Life is what you make it.

It will be alright.

It will be.

Won't it?

xxxx

Three months later Linda and I spent a lovely week's holiday in Whitby, North Yorkshire during Easter 2011. It is a beautiful part of the country and the weather was sensational. Linda and I were staying in a farm cottage with Andrew and Kim, Maia, Violet and Lucas. We had just finished breakfast on Sunday morning and were looking forward to the week away with our grandchildren. Maia was beating me at a game of her new-found joy, Monopoly. We had a lovely morning and were looking forward to a trip out in the early spring sunshine. She stood on a chair to lean over the table. Suddenly and with out warning the chair lurched backwards and then forwards under the pressure from her foot. Maia let out a stifled "ooh". Everyone reacted instantly. "Are you alright Maia?"

"No," she said softly.

"Let me look," said her dad. "Did you bang your leg?"

"Yeees" she said meekly. Andrew Lifted her off the chair to examine her leg as bright red blood began to trickle from a gaping wound in her leg. Andrew ran to the kitchen for a towel as Kim held Maia Linda dashed to the car for the first aid kit.

I tried to distract the other kids, pretending that everything was OK but it was plainly not. If I'm honest I wasn't just tending to the other children. I was running away. I didn't want to see any more blood. Of course I will look after my grandchildren if I have to but if there are others present I am quite happy for them to deal with it. I didn't want to face this. I couldn't face this.

"Granddad are you OK?" Violet's little voice whispered her loving concern as I became aware that I was biting the back of my hand just as I did when I had driven Andrew to hospital all those years ago.

"Yes love of course I am," I lied. "What book shall we read?"

I read a book to two little children, as their sister was being bandaged and prepared by her parents to be whisked away to hospital. Linda closed the car door and it left a trail of dust in its wake. I imagined the satellite navigation system giving out calm instructions as their hearts raced.

Linda came back into the room.

"Will she be alright?" I pleaded.

"Yes. She will be fine. Honest."

Violet's little hand touched my chin, steering my head

back to the book and away from desperate thoughts.

"Now who wants a drink?" asked Linda.

The children put their hands up.

"Orange or milk?"

"Milk please."

"Philip a cup of tea?" I nodded without saying a word.

"She'll be alright."

I nodded and all through the eating of biscuits and drinking of drinks and reading of books we waited.

They returned two hours later. Andrew carried Maia in from the car and placed her gently on the sofa placing protective cushions around her heavily bandaged shin. Everyone made a fuss of her. Whitby hospital is a local community hospital. Maia was attended by nurses as there was no doctor present. They put steri-strips on the wound and glued it for extra support.

"They said it will just leave a thin line on her shin,"

I was relieved. She will have a totally different scar to the ones I have had.

Two days later Maia returned to casualty for a check up. They wanted to ensure that the cut had remained closed and neat. Luckily it had and we were joyously re-assured. Andrew informed the practice nurse about Ehlers Danlos syndrome as he had never heard of it.

"Her skin is very delicate and tears easily."

"I can see that," confirmed the nurse.

"She needs a bandage rather than any adhesive dressing."

The nurse nodded but despite Andrew's request and the nurse's own observation he applied a thick protective pad with its own adhesive surround. A week later my family visited Hull Royal Infirmary on their return from holiday.

The nurses had difficulty removing the adhesive dressing. As they pulled it her skin moved with it and the two sides of the cut parted under the strain. Maia was left with a wide scar on her shin that looks like a Chelsea smile. It is a wide scar just like mine and it could so easily have been avoided. It was so unnecessary. Once again it was a case of professional staff "knowing best" and not listening to the patient. I was so upset that I wrote to the hospital management. They replied saying that unfortunately I was not Maia's next of kin and they requested a communication from Andrew and Kim. They did not pursue it.

Andrew was very busy and they didn't want to cause Maia any further anxiety. I felt it was very important to complain to ensure there would not be a repetition. In reality that member of staff may never see another case again and it wasn't their fault as such. It is virtually impossible to train staff to deal with something so rare.

What is more important is that Andrew and Kim learn to be more assertive in future. This is of course very difficult but it is something they must steel themselves for, if they are to protect their daughter from the care of the unknowing.

"People like us should be seen by a doctor at a major Accident and Emergency Department. Our condition is too unusual to be treated by staff at the average cottage hospital." Andrew nodded in agreement. Very soon events would show how correct that statement was.

Chapter 40 Violet

Three months passed and Maia made a full recovery. It was nearing the end of June and I was in the middle of editing this book as I hid from the burning sun.

Linda and I had spent a lovely weekend together.

On Saturday Andrew and Kim came with Maia, Violet and Lucas. We had a lovely morning and early afternoon with them, which ended with us playing draughts, another of Maia's favourite games. Today, however, Violet, her 4-year-old sister has won. Violet was really chuffed. Maia was not.

An hour after they left we went to Sarah's. They had arrived back from holiday the previous day and were busy unpacking. We returned Zac's kitten, Rascal, who had been nothing like her name for the whole week. We were relieved to see that the hamsters and goldfish were alive and well. We had forgotten to feed them since Tuesday but they seemed none the worse, if a little slimmer. We spent a very pleasant couple of hours with them and then went home to a simple tea of beans on toast before settling down to watch a film. I had a beer or two. Linda had wine.

The weather the next day was glorious so we went for a six-mile walk along Spurn Point. It is a narrow strip of shifting sand that juts out into the mouth of the Humber. On one side is a beautiful beach, which is constantly assaulted by the North sea. It is littered in parts by the remnants of 2nd World War defences and a collapsed road destroyed by the movement of the sand under the pressure of the sea. On the other side river mud flats provide a haven for thousands of migrating birds. The Yorkshire Wildlife Trust charges a fee if you want to drive down but walking is a much better option and produces wonderful rewards that compensate for the pain in my feet. The variety of plants is amazing and on one section heavily scented wild roses border the road on both sides. As Spurn narrows to the now defunct lighthouse the visitor can see huge ships passing round its tip, gliding from the North Sea into the mouth of the river.

We walked along the beach for two and a half hours in the sunshine, deceived by the cooling breeze of the sea until both of us got sunburn. We then had lunch and a cup of tea at a little café full of day-trippers and bird watchers. To finish off a lovely morning we drove back in Linda's little MG sports car with the hood down. It was one of the most enjoyable week-ends I can remember in a long time. It almost felt like we were in love again. On our return we both had a little nap, which was disturbed by the ringing of the phone.

"Hello Dad". It was Andrew.

"Guess where we are."

"Where?" I asked.

"Guess."

"Are you at the sea side?"

"No."

This was impossible. I moved into the conservatory and sat down to view the garden.

"Are you in Hull?"

"Yes. I'll put Violet on. She'll tell you."

A little voice said, "I'm at the 'opital."

"Why?" I sat bolt upright, trying not to sound alarmed. My mind was racing. What the hell had happened to Maia again?

"I cut my head."

I blinked, worried for Violet and pleased it wasn't Maia

"Oh lovely, are you alright?"

"It was bleeding."

"Has it stopped?"

"Yes. They put a bandage on."

There was a rustling as she handed the phone back to her daddy.

"Hello. Sorry to do it like that. I just wanted to make it seem like a bit of a game for her."

I was not angry.

"Is she alright?"

"She fell against the wall and split her forehead. It opened wide like our skin does. She's got it dad."

I closed my eyes. We had always thought that she would be OK.

"Hello?"

His voice jarred me back into action. My son needed my support. There was no place for my getting emotional.

"They say it needs stitching. I wondered what you thought."

I did not know what to say. I could sense his concern not only in his words but in his delivery of them. I wanted to

339

reassure him but all the advice I had ever been given over the last twenty years was to avoid stitching if possible. The skin can break under the pressure as mine often did leaving even bigger scars but steri-strips had not held on Maia even when used with glue.

"I don't know." I said limply. I knew he wanted me to help him protect his little girl. There was a pause of disappointment. I needed to ease his pain.

"How big is the cut?"

"It's big. She's definitely got it. Her skin just burst. It's like there is a big hole."

"Do the doctors know about the EDS?"

"Yes". They said they need to stitch it under anaesthetic and that they'll do a double internal stitch to make certain it holds."

"What does that mean?"

"I don't know".

"Do they know about the tearing?"

"Yes I think so."

"Right go back and make certain they do. Tell them your fears and see what they say. Ask them anything you can think of and then when you're certain they know, take their advice."

"Right."

"That's all I can say."

"Yes I know. Thanks dad."

There was a click and I was left holding the silence. I

couldn't help my son any more than I had done and felt totally useless as I went to the bathroom to disturb Linda's relaxation. I climbed the stairs contemplating dashing to his side but it would have been pointless By the time I had travelled the twenty miles to the hospital they would have finished.

I was wrong.

We sat waiting but no phone call came so I went out for a drink with Robert as I normally do on a Sunday. It should have been a perfect ending to a fine weekend but instead I was sat in a pub worrying about the damage to my granddaughter's head. Robert was, as always, very supportive. Finally the phone rang. It was Linda.

"They have sent Violet home with a dressing applied to the open wound. She is to return the next morning when they will stitch her head under general anaesthetic."

"How big is it?"

"I don't know, I think it's bad," she sighed.

We were held to each other by our lack of words.

"Okay. Well they must be going to do a proper job. Perhaps it'll work out better than Maia's last one."

"Yes. They seem to know what they are doing. They are going to take her into theatre

tomorrow morning and stitch the cut from the inside.

"Stitch it from the inside? How?"

"I don't know but I'm certain she'll be fine. The doctors know about EDS.

Are you OK?"

341

"Yes I'm fine. Are you?"

"Yes."

We were both lying.

I bade farewell to Robert with a hug in the pub car park.

"She'll be alright dad. Don't worry."

I nodded but my mind was in turmoil. All this was happening a week after Indira had dislocated her kneecap in a lesson at school. As I pulled out onto the main road. I waved to Robert and with that he was gone.

The doctor's had reassured Andrew that Violet would be left with nothing but a thin line down the front of her forehead. I was pleased but fearful. I have heard these statements before. It's what they said about Maia's leg and that didn't work out and this was on Violet's face. I drove home on automatic pilot and did not remember anything of the journey so I pulled over to gather my thoughts. There is a stretch of road near where I live that is about a mile long and as straight as an arrow. It is lined by trees and surrounded by fields of a variety of crops. I was crying as I edged the car onto the grass. A faint breeze disturbed the leaves and dappled the fading sunlight. It was beautifully desolate and restful but I could not be at ease.

If only.

If only Linda hadn't wanted children.

If only.

If only I had been stronger and said that we shouldn't.

"It wouldn't be fair on any unborn children."

It was my fault.

I don't blame Linda.

Then I do.

Then I don't.

I understand

Then I don't.

Then I do.

"She was not to know. How could she?"

If only.

If only she'd met someone else.

I wanted it all to stop. I had been through this in my youth and it was then repeated in my children and now it was doing the same again with my grandchildren. It wasn't going to stop. My life, our lives are one long continuous accident. It will carry on.

Then I had a flashback to that day in 1963. I saw the little wall approaching. I felt the bang, the pain. I saw the blood. In the car my head arched backwards as my hand grabbed the long since healed shin. My forehead rested uncomfortably on the steering wheel.

I was trying to reason unreasonable emotions when my phone rang. I fumbled through my bag in the half-light not even thinking to turn on the car's light. I knew it was Andrew even if I couldn't see the phone. My hand shook as I pressed the green button.

"Hello."

"Hi. Is she OK?"

"She's fine dad. She's asleep. She was more concerned that

she didn't get a sticker for being brave. She's asleep. They know all about EDS. They will do it tomorrow. They seem to know what they are doing. She'll be OK"

We said goodbye and he promised to ring me when the operation was complete.

After his confident words I sat in silence as the sunlight finally disappeared and composed myself. She was going to be alright. Things are much better now than they used to be. They will never be stitched without anaesthetic like I was. She would have a pencil line scar that would hardly be noticeable.

I continued my journey home. I drank 2 bottles of beer to send me to sleep.

The doctors performed a minor miracle. Violet was returned home the next afternoon. They did a continuous running stitch on the underside of the cut and then pulled it all together on the outside before adding the extra protection of a few stern strips. She was fine. Eight days later she was making my earlier fears seem foolish as she proudly displayed her wound. It was a pencil line on her forehead exactly as the doctors had described. I felt that a real advance had been made in our care. We all agreed that in future we should take any of our injuries to large hospitals staffed by teams of doctors. The condition is too rare to be dealt with at a local community hospital. They do a wonderful job but are not sufficiently skilled to deal with the problems that we present.

I was happy and relaxed. The following Thursday I played golf in the afternoon. My friend and I had booked a twilight session that costs only £8. I was leaving the house in a bit of a rush and the phone rang. I decided to ignore it.

It was probably one of those annoying companies trying to get us to claim money back from the banks for selling us unnecessary payment protection on loans I have never had. We get about three a day. They are so annoying. I shut the door determined to enjoy my evening.

"If it's important they'll ring back," I thought to myself as I headed for my car.

It was important. Sarah was trying to reach me. She needed me to look after the kids. Someone had stood on Indira's ankle at school. She had been taken to hospital to have stitches inserted in a cut. I didn't find out until 8.30pm when I returned home.

I felt so guilty. I should have answered the phone. How stupid. Sarah phoned at 9.00pm. Indira was OK. Seven steri strips and glue had sealed the wound. I worried about whether it would hold but said nothing. She had to rest and not strain anything. Hopefully she would be fine.

Yet again I went through the process of convincing myself that life is still sweet. I am so lucky, I think, although it doesn't always feel like it. So we go on until the next time, hoping there won't be one, knowing there will be.

Accidents are a fact of life.

Chapter 41 No End

I have been editing the content of this book for the last month. Finishing a book is a strangely dull experience. The author spends about two years writing and re-writing, hoping that it will soon be completed and then, quite suddenly, it is. The ending creeps up and flattens the writer unexpectedly and without warning.

After the shock has diminished he or she can begin to dream of having produced a best seller but the editing process drives away such fanciful notions. The word-smith looks at the work in horror when it becomes apparent that a lot of rubbish soils the pages and much work remains to be done. It is even more difficult to produce a conclusion when the story refuses to end.

October and November produced a beautiful Indian summer. I played golf in ideal conditions with an autumnal sun enlivening the tired fairways. I had just about finished preparing the garden for winter and was pleased with myself. I looked round the garden on the 16th of November with some satisfaction having just cleared my lawn of fallen leaves for the third time and bagged them up to rot down and produce next year's leaf mould.

"When I worked I never had time to do these jobs and I just left leaves to rot on the grass," I thought to myself.

"Now I've retired I can really get ahead of things. I'm really on top of my jobs."

In the morning I finished digging over the bare ground in the vegetable garden in order to let winter frosts break up the soil. Only cabbages and sprouts remained in their raised beds. I bent down and attached the hosepipe to the water sprinkler in order to saturate the parched ground on which the sprouts stood. They are particularly susceptible to drought. I turned on the water and checked to see if the sprinkler was directing water to cover every plant. I was pleased with myself and relaxed. My book was written. The garden was tidy and my vegetables had been bountiful. I moved off the pebbled path that surrounded my growing beds and stepped onto the concrete path heading towards the kitchen for a well-earned cup of tea.

Before I knew it I was lying face down on the floor trying to work out what had happened. My neighbour Geoff was working on a car only thirty feet away completely oblivious to the fact that I was lying amongst the brassicas and completely unaware that a dull throbbing sensation was developing in my right foot.

Unfortunately some of the pebbles which were about an inch in diameter had spilled over onto the firm concrete. I stood on one of them and it rolled my foot over throwing me to the ground. In mid flight I thought, "Shit my ankle is at right angles to my leg."

I lay there shocked for a minute before getting up. I shook myself down before continuing to sweep up leaves from the path.

"I'm OK I think," I said to myself. "God I was lucky I didn't do any damage. Mind you I've gone over before without doing any harm. Maybe being supple has helped me to get away with it. I could have sworn I'd sprained my foot." I continued walking about trying to walk off the discomfort. I was trying to convince myself that I was alright but to no avail.

"Are you OK Phil?" Geoff enquired. I shook my head and

explained to him what had happened.

"You don't have much luck do you?" He smiled sympathetically. I nodded in agreement.

I went in and got some ice cubes out of the fridge, wrapped them in a tea towel and placed it on my raised foot. The phone rang.

"Hello Dad." It was Sarah.

"I was wondering if you could do me a favour?"

"What is it?"

"Are you OK?"

"I'm not sure."

"What have you done?"

I explained to her as I had done to Geoff. She completed the fifteen minute journey in ten. I greeted her in the kitchen.
"Do you need to go to hospital?

"I don't think so. I've had my foot iced and raised and it's not swollen up. I can walk. It's just a bit sooorre." I could walk in a straight line but as soon as I tried to turn I felt the same shredding pain I had felt years earlier on the rugby pitch with the school team.

"I'd better take you to hospital."

I walked to the car but the pain was now getting much worse.

As we drove to hospital I asked her what she had phoned me for. "I was going to ask you to pick up the kids from school but I've got Dorothy to do it instead."

348

She had started out to ask me a favour but now I needed one from her. She sat with me for a while in the packed waiting area but it was proving too much for Aisha her youngest child. Sarah phoned Linda's school and arrangements were made for her to come and pick me up from hospital once again. Linda eventually arrived just as I emerged from the plaster room crutches in hand. She smiled at me sympathetically and kissed me.

"I don't know."

There was nothing else to say. I didn't know either.

"I will have to have the pot on all over Christmas and New Year."

"Oh well it can't be helped."

I felt pathetic, helpless sore and guilty. Yet again Linda was going to have to run round after me. She would have to work, help Sarah as per normal; cook all my meals; buy the Christmas tree; put up the decorations before driving the 540 mile round trip to pick up our mothers. The only defence I had was that it was not my fault. I never asked for this and I'm getting sick of it but it's plainly obvious that, like this book, the story will never end.

I know the accidents won't go away but I am no longer angry. In a strange way I am grateful for the injuries. They have made me the person I am. I couldn't have given the support I have given to my children and been so understanding of others problems had I not gone through those experiences. I look at myself now and despite it all I'm pleased with what I see.

The existence of my children and grandchildren is a great irony in my life. I wanted rugby and couldn't have it. I wanted cricket but it was not to be. I didn't want children but I had them. They turned out to be the best thing in my life and caring for and protecting them became my biggest single driving force. I wanted to make certain that they would never live the kind of life that I have done. I succeeded and for that I am most pleased. I couldn't be a sportsman or a manual worker but I could love and protect others. I have a lot to be thankful for.

Two weeks into my recovery and Maia cut her leg again. She fell over in the school playground and was taken to hospital for several stitches. The following Saturday saw Maia and I sat together looking out onto my garden, one bandaged, the other in plaster. She may be only a child but she has had several injuries and fully understands our situation.

"Granddad does it hurt?"

"It did but not now."

"That's like me."

She smiled.

I held her hand. "I am very happy and do you know why?"

"Why?"

"Because I've got you."

The accidents will continue but we will face them with courage and an insight I never possessed before.

There will be no ending.

Maybe, it's a beginning.

THE E_ _ ?

Previous work by this author

Braver than all the rest
A mother fights for her son

Philip Howard

Dave and Sarah Burgess are devastated when their young son Karl is found to have muscular dystrophy. Then another tragedy hits the family hard. But the family are committed to do the best they can for Karl, who has a passion for rugby league. Karl's determination to get the most out of life, despite his disability, inspires those around him.
Published in 2010 at £9.95. special offer £9.00 direct from London League Publications Ltd. Credit card orders via www.llpshop.co.uk , orders by cheque to LLP, PO Box 65784, London NW2 9NS

"A powerful and emotional debut novel; a book that will haunt me for some time to come." ...Hull Mail
"While this isn't a book about the clinical symptoms Philip Howard demonstrates a true empathy in his writing for those dealing with disability" ... "Able" magazine.

74230254R00204

Made in the USA
San Bernardino, CA
13 April 2018